ANCHOR BREWING CO.
SAN FRANCISCO CAL.
OCTOBER 1906

A. MARITZEN.
ARCHITECT & ENGINEER
SAN FRANCISCO CAL.
· October 30th, 1906 ·

ANCHOR BREWERY

Galv. Iron Cornice.

OFFICE

ELEVATION 18TH ST.

There are few things from this town which are unique. . . . There is, however, Steam Beer. We can be proud of it. . . . How shall one describe this brew, which is made at The Anchor Brewery . . . and no place else? . . . Steam has been neglected by booze authorities. . . . Yet Steam had as much to do with building San Francisco and Northern California as the Christian virtues, good stout Levi's, shovels, and the saving presence of whores.

—**Charles McCabe, columnist, *San Francisco Chronicle*** (1970)

THE ANCHOR BREWING STORY

AMERICA'S FIRST CRAFT BREWERY & SAN FRANCISCO'S ORIGINAL ANCHOR STEAM BEER

DAVID BURKHART

FOREWORD BY FRITZ MAYTAG

TEN SPEED PRESS
California | New York

To Fritz Maytag
and all those who share our joy of beer, brewing, and San Francisco.

The longer I live, the better I understand the kindness of thy heart and the high quality of thy mind.

—Louis Pasteur (1879)

VIEW OF SAN FRANCISCO, FORMERLY YERBA BUENA, IN 1846-7
BEFORE THE DISCOVERY OF GOLD

The texture of a city is drawn from its beginnings, and the tapestry that is San Francisco is strong with legends.

—Herb Caen, columnist, *San Francisco Chronicle* (1965)

CONTENTS

PART THREE: FRITZ MAYTAG'S REVOLUTIONARY OLD BREWERY

PART FOUR: FRITZ MAYTAG'S REVOLUTIONARY NEW BREWERY

PART FIVE: GOLDEN PROSPECTS

FOREWORD

I was twenty-seven years old when I first set foot in a historic little San Francisco brewery known as Anchor, the makers of Anchor Steam Beer. Struggling and on the brink of bankruptcy, the brewery had had nine owners since 1871. On August 2, 1965, that very same day, I became its tenth.

My career as the guiding force at Anchor lasted forty-five years, almost a third of the company's long history. When asked about it I always say, "I had a wonderful time . . . I was made for it!" The combination of biochemistry, simple physics, and chemistry had been my passion ever since my earliest years. In 1965, I stumbled into a perfect world to explore these passions.

I have often been called "the godfather" of the craft brewing movement. But I have also been referred to as "the alchemist of steam," which especially delights me. Alchemy, sometimes called the mother of chemistry, is rooted in the search for a means of transmuting a base metal such as lead into its highest form, gold. It is the ancient and mysterious art of transformation—of something ordinary into something extraordinary, of something mundane into something wondrous.

Running the brewery, I gradually realized that my childhood dream of being a research chemist was wrong. Rather, it was the magical transformation of raw materials into successful products that was my destiny and my purpose in life.

I love looking at all those marvelous old illustrations and paintings of ancient alchemists, hard at work in their tools-of-the-trade-filled

Christoph Weigel the Elder
The Alchemist or Goldmaker
Copperplate engraving (1699)

The Alchemist or Goldmaker.
The toil often is nothing but cow dung.
Use these arts,
    prepare medicines,
    and help nature;
But if you want to get gold,
    it will go up in smoke[:]
Honor, Wit, Money and Mercury.

David Teniers the Younger
The Alchemist
Oil painting (1650)

laboratories. There, I often see a second person hard at work—an apprentice or an assistant perhaps—and that was an all-important feature of my transforming Anchor. I had a wonderful team of colleagues, who compensated for my shortcomings in countless ways.

People now ask if I miss the brewery, and I always say, "I miss sitting in my office with my team of Linda, Mark, and Gordon, the brewery humming along all around us, and knowing, as I said often, "We are the Anchor Brewing Company; we can do anything."

Dave Burkhart was on our team. My close colleague of many years, Dave shares my sense of curiosity and wonder about the world and has a great love and respect for tradition and history— especially the traditions and history of Anchor and its hometown, San Francisco.

So I'm not surprised that *The Anchor Brewing Story* is such an honest, thorough, insightful, and engaging insider's guide to Anchor Brewing Company. Here, Dave has shown that he too is an alchemist, having distilled 150-plus years of history into a compelling narrative that reveals not only what makes Anchor Brewing and its beers unique, but what makes working at Anchor so special. It's a book that's worth its weight in gold!

—*Fritz Maytag*

INTRODUCTION
HISTORY IN A GLASS

While there are countless beers that are weird for the sake of being weird or because their odd combination of ingredients works, there's something unique about quirkiness rooted in the past.

—**Zak Stambor**, *Chicago Tribune* (2014)

Welcome to San Francisco! And thanks for including Anchor Brewing on your itinerary. Time for a beer, right?

Here you go. Let's have a seat. You know, people have been having friendly conversations over beer for thousands of years. So here's to Ninkasi, the ancient Sumerian goddess of beer! But more about her later. Let's talk a little about that Anchor

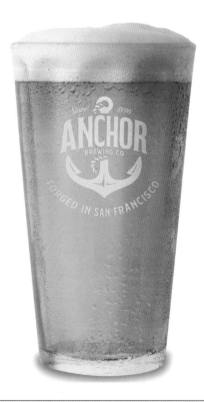

Steam in your glass and slow everything down so we can fully experience it from start to finish. First, lift your glass up to the light, twist it slowly back and forth. Note the deep amber and coppery colors and the bubbles wending their way to the surface, where they join a thick, creamy head of foam.

Tilt your glass a little and then back upright. What remains on the side of your glass is called *lacing*, one of the hallmarks of a naturally carbonated beer. If you don't see lacing on your Anchor at home, by the way, start washing your beer glasses with hot water, but no soap, which destroys the head on a well-made beer.

Now swirl the beer around just a little and bring the glass up to your nose. What do you get—besides thirstier? There are no wrong answers. For me, it's subtle aromas of fresh mint, evergreen, and wood outside an old-fashioned bakery; a synergistic complexity, with hints of caramel, fresh herbs, spices, fruit, and even flowers.

Bring the glass to your lips and take a small sip. Savor the mouthfeel and taste. Are they what the aromas invited you to experience? I get the gentle nip of lively bubbles, followed by velvety smoothness. There's fullness and richness without heaviness, a marvelously refreshing balance of bitter and sweet. It's biscuity, caramelly, a little fruity, with just a hint of savory herbal spiciness.

Now take a bigger sip to experience the finish. Does it linger? I get a hint of toffee-like sweetness, caught in a balancing act with mellow bitterness, followed by a farewell wave from the bubbles. Does it quench your thirst but beckon you to have another?

You probably noticed that I didn't use the ingredients themselves to describe the beer—no "malty, hoppy, yeasty" or—God forbid—"watery." That would be a cop-out. But one of the great joys of drinking beer is that we don't have to wait for an expert opinion. We get to describe it however we see fit—and debate it over a second glass! Indeed, beer may just be the most democratic of all beverages.

To me, Anchor Steam is the uniquely extraordinary, everyday beer. No wonder it's the sole survivor of the first Golden Age of San Francisco brewing. It's history in a glass, and it never gets old.

As Anchor's own brewery historian, I must confess that I have gotten a little older since my first day at Anchor, May 20, 1991. In those days, everyone started out in production—on the bottling line or filling kegs—and eventually learned how to do just about every job at the brewery on their way to finding the job that suited them best. From day one, I was curious about the brewery's unique history and asked a lot of questions, including many of Fritz Maytag. Fritz, great-grandson of the founder of the eponymous appliance company, was owner, president, and brewmaster of Anchor for forty-five years. I got to work alongside him for two decades, and he was always generous with his knowledge, wisdom, and insight. But even he didn't have all the answers, which only added to my enthusiastic determination to learn more. So what makes Anchor's story so special?

Traditionally, beer is made from four basic ingredients: barley malt, which gives it sweetness, body, and color; hops, which gives it bitterness and aroma; water, of course; and yeast, the hardest-working organism in the brewery. Yeast feasts on the malt's sugars, transforming them into alcohol and CO_2 (booze and bubbles) during fermentation, the yeast's reproductive cycle.

Ever wonder why Grape-Nuts cereal tastes a little sweet, even though sugar isn't listed as one of its ingredients? It gets its sweetness from malted barley. First, barley is steeped in water and allowed to germinate, releasing enzymes that convert its complex starches into more simple sugars—aka yeast food! The malt is then kiln dried, a bit like roasting coffee, giving it different colors and flavors according to the time in and temperature of the kiln.

Like a master chef—who might use Arborio, basmati, or jasmine rice; lemon, lime, or grapefruit juice; olive oil, butter, or sesame oil; a saucepan, a sauté pan, or a wok—one of the great joys of brewing comes from the myriad choices we have of ingredients and methods, combined in a distinctly distinctive way. For Anchor Steam, the ingredients are 2-row pale and caramel malt, whole-cone Northern Brewer hops, San Francisco tap water, which comes to us all the way from Hetch Hetchy

Reservoir in Yosemite National Park, and our own special yeast. (More about these later.)

Do you like IPAs? They're all the rage today, in almost as many varieties as there are IPA drinkers. Well, in the mid-1800s *lagers* were all the rage, especially in the parts of Europe and North America with cold winters and lots of ice available year-round.

Yes, ice. By definition, lager beers are made with lager yeast, a type of yeast that does its best work at very cold temperatures over long periods of time. The word *lager* comes from an old German word meaning to store, lie down, or rest, and that's just what Germans did with their lager beers: After an initial cool fermentation they lagered (stored) their lagers for months at a time in alpine caves or deep cellars, often literally on ice harvested from nearby lakes and ponds and kept available in icehouses year-round. It is during this *lagering* process—this slow secondary fermentation—that *lager beer* develops its characteristic crisp, clean flavors.

After the discovery of gold in California in 1848, German beer drinkers and brewers flocked to San Francisco, bringing with them the thirst for a good lager and the ingenuity to make one. In those days, as Mark Twain reminisced in *Life on the Mississippi*, ice "was jewelry. None but the rich could wear it." During the California Gold Rush, ice was sometimes packed in sawdust and brought in by ship from Sitka or around the Horn from Boston or New York, at a price too dear for beer. There was plenty of ice in the Sierras, of course, but no practicable way to get it to San Francisco until the completion of the transcontinental railroad in 1869. And ice-making technology and modern refrigeration were decades away.

But San Francisco was—and is—the cradle of creativity. "Brought into the world recklessly. Brought up recklessly. And now recklessly alive," declared Californian William Saroyan with pride. "It is a city with no rules. Like nature itself, it improvises as it goes along. It does what it needs to do at the time and under the circumstances." So

brewers—like our first brewmaster, Gottlieb Brekle—being short on ice but long on ingenuity, ad-libbed, each in their own way, to create *California common beer.*

Fritz Maytag explained to a fervent fan that California common beers—also called *quick-brewed*, *present-use*, or *ordinary* beer—are not "specific 'types' of beers that can be clearly defined, because what scant evidence exists indicates a very wide range of brewing methods and materials, just as we would expect under pioneering and rapidly changing conditions. Brewers in those days did not follow textbooks; each would do the best he could to make and sell beer quickly and cheaply in the absence of modern technology." Wooden barrels of California common were delivered by horse-drawn wagon to local saloons as soon as three to five days after brewing. These weren't lagers in the traditional sense, but during the Gold Rush, Gottlieb Brekle and his fellow San Francisco brewers chose to call them lager anyway. And in those days there were no imported lagers to which they might have been unfavorably compared. So *lager* became the catchall term for nearly all of the beers brewed in California other than ale or porter. And it didn't take long before Californians began asking for these California commons—these so-called lagers, brewed under primitive conditions and without ice—by their catchier, quirkier, colloquial nickname: *steam beer.* And for many decades, Anchor alone—the lone survivor of this bygone era—has used the quaint name *steam* for its unique beer. Today *Steam Beer* is a trademark of Anchor Brewing Company.

But why the mysterious moniker *steam*? Fritz Maytag is the world's foremost expert on the subject, and even he doesn't know for sure! In my own thirty years at Anchor, I've learned there are many plausible origin theories, perhaps best told through the lens of the brewery's own story. History isn't always about answers, sometimes it's about possibilities. And you get to choose your favorite—just as you get to choose your favorite Anchor brew.

Though our first brewery, dating to 1871, was destroyed in the 1906 San Francisco earthquake and fire, some pre-quake documents and photos survived. Moreover, the way in which the brewery was subsequently rebuilt also reveals a lot about how *we* made California common beer *as early as 1871*, because post-quake, rather than rebuilding the brewery *looking forward* to the *twentieth* century, with ice and modern refrigeration, our company opted to rebuild *looking back* to the *nineteenth* century and its Gold Rush brewing heritage. It was a radically traditional decision. Amazingly, the 1906 blueprints for the second brewery, here transformed into a cutaway view, show this with remarkable clarity.

At Anchor, the making of California common began in the brewhouse like that for any traditional German lager. The nickname *steam* had nothing to do with using steam power or steam heat. Rather, it was when the *wort* (the sweet, hot, syrupy liquid that is created in the brewhouse) left the brewhouse for cooling,that Anchor's lager beer took its steamily Gold Rushian turn. The following are the four likeliest theories for why California common beer may have gotten the nickname *steam*, based on what we know about Anchor and its history:

THEORY #1: THE COOLSHIP

Pitching (adding) lager yeast to the 200°F+ (93°C+) hot wort would kill the yeast. But if allowed to cool down all by itself, the sugary liquid would succumb to bacteria and spoil long before the yeast could be pitched. How then, without ice or modern refrigeration, could the wort be cooled as quickly as possible? The answer was San Francisco itself.

Thanks to the natural air-conditioning of its sea breezes, fog, and hilly terrain, San Francisco's mean temperature in the 1850s and '60s was a cool 56.5°F (13.5°C). So, after transferring the *hot wort* from the brew kettle to the *hop jack*, which acts like a strainer to remove the hops, we pumped it up to our brewery's enclosed rooftop. There, elevated so that air could pass freely above and below it, sat a very shallow, open pan called a *coolship* or *cooler*. Evidence in San Francisco of this adaptive technology dates to about 1852, and these coolships may have been inspired by similar vessels in Germany called *Kühlschiffe*. Both before and after the quake, Anchor's coolship was flanked on all four sides by louvered windows, allowing cool breezes and fog in, while keeping sunlight and birds out. Above, a slanted roofline kept condensation from dripping back into the cooling wort. In 1907, our coolship was 28 by 30 feet and *just 6 inches deep*, its huge surface area dissipating heat both quickly and efficiently, cooling the wort (it's not called beer until the yeast is added) to the ambient temperature of San Francisco.

Imagine looking up at our original brewery or post-quake brewery from the street. As cool air met hot wort, what looked like steam wafted from the louvers—one possible origin of the nickname *steam beer*.

THEORY #2: THE FERMENTATION

After this step, the wort, having cooled to about 58°F (14.5°C), was dropped one floor below to the *starter fermentor*, which looked like the top half of a monstrous, upright wooden barrel, open at the top. 58°F is closer to a traditional ale fermentation temperature than a traditional lager fermentation temperature, but it worked, resulting in an extraordinary marriage of the flavors and aromas of a crisp, clean lager (thanks to the lager yeast) with a fruitier, esterier ale (thanks to the ale temperatures). Esters are the volatile flavor compounds created when organic acids interact with alcohols during fermentation, which can taste or smell of fresh flowers, fruit, or even

vegetables. Into this enormous tub we pitched the yeast, a beige-colored slurry used again and again from generation to generation like sourdough starter. Although the original California common beer yeasts used were probably conventional lager yeasts, once used repeatedly at these higher, ale-like temperatures, they took on their own unique character. So lager yeast could be used for steam beer, but steam beer yeast became an evolved type, no longer usable for traditional lager. Of course, that didn't matter at the time, because there were no traditional lagers on the West Coast!

After seven or eight hours, the remaining wort was dropped into the starter fermentor, creating a vigorous fermentation. Next, we transferred the beer to a shallow, open-pan fermentor, sometimes called a *clarifier*. In 1907 there were two, each 13.5 by 23 feet and *just 12 inches deep*, allowing heat

---

by as much as 10°F (6°C) or more, much higher than a traditional lager.

Next, the beer was dropped into a lineup of wooden barrels below, filling each about 85% full. Then we topped off each barrel with younger beer in *high kräusen* (from the Middle High German *krūsen*, to curl, because the fluffy white head on the fermenting beer curls like cauliflower), the cappuccino-looking midway point of primary fermentation. This would jump-start a lively secondary fermentation inside the barrel, like champagne in a bottle, the CO_2 going right into solution. The wooden barrels were heavy six-hoopers, specially fitted with threaded iron bungs, so they wouldn't blow out like wooden ones. There are a few of these barrels on display today in Anchor's taproom.

The secondary fermentation of traditional lager—in wooden barrels or large wooden casks—took months, at temperatures just above freezing.

and carbon dioxide—the natural by-products of fermentation—to escape. During its three to five days of primary fermentation, the beer went from looking like espresso to cappuccino and back again, as the temperature in the fermentor climbed

THE ANCHOR BREWING STORY

Newly filled barrels of California common, however, to preclude spoilage, were delivered by horse-drawn wagon up and down the streets of San Francisco to the city's saloons after as little as a few days. Savvy bartenders knew to let the kegs rest a few more days before tapping, since the beer was still fermenting and the barrels were quite volatile. Even so, when tapped, they often hissed and sprayed like a steam engine—another possible origin story for the sudsy sobriquet *steam beer*.

THEORY #3: THE POUR

Unlike traditional lager, served two months or more after brewing, so-called California commons took two weeks or less from brew kettle to glass, and they could be hell to pour. For good reason in those heady days, skilled "steam beer tapsters" were often better paid than the bartenders who dispensed hard liquor. They would slowly fill a glass from as many as three different barrels (each at progressive stages of secondary fermentation) to achieve the perfectly effervescent *head of steam*—a third possible origin of the term—that their customers craved.

THEORY #4: THE BUZZWORD

In the nineteenth century, steam was the dynamic new technology that powered steamships and locomotives. Soon the word *steam* became au courant—just as *atomic* would in the 1950s, *digital* in the 1980s, *dot-com* in the 1990s, *i-anything* in the 2000s, and the word *craft* in the 2010s. This is borne out by early advertising for San Francisco steam book and job printers, steam laundries, steam flour mills, steam bakeries, steam cracker factories, and even steam candy-works, regardless of whether steam was actually involved. Associating the word *steam* with your company or product imbued it with the cachet of cutting-edge modernity, which, in the case of *steam beer*, helped propel the amber rush that swept the Golden State.

This is the definitive story of America's first craft brewery and its legendary brews, from the Gold Rush to today. It is an operatic, only-in-San-Francisco tale of pioneering entrepreneurs and their dedication to quality and integrity—a century and a half of curiosity, enthusiasm, creativity, determination, perseverance, and resilience against all odds.

I could not have written this without its thirty years of research nor the joyful honor of working side by side with Anchor's greatest champions. Most of the book's quotations and anecdotes come directly from personal conversations and interviews unless otherwise noted. Some come from the Anchor archive, which includes everything from brew charts to ledgers, notebooks to correspondence. As such, they—like many of the images in this book—are appearing for the first time. New also are recipes for homebrewing four of Anchor's classic beers.

I sincerely hope that you get as much joy reading *The Anchor Brewing Story* as I did writing it. Both endeavors, I've discovered, are best done with a cold Steam nearby.

FROM A SKETCH by J.C.WARD. ESQ.   LITH. OF SARONY & MAJOR.

SAN FRANCISCO IN NOVEMBER, 1848.
NEW YORK. GEO. P. PUTNAM

BAYARD TAYLOR.   LITH. OF SARONY & MAJOR. N.Y.

SAN FRANCISCO IN NOVEMBER 1849.
NEW YORK. GEO. P. PUTNAM.

PART ONE

GOLD RUSH ROOTS

BREWER'S GOLD
(1848–1871)

*It was a splendid population—for all the slow, sleepy, sluggish-brained sloths staid at home—
you never find that sort of people among pioneers—you cannot build pioneers out of that sort
of material. It was that population that gave to California a name for getting up astounding
enterprises and rushing them through with a magnificent dash and daring and a recklessness
of cost or consequences, which she bears unto this day—and when she projects a new surprise,
the grave world smiles as usual, and says "Well, that is California all over."*

—**Mark Twain**, ***Roughing It*** (1872)

Modern-day Anchor brewer Ollie Lagomarsino

Gold was the catalyst—the magnet and the leaven—that transformed a quiescent hamlet of 459 souls into a burgeoning cosmopolis, teeming with reckless enthusiasm and pioneering spirit. Overnight, San Francisco's pop-up population became an instant city, destined to become what Richard Henry Dana Jr. dubbed "the sole emporium of a new world, the awakened Pacific."

On January 24, 1848, a millhand scribbled in his diary, "This day some kind of mettle was found in the tail race that looks like goald, first discovered by James Martial, the Boss of the Mill." Millwright James Marshall had partnered with land baron John Sutter to build a water-powered sawmill at Coloma, on the South Fork of the American River. Every night, Marshall ran water through the *tailrace*, the channel they had dug below the mill, in order to widen and deepen it. On the morning of January 24, he shut off the water as usual and stepped into the race. A glint caught his eye. About six inches below the surface, on a small, muddy rock, rested a few pieces of shiny metal. Marshall dipped his hand into the cold water and picked them up. He had discovered gold.

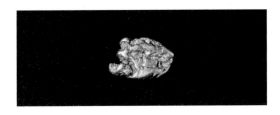

From California gold to the Dead Sea Scrolls, discoveries are sometimes the result of simply being in the right place at the right time. Great enterprise, however, is no accident.

A THIRST FOR GOLD

On March 15, 1848, the *Californian*, one of only two newspapers operating in the sleepy Mexican territory of Alta California, matter-of-factly printed the news of Marshall's find. Mormon pioneer Sam Brannan, who owned the *California Star*, San Francisco's first newspaper and the *Californian*'s only competition, had been scooped. But he had a store near Sutter's Fort, and decided it would be a lot more profitable to mine the miners than mine the mines. So Brannan reinvented himself—as the Gold Rush's first entrepreneur.

In mid-May, having bought up every pan, pick, and shovel he could find, Brannan launched a guerilla marketing campaign in San Francisco. Waving a bottle of gold dust in one hand and his hat in the other, the Mormon missionary turned bayside barker paraded down Montgomery Street (less than two miles from today's Twitter headquarters), chirping, "Gold! Gold! Gold from the American River!" The exodus was feverishly immediate: to Brannan's store for supplies—then off to the mines! The rush was on.

Mining for gold in those early days was a solitary endeavor, a man with a pan and a plan. But the more gold one panned, the harder it became to extract, necessitating novel, jerry-rigged devices with colorful names like *rocker*, *cradle*, *long tom*, and *sluice box*. Requiring two to four goldseekers

working in harmony, the devices gave birth to the "miner's partnership," a sociological phenomenon at the core of future California partnerships, from the humble beginnings of Anchor Brewery to the Comstock Lode's Silver Kings, the Central Pacific Railroad's Big Four, and Apple's Jobs and Wozniak. "Recklessness is in the air," observed Rudyard Kipling. "The roaring winds off the Pacific make you drunk with it. . . . Young men . . . embark on vast enterprises, take partners as experienced as themselves and go to pieces with as much splendor as their neighbors."

A THIRST FOR BEER

For many Gold Rush partnerships, the only liquid assets were a pitcher of beer and the camaraderie it facilitated. Equally enjoyable in boom or bust, beer was nutritious and often safer to drink than water. And it went great with gambling. No surprise, then, that beer became the drink of choice for many of California's goldseekers, whether they had a "pocket full of rocks," as they called their golden cache, or a pocketful of dirt.

But there was just one brewery at the time, belonging to Francis (Franz) Hoen. The son of a Bavarian brewer, Hoen arrived in California with the Swasey-Todd caravan in 1845. By 1847 he had opened San Francisco's first brewery, at the northwest corner of Pacific and Dupont (now Grant) Streets. It was still in business on June 22, 1851, when it suffered $10,000 (over $335,000 today) of damage in the last of San Francisco's seven big Gold Rush fires. All the repeated burning and rebuilding led to the inclusion of a symbolic phoenix on San Francisco's first city seal in 1852. Hoen chose not to rebuild and flew the coop, making his way to New York. There he boarded a ship bound for Bremen in 1854, never to return. It would be of great consequence if any evidence ever surfaced of Hoen brewing California common or "steam" beer, but it hasn't, leaving unresolved the question of

Bar Room in the Mines

who was the first. Suffice it to suggest, perhaps, that what really matters is whose brewery was the *last* to make "steam beer."

Other than Hoen's and a few subsequent breweries' brews, the first wave of gold miners drank imported ales, porters, and stouts, brought around the Horn by ship to San Francisco at great cost, from as far away as Liverpool and Dublin. Most of

the ales were India Pale Ales—IPAs—made a little stronger and more bitter than ordinary pale ale, to which British brewers added dry hops in the barrel for the long voyage to colonial India, a technique that became known as *dry-hopping*. The hops helped preserve the ale in the ship's hold and, coincidentally, gave it a pronounced aroma, the hallmark of a well-made IPA. All the great English India Pale Ales were available during the Gold Rush, including Allsopp's from Burton-on-Trent. In the Sam Brannanian spirit of mining the miners, though, a bottle of IPA cost as much as $8 ($270 today).

Porters were working-class brews, originally favored by London porters after a day of hauling goods around town. The stoutest porters (the beers, not the workers) were called *stout porters* and *stouts*, and the stoutest stouts, *export stouts*. The higher alcohol content of these pitch-black brews helped them survive the months-long voyage to California, where parched prospectors lapped them up along with IPAs as a safe source of hydration and nutrition—if not revelry.

By the late 1840s, lager had captured the fancy of beer drinkers in Europe as well as the eastern United States, where German immigrants had introduced it. Lower in hops than IPAs and lower in alcohol than export stouts, lager spoiled easily and didn't travel well, so its availability was dependent on *local* brewing. Although San Francisco had no readily available, let alone year-round source of ice with which to successfully cool and then store cold-fermenting lager beer in the traditional manner, the demand for it begged for a supply. So, under primitive conditions and without ice, San Francisco's German brewers began turning out a quick-brewed beer that they called lager, since there were no genuine lagers around to which it might be unfavorably compared. In actuality, it was *California common beer*, colloquially known to their customers by its quaint nickname *steam beer*. It sold for a nickel a glass, usually including a free lunch. The unique-tasting, frothy Gold Rush brew, with its magnificent *head of steam*, became the beverage of choice for San Francisco's working class, a makeshift beer for a makeshift town.

One such working-class San Franciscan was a German carpenter who reinvented himself as a San Francisco brewer. And because the brewery he built in 1871 became Anchor Brewery in 1896, he is the first in a 150-year-old line of Anchor brewmasters.

ANCHOR'S FIRST BREWMASTER

Born Johann Gottlieb Breckle on March 18, 1819 in Ossweil—a district of Ludwigsburg in southwest Germany—he was the eldest son of townsman/carpenter Gottlieb Breckle Sr. and Catherine Barbara Mergenthaler Breckle. History records him by a number of names in a variety of spellings. Since it was common in those days for Germans to go by their middle name, he was known as Gottlieb. The spelling of his surname was not nearly as

Ossweil.

important to him as it would be today, but he ultimately went with Brekle, which his descendants and Anchor brewers ever since have used and rhymed with *freckle*. Gottlieb Brekle became one of the so-called "Forty-eighters," which, surprisingly, had nothing to do with the Gold Rush. Rather, it was a group created by the political and economic consequences of the failed German Revolution of 1848 and 1849. Prospectors for freedom rather than gold, these "new argonauts" sought "the golden fleece of liberty" in America and elsewhere. Gottlieb chose Chile.

In 1843, a Chilean expedition had taken possession of the Strait of Magellan. To maintain sovereignty over its remote conquest, Chile granted cheap land and tax-free living to German immigrants in exchange for their establishment of German colonies in Southern Chile. Unlike

America, where Germans assimilated, in Chile, they were promised, they could preserve their language and nationality and live unaffected by foreign influences.

So, on July 31, 1852, Gottlieb Brekle, thirty-three, and Marie Hedwig Betz, thirty-four, from nearby Eglosheim, and fifty other passengers boarded the three-masted, 115-foot ship *Hermann* in Hamburg, bound for Chile. The cheapest tickets were 80 thaler (about $2,000 today): pricey, but far less than the 180 thaler it would have cost each to sail all the way to San Francisco. In December 1852, after an arduous voyage, they arrived in Valdivia, Chile, where they joined the small German colony there. It probably didn't take Gottlieb long to find the local brewery, Chile's first. Fellow German emigrant Karl Anwandter had opened it the year before, and it is easy to imagine Brekle working there. On July 5, 1853, Gottlieb and Marie were married. Ironically, despite all the talk of preserving German identity, their names were entered in the Valdivian church register as Maria and Teófilo, the latter a literal translation of Gottlieb's name, meaning *loved by God*.

The happy couple could have lived out their days in Chile, but for the siren song of gold. Estimates of California's total gold product through 1853 were $288,495,000 (over 9.7 billion today). The City by the Bay was 10% German, with nine breweries in 1853, and as California historian Hubert Howe Bancroft recounts, "There were in San Francisco 537 places where liquor was sold, 46 of which were public gambling houses, 743 bartenders officiating." And perhaps, as Mark Twain wrote about Virginia City, "some talk of building a church."

In late 1853 or early 1854, Gottlieb Brekle and his new bride disembarked into this irresistibly bountiful paradise of gold, beer, and community. The Germans, according to the *Annals of San Francisco* (1855), "have a society for the protection of immigrants, and various other benevolent and social institutions. Many of their naturalized citizens manifest a lively interest in the politics of our country, which they discuss with much warmth in their favorite beer-house." On August 5, 1854, Gottlieb Brekle formally declared his intent to become a US citizen at some future date.

The earliest surviving evidence of Brekle as a brewer is through his partnership with German goldseeker Frederick A. Ballhaus, who in 1856 established the Golden Gate Brewery on Russian Hill's Union Street, a few blocks west of Washington Square. The demand for beer had continued unabated, and by 1858 San Francisco breweries numbered nineteen, employing about a hundred workers altogether. That same year, another gold discovery, on British Columbia's Fraser River, lured Ballhaus there, where he spent three months losing money. Brekle bought out his absent partner and became, for the first time, the sole proprietor of his very own brewery.

On March 5, 1848, back in Ossweil, Brekle's sister had given birth to a son, Carl Friedrich Brekle, out of wedlock. Years later, Gottlieb Brekle reached out to another sister, Louise Pauline, to see if she could bring his seven-year-old nephew, now Carl Friedrich Deng, to San Francisco. On November 14, 1855, after nearly seven months at sea, Louise and Fritz, as he was called, reached San Francisco. Louise stayed on to marry a French butcher, and Gottlieb and Marie adopted Fritz as their own. The boy would grow up to become Frederick Brekle, Anchor's second brewmaster—and first Fritz!

By 1860, the brewing business was a crucible of competition. That year, the owners of San Francisco's breweries, including Gottlieb Brekle, united to form the local, nearly all German, Brewers' Association, which would play a significant role in future disputes with organized labor.

By 1861, twenty-four breweries were operating in the city, averaging six employees per business, and producing, on average, about two thousand barrels per year.

Beer was measured by the 31-gallon barrel but usually sold by the half barrel. The lion's share came from just one brewery, the Philadelphia, makers of prize-winning "lager beer," which is what California brewers still called their immensely popular California common beer. Seven new breweries opened in 1861, but eight breweries closed, including Gottlieb's Golden Gate Brewery, which burned to the ground on August 3, just as another brewery, Hoen's, had ten years before.

The *Daily Evening Bulletin* carried the story of the conflagration. Filled with melodrama and schadenfreude, it implied, without proof, that the fire had been arson, which was highly unlikely. In those days, California common brewers like Gottlieb Brekle lived with their families in or next door to the brewery, enabling them to monitor the cooling and fermentation of their beers. Burning down his brewery would have meant burning down his family home. Brekle was insured, but for just $2,000 (about $62,000 today) of the estimated $10,000 ($312,000) damage.

Gottlieb was at a crossroads. His brewery in ashes, he decided, having declared his intent years before, to become a US citizen on September 21, 1861. He was strong and healthy, with a full head of black hair, but at forty-two he would have been one of the older—and, at five foot six and a half, shorter than average—soldiers to fight in the Civil War. He knew that his father was still living, and young Fritz, now thirteen, had not seen his own birth parents in over six years. Gottlieb had the insurance money from the fire and, thanks to his citizenship, a new passport. After nine years abroad, it was time to try Germany again.

HOME AND BACK AGAIN

The Brekles returned to Ludwigsburg in late 1861, where they were warmly received. Gottlieb bought an old brewery in an attempt to revive it, but it

or not, nobody will be mustered into the service or whose loyalty or capacity there is the slightest doubt.

Fire on Russian Hill.

Fire broke out in the Golden Gate Brewery at 11¼ o'clock on Saturday night. The brewery stands, or rather the ash-heap that now represents it, stands on the northwest corner of Jones and Union streets, Russian Hill rising with a steep slant just to the west of it, and falling off sharply to Powell street on the east. How the fire was kindled does not come out. The alarm was prompt, and the firemen were prompt, and they promptly stretched their rotten hose up the hill, and got three streams on to the flaming beer barrels, hop bags and dry tindery stuff that composed the building. But the combustibles were too well under way to be stayed, and all was consumed, including the hay house adjoining the brewery west, and the stable in the rear. The loss is estimated loosely at $10,000, on which there was $2,000 insurance. The occupant of the premises, C. Breckel, lost most of his stock.

The fire was another of those beautiful illuminations which the Northsiders have enjoyed so liberally of late. The windows and housetops of the vicinity were full of people, delighted with the spectacle—of course they presumed that nobody but the insurers were suffering—and we noticed on Sunday that about every female from north of Green street, that we met, was sneezing The fire bred an influenza.

COURT OF SESSIONS.—Anna Mulhare has been admitted to bail in $3,000.

turned out he was better with barley than balance sheets. By early 1868, Gottlieb's *Bierbrauerei* was on the auction block, for sale in an out-of-court debt settlement, including horses, sleigh, hay, malt, and hops. The Brekles undoubtedly pined for San Francisco, where such a failure would have been considered a mere bump in the road to success. And in Germany they undoubtedly discovered just how American they had become. Like most of his fellow gold rushers, Gottlieb was not born in California; California was born in him. So, in 1868, the Brekles headed back to the New World—but not before posing for photographs in Ludwigsburg. Both photos are believed to be of Frederick, though it's possible that the formal one may be of Gottlieb (see page 26).

Impoverished but undaunted, the Brekles moved into a boarding house on Russian Hill, at the northwest corner of Mason and Broadway, above a corner grocery. There were about 1,200 such "groceries" in San Francisco, one for every seventy adult males. The groceries were up front and the "sample room" in the back, a "loafing place" frequented by working-class men from the

Photograph Weigel   Ludwigsburg

neighborhood. And yet, despite the popularity of these haunts, as one observer wrote in 1869, "drunkenness is not by any means a rule in these places. . . . For the town works, and the morrow brings its labor." Brekle bought the grocery.

On March 4, 1869, Spring Valley Water Works, which had two reservoirs on Russian Hill, hooked up the water at 1501 Mason Street, facilitating the grocery's transformation into a small saloon/brewery, known variously as Mason Street Brewery, Breckle's Brewery, and Germania Brewery. "The sturdy German," wrote San Franciscan Benjamin Lloyd in 1875, "does not forego the *Bier Halle*; the fragrant fumes from his favorite *weed* [hops] tempt him to traffic in that article. . . . A brewery would be incomplete without its German proprietor, and the beer garden without its German patrons. . . . His presence in San Francisco . . . is indispensable."

Situated a few blocks up from the notorious "deadfalls" of the Barbary Coast, the "low beer and dance cellars" where toothsome "beer-slingers" welcomed the curious into San Francisco's seedy underworld of gambling, prostitution, and shang-haiing, Gottlieb and Frederick had plenty of places to sell his kegs, enlisting the help of two young men who roomed with them, Jacob Kihlmeyer and Frederick Blankenhorn. Despite sales of just 163 barrels, their nascent brewery still finished 1869 twenty-second out of San Francisco's twenty-eight breweries.

Unbeknownst to his customers, Breckle's Brewery was a dress rehearsal for a more ambitious production.

GOLDEN CITY BREWERY
(1871–1888)

*Recklessness is in the air. . . . The roaring winds off the Pacific make you drunk with it. . . .
The young men are experienced in business and embark on vast enterprises, take partners as
experienced as themselves, and go to pieces with as much splendor as their neighbors. . . . As
far as regards certain tough virtues, they are the pick of the earth. The inept or weakly died
on route or went under in the days of construction.*

—Rudyard Kipling, letter from San Francisco (1889)

On May 10, 1869, at Promontory Summit, Utah
Territory, railroad baron Leland Stanford swung at
a ceremonial golden spike, symbolizing the completion of the transcontinental railroad. He
missed, but manifest destiny's iron horse was a hit,
connecting the mushrooming metropolis of San
Francisco, America's tenth largest city in 1870, to
the big cities of the East. California was shifting
from a mining economy to an agricultural one, its
hops and barley now among the lauded crops
transported by rail. The railroad, as it turned out,
brought more workers to California than there
were jobs. But entrepreneurial brewers like Brekle,
who had seen people drink beer in good times and
bad, remained hopeful.

> San Francisco had twenty-eight breweries in
> 1870, employing 212 people, producing
> 140,700 barrels of beer annually—215 pints
> per capita.

In the summer of 1871, before the economy
went south, the ever-enterprising Gottlieb Brekle
had a bold idea for a bigger, better brewery. To
make it a reality, he needed a new location, a new
partner, and a new name.

In 1863, German immigrant Charles Grimm
had opened a watering hole on the western slope of
Russian Hill, on the south side of Pacific, between
Larkin and Hyde, one of 878 places in the city where

Russian Hill, from Gough St.
The steeple is at Larkin & Pacific. ›

View from Telegraph Hill (1873)

alcoholic beverages were sold at the time. Charles and his son Henry tended bar at Grimm's beer and billiard saloon, just four blocks west of Brekle's Germania Brewery. By 1871, though, Charles had become a special policeman and was looking to sell.

Bavarian immigrant and former Union soldier William F. Noethig worked at John Wieland's Philadelphia Brewery as a driver/salesman, marrying the owner's niece, Frederika Wieland, in 1867. He was looking for a business partner.

On September 18, 1871, Brekle—having sold his Germania Brewery to one of his brewers, Frederick Blankenhorn—partnered with Noethig to buy Charles Grimm's beer-and-billiard saloon for $3,500 (about $82,000 today), transforming it into the brewery/saloon that, twenty-four-plus years and several names later, would become Anchor Brewery. In early January 1872 they advertised their

newly christened Golden City Brewery—a nod to San Francisco's mid-century sobriquet—in one of San Francisco's German-language newspapers, the *California Demokrat*. The "best Lager Beer" that they made, of course, was similar to the other so-called lagers on the Pacific Coast; it was in actuality California common beer.

When Noethig—who was doing Brekle a favor by lending his money and Wieland know-how to this start-up—left to establish his own successful enterprise in the Mission District, the Humboldt Brewery, "Gottlieb Breckle & Co." (that is, Gottlieb and Marie) became sole owner of the Golden City Brewery. An early 1873 ad in another German-language newspaper, the *Humorist*, proudly affirms this. There were just three employees: Frederick Brekle, brewer; Frederick Kurtz, brewer; and Wilhelm Netie, driver/salesman.

Golden City Brauerei,
1431 Pacific Strasse, nahe Larkin
Gottlieb Bredle) Eigenthümer
Wilhelm Röthig)

Dem Publikum zur gefälligen Notiz, daß wir in unserer Brauerei stets das beste Lagerbier haben und daßelbe transportfrei nach irgend einem Theile der Stadt liefern. Mit der Brauerei ist eine Bar verbunden. — Um zahlreichen Besuch bitten ergebenst

no2t3mt   **G. Breckle & W. Röthig**

GOLDEN CITY BREWERY.
1431 Pacific Street, near Larkin
Gottlieb Breckle
Wilhelm Nöthig   Owners
To the public for their pleasing notice, that we always have the best Lager Beer in our brewery, and its delivery to any part of the town is free of charge.
There is a bar connected to the brewery.
—For numerous visits we humbly ask,
G. Breckle & W. Nöthig

GOLDEN CITY BRAUEREI.
1413 Pacific Straße, nahe Larkin
Gottlieb Breckle & Co,
Eigenthümer.

Diese neue und großartige Brauerei des alten Pioneer Brauers nimmt jetzt Bestellungen entgegen und können Alle sich einer vorzüglichen Qualität des abgelieferter Bieres versichert halten,

GOLDEN CITY BREWERY.
1413* Pacific Street, near Larkin
Gottlieb Breckle & Co.,
Owner.
This new and magnificent brewery of the old pioneer brewer takes orders now and all can be sure to receive an excellent quality of the delivered beer.

*The address was 1431. "1413" was Anchor's first typo.

In early 1872, young Frederick, who continued to work alongside his father, married. By the following year he had a son, Frederick Jr., who would grow up to become a third-generation brewer.

> In 1873, Golden City ranked twenty-ninth of San Francisco's thirty-four breweries, producing 585 barrels of beer—just 0.3% of the city's total. Coincidentally, in addition to being the inaugural year of the cable car, 1873 was the year that America had more breweries—4,131—than ever before—or ever again, until 2015.

Based on his property valuation and taxes, Gottlieb Brekle was described in 1873 as one of San Francisco's financially "heavy men," tied for fifteenth "heaviest" brewer. But his "weight" was heavily mortgaged, and, while saving for a new steam engine and boiler, Brekle's debts caught up with him in a nearly tragic way. There had already been one stabbing at the brewery in 1873. On Saturday night, April 12, one of the assailants returned with two friends to get the money Brekle owed him.

Christopher Woerner [sic] was one of 150 men employed at the city's two barrel manufactories, producing 235,000 barrels, half-barrels, and kegs annually. One of the cooper's accomplices got away, one got off, and Woerner pled guilty to assault in Municipal Court.

The Wall Street Panic of 1873 precipitated a nationwide depression. Over the next two years 150,000 migrated to California. In search of work, they found themselves in competition with the Irish and Chinese, who had built the very railroad that brought these new "immigrants" west. Just when the 1870s couldn't look any bleaker, the Bank of California collapsed in 1875. But San Francisco's brewing industry not only survived but thrived, as breweries are wont to do, during the tough economic times of the mid- to late 1870s. Golden City Brewery's growth, from 585 barrels in 1873 to 2,265 barrels in 1876, was one of those success stories. But until that year, Brekle and his fellow brewers remained blissfully unaware that a new, and ultimately more implacable foe was fermenting just a few hours by rail to the northeast: real lager beer.

GENUINE LAGER'S CALIFORNIA DEBUT

For nearly three decades, the brewers of the Golden State had been able to call their product "lager" without fear of contradiction or competition. Everything changed when a new brewery staked its claim as the maker of California's first and only *genuine* lager beer. "A formidable outside rival," warned the *San Francisco Chronicle*, "has sprung up in the Second District of Truckee, from which is supplied the suddenly popular beverage styled BOCA BEER . . . conducted on the system of the Eastern lager-beer breweries . . . with extensive ice-banked vaults, for producing the effect of slow fermentation."

Boca was the name of a California mountain town, about two hundred miles northeast of San Francisco, where the mouth (*boca* in Spanish) of the Little Truckee River flows into the Truckee River. It originated as Construction Camp 17 for

the Central Pacific along the eastbound route of the transcontinental railroad. A sawmill there provided lumber for snowsheds, telegraph poles, and railroad ties. When the camp's logging pond froze over, an opportunity presented itself for the harvesting of natural ice.

Boca Brewing Co.

Bottled

The BOCA BOTTLED BEER is made from the Superior California Barley So Eagerly sought for By EASTERN BREWERS

Lager Beer

BREWERY, BOCA, CAL.

GENERAL OFFICES

DEPOT AND BOTTLING DEP'T.

SAN FRANCISCO, CAL.

In the summer of 1875, Latimer Emery Doan of the Boca Mill and Ice Company realized that he had both the lumber to build a brewery and enough ice to lager beer for months at a time year-round. Boca Brewing Company incorporated on August 5, 1875, "for the manufacture of Beer, Ale, and Porter." In April 1876, Boca shipped its Boca Beer by rail to San Francisco, where it was successfully test marketed in anticipation of the city's bibulous celebration of America's centennial. Lagered at near-freezing temperatures for months on end, this genuine lager beer was unlike any beer ever made in the Golden State. The California lager revolution had begun.

Unrivaled in California and Nevada, Boca billed itself as "the only lager beer brewery on the Pacific Coast," disparaging all other so-called lagers, aka *steam beers*, with the lukewarm epithet "underbrewed beer." San Francisco brewers, who had been calling their California commons *lagers* for years, were exposed. Before long, the quality and popularity of Boca's golden elixir prompted the San Francisco Bay Area's biggest breweries to make the substantial investment in ice-making

equipment and mechanical refrigeration. In 1884, San Jose's Fredericksburg Brewing Company became the first California brewery to compete with Boca in the "true lager" category. The following year, San Francisco's National Brewing Company entered the race, with long-standing volume leader Philadelphia Brewery nipping at its heels.

By the time the Boca Brewery burned down in a suspicious fire on the evening of January 9, 1893, nearly every sizable brewery in California was making genuine lager beer, whether they harvested, bought, or made their own ice. The Boca Brewery was never rebuilt, but its erstwhile competitors flourished. Most continued making the old California common beer alongside the new, true lager beer. Since the former could no longer be called lager, the colloquial nickname *steam beer*, already in use by imbibers, was embraced by brewers as well, to distinguish the two brews more clearly.

THE ANCHOR BREWING STORY

THE REAL COSTS OF BREWING

In those days, saloonkeepers bought a barrel of steam for $5 to sell at 5¢ a glass, while a barrel of true lager could be had for $8 and sold for 10¢ a glass. The algebraically adept barkeep steered his patrons toward lager over steam, increasing his profit per glass and setting in motion the slow decline of steam beer. Breweries like Golden City couldn't afford to "upgrade" to true lager production. But it maintained its reputation for quality, selling 1,653 barrels in 1884.

But without real growth, Golden City couldn't take advantage of economies of scale, and without lager, they couldn't raise their prices to offset the increasing cost of raw materials, labor, and taxes. All this made the Brekles's mortgage even more burdensome than it already had been. To bring in more money, Frederick moonlighted as a cable-car brakeman. But in 1885, Gottlieb and Marie, having borrowed against their mortgage too many times, defaulted. In November, real-estate tycoon Alexander Montgomery, who once advertised in the *Chronicle*, "I HEREBY NOTIFY THE PUBLIC NOT to trust my wife on my account," sued the Brekles for $8,500 ($265,000 today) for recovery of accrued interest and costs related to their mortgage. With nominal assets and over $6,000 in liabilities, their mortgage was foreclosed. Gottlieb Brekle filed for insolvency in Superior Court,

whereupon the sheriff took possession of Gottlieb and Marie's estate.

A sheriff's sale on December 14, 1886, included the 54-ft by 137.5-ft lot on which Gottlieb and Marie's brewery stood, its adjacent alley—called Brekle's and Grimm's Place—and "all vats, machinery, steam engines, elevators, pumps, pipes, granaries, cooper-shops, and stables." 1887 was an even more tragic year for Gottlieb and his family. Marie died on April 19, 1887. And by the end of June

1887, Montgomery's acquisition was final. He owned everything, at a cost of $10,345 (over $322,000) for the brewery and $5 for the alley.

But forty-niner/capitalist/philanthropist Alexander Montgomery was in the business of real estate, not brewing. So he did the shrewd and refreshingly compassionate thing: he hung onto the property and leased it back to Gottlieb, who died at sixty-eight on January 25, 1888, at peace knowing that the brewery he built would live on.

CO-OPERATIVE BREWERY
(1888–1896)

The Co-operative Brewing Association ... was started mainly to aid the lock-out of the Brewery Workmen, as many dealers in steam beer claimed they could not get supplied by any other than the boycotted breweries. ... It is claimed [the brewery] can turn out as much steam beer and porter as any other brewery on the coast.

—San Francisco Chronicle (1892)

Although Frederick Brekle—assisted by teenage son Frederick Jr. and three workers, all of whom lived at the brewery—kept Golden City afloat into the early 1890s, he lacked the wherewithal if not the interest to convert his brewery to the production of genuine lager beer. Small, antiquated, anachronistic, Golden City was becoming an amber eddy in a golden sea.

In 1890, a newly formed syndicate of English capitalists—San Francisco Breweries, Limited— took no interest in Golden City nor any other small brewer, choosing to invest in ten of the Bay Area's largest breweries. The syndicate's long-range goal, revealed by the *Chronicle* but never fully realized, was one of total consolidation, such that "every customer will be served with Philadelphia [Wieland], Fredericksburg, National Brewery, or any other brand which he may desire and all of the different beers will be brewed in one great establishment." Instead, as it played out, the syndicate's breweries remained in separate locations, their original owners retaining one-third interest as an incentive not to compete. San Francisco Breweries' cash helped its breweries recoup their investment in refrigeration for the production of genuine lager, compete with refrigerated railcars full of beer from places like St. Louis, and weather tumultuous labor disputes that, surprisingly, propelled the city's pint-sized Golden City Brewery into a starring role.

THE DIGNITY OF WORK

Forty-niners learned to value the dignity of work in the goldfields, where, regardless of past, present, or future class, goldseekers toiled side by side with the hope of striking it rich. There the

Executive Commiitee

United Brewery

Workmen's Union

Of the Pacific Coast.

UNITY IS STRENGTH

the rising union star of both: German sailor Alfred Fuhrman.

In June 1886, Fuhrman organized the local Brewers' and Maltsters' Union of the Pacific Coast. In early 1887 it became Local 16 of the newly organized National Union of United Brewery Workmen of the United States. Although its name would evolve over the years, its mission from the beginning was to guard "the noble trade of the brewer's craft."

Wages at the time ranged from $50 to $60 a month ($1,550 to $1,850 today), with workers expected to work ten-to-fourteen-hour days Monday through Saturday and three to nine hours on Sundays.

80% of beer on the West Coast at the time was California common and 20% genuine lager. Those who made the former usually lived at the brewery at their own expense, frequently working excessive, nonconsecutive hours to cope with unpredictable fermentations.

In May 1887, under Fuhrman's leadership, the workers' union voiced its demands to the Brewers' Protective Association, which represented the brewery owners. With the exception of Golden City, embroiled as it was in financial troubles, the owners had girded themselves for this fight by joining the national United States Brewers' Association (USBA). The union position was that only union men should be hired (the so-called closed shop); that workers had the right to live and board wherever they wanted to; that they should be paid weekly, with ten-hour days, six-day weeks and no more than three-hour Sundays; that the apportionment of hours in the steam beer breweries be agreed upon between the owner or foreman and the workers; that a board of arbitration should be established to settle disputes; and that they were entitled to free beer.

common bonds of the self-employed miners were more sociopolitical than socioeconomic. In Gold Rush San Francisco, on the other hand, there were plenty of traditional jobs—high-paying ones—and few workers. Frequent fires necessitated frequent rebuilds, leading to a strike by carpenters in 1849, followed in 1850 by the organization of the city's workers—from teamsters to typographers. Over the next three decades, California's unions, mostly unaffiliated with their national counterparts, waxed and waned in tandem with California's isolated economy, as San Francisco evolved from a frontier town, dependent on its harbor for goods, to a more self-sufficient manufacturing city.

As San Francisco emerged from the economic doldrums of the 1870s, many of its industries unionized, especially those with large workforces, where the capital was more variable (the cost of labor) than constant (the cost of plant, equipment, and raw materials). In 1880, averaging just seven workers per brewery and with no national union to encourage and support them, the city's brewery workers remained reluctant to organize, despite deplorable conditions, long hours, and relatively low wages. But as they witnessed the mounting successes of the Federated Trades Council (San Francisco's union umbrella organization) and its Coast Seamen's Union, they decided to hitch their beer wagons to

Brewery owners acceded to all of the demands except the critical one—not free beer, which was de rigueur in those days, but the closed shop (union members only). So the union employed their two most powerful weapons: strike and boycott. Their strategy was to go on strike one brewery at a time. They started at Wieland's Philadelphia Brewery, encouraging the beer-loving union town's thirsty laborers and their bartenders to boycott Wieland's "scab beer." Thanks to the national union, strike benefits between $6 and $10 ($187 to $312) per week empowered the striking Wieland workers, and those who followed in their footsteps, to hold out.

The scheme worked, and a mere two months later the owners were defeated, agreeing to increase wages to $14 to $16 a week and all other demands. The battle was won, but the war was far from over. The owners, backed by an emboldened USBA, broke their agreement in 1888, implementing their two most powerful weapons: the lockout (discharging union employees) and the blacklist (so they could not work elsewhere). The workers fought back, this time boycotting the United States Brewery. Breweries in San Jose and Sacramento helped supply union beer to San Francisco's saloons, contributing to another union victory in June 1889.

In October 1891, in preparation for another skirmish with the employers, the local union, at Fuhrman's behest, assessed each of the union's six hundred members $20 ($624), more than a week's wages. The union then used the assessment to

acquire the Golden City Brewery in February 1892, its building and property still owned by real-estate magnate Alexander Montgomery and run by Frederick Brekle and son Fred Jr. With some sense of relief, perhaps, Fred Sr. moved on, going into the beer bottling business with his son-in-law, Adolph Manfredini. Fred Jr. worked with them for a few years, eventually opening his own establishment, the short-lived Richmond Brewery, near the Cliff House.

CO-OPERATIVE BREWING

On February 28, 1892, Golden City Brewery got a new name when it was incorporated as the Co-operative Brewing Company. Its directors, all involved in organized labor and nearly all attorneys, included England-born lawyer Harry William Hutton, president, and Alfred Fuhrman, treasurer. The new board focused its attention and the union's money on upgrades to the twenty-year-old Golden City Brewery. Ironically, despite the growing popularity of genuine lager, they chose not to install mechanical refrigeration. Rather, they added a fourth story and made improvements to the physical plant, reportedly enabling the newly christened Co-operative Brewery to turn out a hundred barrels a day. About a thousand attendees turned out for free beer, sandwiches, and union talk at a housewarming April 13. And that year's Labor Day parade featured an elaborate Co-operative Brewery float, representing a functioning brewery overseen by Gambrinus, mythical ruler of the Kingdom of Beer.

There were three kinds of breweries in San Francisco in the summer of 1892: those that refused to employ union men; those owned by San Francisco Breweries, Limited, which employed both union and nonunion workers under a "don't ask, don't tell" policy; and a single union stronghold, the Co-operative Brewery, offering the local union alternative to boycotted beer. "We reminded

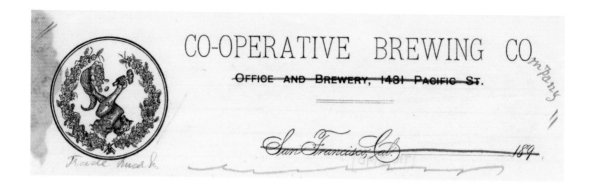

the saloonkeepers," recalled Fuhrman, "of the fact that their patrons consisted principally of working men, and that it was the desire of working men that they should not have scab beer there, and it would be a favor to labor to dispense with that beer and take union beer."

German brewer/maltster Ludwig Berg landed a job in the basement malthouse of the Co-operative Brewery at $17 a week. Constantine (Constant) Harth, who had been cellarman at the Chicago Brewing Company on Pine Street, became the Co-operative's foreman. At a union meeting in February 1893, Harth nearly gave his life for the cause. Frank Bucher, who had succeeded Fuhrman as the union's general secretary, was accused of collusion with the boycotted breweries' owners. A fracas ensued. Ordered to leave the meeting, Bucher

drew his revolver, pointed it directly at Harth's chest, and pulled the trigger. The gun did not fire, but Bucher was still in big trouble. On top of attempted murder, he was accused of embezzling $7,000 (over $218,000) of the union's promissory notes from the Co-operative Brewery, sadly hastening its eventual dissolution.

Harth, in addition to his malting and brewing skills, was a talented inventor. Notably, in 1893, he applied for a patent for an improved "steam beer faucet" of his own design. From the days of the gold rush, California's lively common beer had a reputation for being difficult to pour. Indeed, inventors had been devising "steam beer" tapping mechanisms since the early 1870s, their patents representing the earliest known use of "steam beer" *per se* in print. Locally, the tricky process was

so familiar that it served up an easily understood simile. In 1890, the *Chronicle* observed that former president Grover Cleveland seemed "to keep a certain stock of political platitudes on tap, and whenever the faucet is turned the right way they gush out, like steam beer, with more froth than body." So confident was Harth in the potential of his faucet that he presold the exclusive East Bay rights to it in advance of receiving his patent on February 27, 1894. It was a hit, but soon eclipsed by the *ne plus ultra* of faucets, pictured here.

A CASUALTY OF WAR

By providing local union beer, the Co-operative Brewery and resourceful men like Harth and Berg made a significant contribution to the union cause. But the union had miscalculated, thinking that the Co-operative Brewery's union-made steam beer would continue to be viewed by an increasingly fickle public as an acceptable substitute for non-union genuine lager. And they didn't plan on the non-union brewery owners denying the saloon-keepers, and thus their parched patrons, any beer at all if they chose to serve Co-operative beer. Its boycott losing steam, the union soon lost the battle. The brewery owners had also miscalculated, spending most of their energy and war-chest on crushing the Co-operative Brewery instead of the union itself, which rose again, stronger than ever. By the end of the decade, San Francisco's breweries would be completely unionized.

A casualty of war, the Co-operative Brewery was sued for $9,612 ($311,000 today) in November 1894, by its biggest creditor, maltster Frank A. Lux. On December 10, 1894, in the brewery's second sheriff's sale in eight years, Lux purchased the stock and plant of the Co-operative Brewery for $7,400 ($240,000). He thus followed Gottlieb Brekle, Frederick Brekle Sr., and then the brewery workers of San Francisco, as the brewery's fourth owner. Berg continued working for the brewery

until 1896, Harth until 1897, two examples of the unbroken continuity of Anchor's enduring brewing tradition.

Alsatian immigrant Francois Antoine Lux went by Frank A. Lux to better fit into the Teutonic world of San Francisco brewing. Naturalized on May 14, 1857, in gold country's Placerville (better known as Hangtown, culinary home of the Hangtown Fry), Lux was first a miner, then a brewer, then a maltster. His acquisition of the Co-operative Brewing Company was neither dream nor destiny. Incorporated on April 15, 1895, F. A. Lux Brewing Company was sold by its eponymous owner less than a year later. Sadly, Lux died February 28, 1897 and Frederick Sr. died July 30, so neither got to see their brewery flourish under new management.

PART TWO

RAISING ANCHOR

ANCHOR BREWERY
(1896–1906)

Upon the surface of amber-colored beer floated foam as evanescent and light as thistle down. The receptacle holding the beer was as deep and as musical, as it was clinked against another, as a bell of Shandon. . . . Clearly through its translucent sides could be observed the sparkling effervescence, the riotous ascent of sparkling globules which conferred, as a reward for patronage of a plebeian beverage, a delightful tang, in which was all the lusty flavor of sun-kissed fields of bearded barley, waving and rustling in the wind. . . . The beer percolated softly as cool spring water drips from a mossy spring down a grateful throat, not staying nor speeding the clouds of yesterday vanished as a wraith. The present became radiant with expectation, money was dross and the future . . . was filled with premonitions of pleasing accomplishment.

—**San Francisco Call**, July 12, 1896

L: Pre-Prohibition glass, R: Post-Repeal glass

In the summer of 1896, the *Call* published a story by an anonymous reporter called "A Prince for a Day in San Francisco on Two Bits," chronicling the hidden joys of being a spendthrift in the Paris of the West. The day begins in a saloon on the Embarcadero, where a nickel buys "three shiny frankfurter sausages, bread ad libitum, and potations from a deep glass in which foamed the amber liquid popularly known as steam beer." Six and a half months earlier, he might have been writing about Lux Steam Beer. Instead, his flowery portrayal of this heady elixir might well be the earliest known tasting notes for Anchor Steam Beer, which owes its name to Ernst F. Baruth.

Ernst Friedrich Baruth was born on April 28, 1843 in Oxstedt, Germany. Like Gottlieb Brekle, Baruth was a carpenter, German immigrant, and aspiring entrepreneur. In 1868, he opened a grocery and liquor store with his brother-in-law at Post and Hyde, just a few blocks from Grimm's saloon. Fast-forward to 1884, when Baruth, now a saloonkeeper, saw a business opportunity that looked like a gold mine: bottled soda water. He partnered with grocery and liquor store owner Henry Goetze to form Goetze & Baruth and the California Soda Works. Located at Octavia and Ivy, it even had its own trademark, which they registered on June 30, 1886.

STEAM BEER IN THE LATE 1890S

A tattered reprint of "The Ballad of Steam Beer," written by San Francisco–born William Sanford Barnes, resides in Anchor's archive. The sudsy sonnet was first published in 1897 in *The Wave*, a San Francisco weekly, alongside excerpts from a new Frank Norris novel. *McTeague* is Norris's tale of a concertina-playing, steam-beer-swilling, Polk Street dentist, who regularly takes his to-go pitcher to a nearby saloon for a refill. Both could easily have been written about Anchor.

E. F. BARUTH
1886

Californians had been registering and disputing trademarks since the early 1860s, and California Soda Works became one of a dozen soda companies sued in 1890 for imitating a "Sarsaparilla and Iron Water" trademark. Goetze & Baruth lost their case and $3,040 ($95,000). Tapped out, they ended their venture. Baruth, smoothly transitioning from the bubble business to the foam trade, next partnered with Henry C. Kroenke, proprietor of Oakland's Tivoli ("I Lov It" backward) Saloon. In March 1892, they purchased the venerable Lafayette Brewery, which had amassed liabilities of $25,800 ($805,000) and a host of creditors—including maltster Frank Lux. Renaming it the American Brewery, Baruth & Kroenke used their business acumen to steer it back into the black.

Meanwhile, Ernst and Doris Baruth's daughter Ida had fallen for Otto Schinkel Jr. Born in Germany on April 9, 1869, he was a clerk at his father Otto's grocery/liquor store. They were married at the Baruth's on November 26, 1890. Ida's "dowry" would be a job for Otto Jr. as driver/salesman for Baruth & Kroenke's American Brewery.

In early 1896, Baruth sold his interest in the American Brewery to Kroenke to create a partnership with his son-in-law, called Baruth & Schinkel. In January or early February—the exact date is unknown—they bought Frank Lux's twenty-four-year-old brewery at 1431 Pacific, leasing the lot from the Alexander Montgomery estate. They christened their eight- to ten-thousand-barrel brewery Anchor, its fourth name to date. Above its entrance, they hung a handmade sign. It featured an anchor nestled between ANCHOR and BREWERY, as if to highlight the name's powerful allusion to the port of San Francisco. Inside, the brewery continued making California common and porter, but now as Anchor Steam Beer and Anchor Porter. Most of Lux's employees stayed on, including a Frenchman, brewer Louis Raspiller. He was promoted to foreman by Baruth, for whom he had worked at the American Brewery.

By 1899, there were twenty-four breweries in San Francisco, down from 1896's twenty-seven. Despite the growing popularity of genuine lager beer, fin de siècle San Francisco still embraced its indigenous steam beer—common beer for the

OTTO SCHINKEL
BREWER
Proprietor Anchor Brewery. Born Germany. Arrived
in California 1876. Address, San Francisco.

ERNST F. BARUTH
BREWER
Proprietor Anchor Brewery. Born Germany, 1843.
Arrived in Cal. 1867. Address, San Francisco.

common man and woman—as one of its quirkily original local charms. Anchor was in its heyday in 1899, its fifteen employees now producing Anchor Steam Beer exclusively, at a rate of ten thousand barrels a year. That same year, a boosterish publication touted the city's many charms, ranking San Francisco with Milwaukee "as one of the greatest beer producing cities in the Union," its steam beer "the favorite beverage of the people," containing a "snap and flavor found in no other drink of this character." Hailed as "wide-awake, progressive businessmen," its owners Baruth and Schinkel "believe in up-to-date ideas in the brewing" of their very traditional beer, and take "great care" to maintain its "uniform quality," an Anchor leitmotiv first noted in Gottlieb Brekle's advertising twenty-seven years before. The brewery, they continued in chamber-of-commerce type fashion, is "fitted out with the very latest improved machinery, and nothing is left undone to place beer on the market to perfection." In short, when one drinks steam beer as "it is brewed at the house Anchor Brewery, it is truly a delicious beverage."

As a driver at Anchor, Otto Jr. was in a position of great responsibility—delivering beer, retrieving empty kegs, collecting payments, and making sales calls. But he liked to play the ponies and wasn't very good at it. In May 1905, his gambling caught up with him. Baruth became suspicious of his son-in-law's activities and insisted on signing all the company checks. When two checks Baruth didn't sign—totaling $1,100 ($34,000)—bounced, Baruth sued to dissolve their partnership and sell the otherwise successful business. By that time, Schinkel had already appropriated $5,000 ($156,000) more than his interest in the company. In the end, however, Baruth's love for his daughter triumphed over his distrust of his feckless son-in-law. Instead of dissolving Anchor Brewery, Baruth incorporated it on July 7, 1905, bringing more trust and accountability to an expanded organization. Of the 2,500 shares—at $15 per share—830 (valued at $12,450, $388,000 today) went to his son-in-law and 5 shares each to Otto Schinkel Sr. and Ernst; the remaining 1,660 shares were divided evenly between two new investors, Albert Graf, who had been a San Francisco brewer since 1878 and Anchor brewer since 1903,

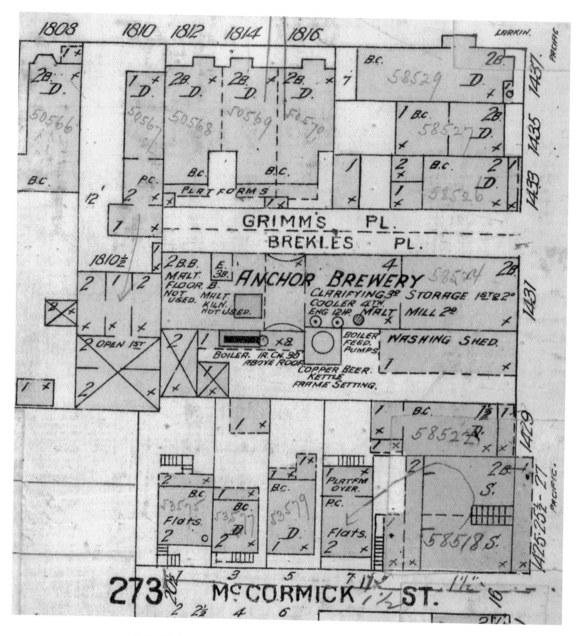

This 1905 fire insurance map shows the layout of the brewery.

and baker Nicholas Wirtz. In late 1905 or early 1906, a grand photo commemorated the brewery's incorporation (see page 40). Otto Jr. is driving the lead wagon. His father and his daughter Alice are in the carriage. Baruth is behind it.

Baruth had not bought a modern brewery from Lux, equipped to make genuine lager. But thanks to the Co-operative Brewery upgrade in 1892, he had a state-of-the-*old*-art California common brewery, ready and waiting for an astute entrepreneur like him, who understood both business and brewing. Sadly, a heart attack felled Baruth on Saint Valentine's Day 1906. Otto Jr. took over the brewery and, thanks to Baruth's wisdom and foresight, its

incorporation precluded further misconduct. But San Francisco, in the words of photographer Edwin Rosskam, "was born out of gold-hunger and nursed on catastrophes." Nothing could possibly safeguard Anchor or the City by the Bay from what lay in store.

EARTHQUAKE

On Wednesday, April 18, 1906, at 5:12 a.m., San Francisco shook like a runaway stagecoach. It was a temblor of biblical proportions, a momentous magnitude 7.9 earthquake lasting between forty-five and sixty seconds and rupturing 296 miles along the San Andreas Fault. In San Francisco, buildings collapsed, water mains burst, and fifty-two fires broke out. San Francisco was, according to eyewitness Jack London, "like the crater of a volcano." The fires were still burning Saturday morning, three days after the quake.

Fully 508 city blocks—4.7 square miles—and 28,188 buildings were destroyed. The damage was estimated at $400 million (nearly $13 billion) and left 225,000 of San Francisco's 400,000 inhabitants homeless. Although contemporaneous reports cited between 478 and 498 killed, in reality the death toll exceeded 3,000.

Of San Francisco's twenty-seven breweries (including both Jackson Brewery plants), eleven were destroyed and eight damaged. Hermann Noethig—son of William Noethig, Brekle's original partner in the Golden City Brewery nearly thirty-five years earlier—worked for one of the survivors: The Union Brewing & Malting Company, at Eighteenth Street and Florida, was outside of the fire zone and only slightly damaged by the quake. An amateur photographer, Hermann walked the rubble-filled streets, photographing what remained of the city's beer industry, including a particularly poignant view of Anchor Brewery (see above). Its wood-frame building had helped Anchor ride out the quake, but it was obliterated when fire swept through its Russian Hill neighborhood on April 19. Fellow brewer and amateur photographer Theodore Rueger recalled, "We saw a kettle standing on the side of a hill, the only thing to indicate that the Anchor Brewery had been

there." Had Anchor been located just a few blocks away, near some houses at the summit of Russian Hill, it would have survived.

San Francisco's Mayor Eugene Schmitz ordered all of the city's saloons closed, a microcosmic prequel to nationwide prohibition. Breweries in a position to do so were permitted to ship their beer out of town, while, according to the sanguine Brewers' Protective Association, "the sufferers are making ready to rebuild, and, I dare say, we shall have better and more completely equipped Breweries in this city than we had ever before."

SOUTH OF THE SLOT
(1906–1920)

Old San Francisco, which is the San Francisco of only the other day, the day before the earthquake, was divided midway by the Slot. The Slot was an iron crack that ran along the center of Market street, and from the Slot arose the burr of the ceaseless, endless cable that was hitched at will to the cars it dragged up and down. . . . North of the Slot were the theaters, hotels, and shopping district, the banks and the staid, respectable business houses. South of the Slot were the factories, slums, laundries, machine-shops, boiler works, and the abodes of the working class.

—**Jack London, "South of the Slot"** (1909)

To preclude a drunken revel, Mayor Schmitz waited until the morning *after* Independence Day, 1906, to lift the emergency ban on alcohol that he had imposed in the aftermath of the earthquake and fire. San Francisco's long thirst was broken, as San Francisco's six hundred saloonkeepers helped return the temporary temperance town to its frisky pre-quake ways. Not until April 18, recalled the *Call*, had San Francisco ever been "known as a town patterned after the dreams of the prohibitionist. From ocean to ocean our city has been celebrated for the elegance of its liquid emporiums, its jovial bartenders, its choice cocktails, and world-renowned steam beer. Every tourist swore our steam beer was worthy of such an original metropolis of the Golden Gate." Now, after nearly three long, dry months, the city rejoiced in its return, especially "down in the south of Market street districts," where "the big steams are just as popular as before the fire."

His brewery destroyed and his father-in-law dead, Otto Schinkel Jr. had little to celebrate. Undaunted and resilient, he set about finding a new location and a new partner. Although upbuilding, as San Franciscans called it, was already underway on Russian Hill, Schinkel looked "South

of the Slot" instead. After all, that was where most of his working-class customers lived and worked. And for a new partner he chose Joseph Kraus, born August 18, 1869.

German farmer Kraus reinvented himself as Bay Area brewer Kraus in 1888 at the Oakland Brewery, "pioneer paradise of the thirsty way-farer." Over the next fifteen years, the itinerant brewer worked for five breweries, including, from 1898 to 1903, Oakland's Anchor Brewery. Founded in 1894 at 49th and Shattuck, it was a completely separate entity and unrelated to San Francisco's Anchor Brewery, though the two breweries have Kraus in common. In 1903, he returned to San Francisco to brew at the Milwaukee Brewery, whose wood-frame building, like Anchor's, was destroyed by fire after the 1906 quake. Although the Milwaukee Brewery would also be rebuilt, Kraus opted after the quake to start fresh with Schinkel, a decision that cemented his connection with Anchor for the next forty-five-plus years.

As luck would have it, Schinkel had been buy-ing malt for Anchor from Joseph Schweitzer of Bauer & Schweitzer Malt House in North Beach, which was also recovering from the quake and fire. Schweitzer had a lot South of the Slot, which he generously leased to Schinkel and Kraus for ten years at $720 per year. It was at the southeast cor-ner of 18th Street and Hampshire, across the street from where the old Viking Brewery once stood. As architect they chose August Maritzen, who had moved to San Francisco from Chicago in 1902. His Jackson Brewery, a Midwestern-style brick-and-mortar edifice under construction when the quake hit, was ravaged, its majestic tower collapsing in a fatal heap. Lesson learned, Maritzen designed a noble wooden structure for Schinkel and Kraus, but with a significant twist (see page 15 and endpa-pers). Anchor's competitors were rebuilding their breweries as state-of-the-art *twentieth*-century breweries, incorporating the latest innovations and equipment. Schinkel and Kraus chose to rebuild Anchor as a *nineteenth*-century brewery, reprising the throwback San Francisco technologies—coolships; shallow, open-pan fer-mentors; in-barrel kräusening—instead of modern refrigeration, closed fermentation, pasteurization, and bottling, all of which would have taken longer, cost more, sacrificed Anchor's legacy, and forced Anchor into direct competition with the big lager breweries in town.

LOSES BALANCE AND IS CRUSHED BENEATH CAR

OTTO SCHINKEL JR.

J. KRAUS   AUG. F. MEYER, MGR.   HENRY TIETJEN

STEAM BEER

Anchor Brewing COMPANY

18TH & Hampshire Sts
San Francisco.

TELEPHONE
MISSION 2488

Maritzen completed his design for the new Anchor Brewery just six months after the quake. The building was still under construction on January 26, 1907, when Schinkel saw it for the last time. Hours later, as he boarded a Bryant Street streetcar, it lurched forward, throwing him into its lethal path. Just thirty-seven, Schinkel had been an Anchor Brewery owner for eleven years. In his pocket was a checkbook showing a balance of $40,000—well over $1.2 million today.

After Schinkel's tragic demise, his extended family showed no interest in the brewery. So Kraus partnered with German-Americans Henry Tietjen, who had a saloon thereabouts, and brewer August Frederick Meyer. On August 15, 1906, Meyer's Shasta Brewing Co., on Treat near 19th Street, had become the first of the city's burned-out breweries to brew again. At the beginning of their partnership in 1907, in a nod to Meyer's brewery, they called their business the Anchor-Shasta Brewing Co., but by 1908 it was back to Anchor Brewing Company (ABC).

In 1909, the Portolá Festival—a dress rehearsal of sorts for the 1915 Panama-Pacific International Exposition (PPIE)—feted the 140th anniversary of the sighting of San Francisco Bay by the Don Gaspar de Portolá Expedition. But it was mostly an excuse to celebrate the phoenix-like rise of the resilient "City That Knows How" from the ashes of 1906. "The hardy sons of pioneers," trumpeted the Festival Committee, "now pioneers themselves, rebuilt, and today present to the world a modern metropolis." As evidence of Anchor's own phoenix-like ascension, Kraus, Meyer, and Tietjen took out an ad in the program, featuring the brewery's first Anchor Steam Beer logo. It featured an anchor, rope, life ring, the words STEAM BEER, and Mount Shasta (Meyer's suggestion, no doubt). The following year, 1910, Anchor joined with fourteen San Francisco breweries and others to contribute $50,000 to the "San Francisco for 1915" Exposition Fund. But as opening day of the PPIE approached, the brewers' boosterism was increasingly tempered by growing concern for the future of brewing in America.

THE DRYS VS. THE WETS

In 1898, the Anti-Saloon League had set up shop in California. For the first ten years they made little progress toward outlawing alcohol. Nevertheless, their continuing activism prompted the organization of the California State Brewers' Association in 1909, to defend against legislation antagonistic to their livelihood and to counter the relentless propaganda of the Woman's Christian Temperance Union, the Anti-Saloon League, and other, even more radical proponents of Prohibition. Forced into rearguard action, California's brewers soon decided to abandon their efforts to save the saloons, despite the fact that most of their product was sold there, in favor of saving beer itself, arguing that—in contrast to distilled spirits—beer was a perfectly acceptable beverage of temperance.

The battle between the "drys" and "wets" was in many ways a conflict between rural and urban America. Because the wetter cities were growing fast, Prohibitionists wanted a constitutional amendment passed before the 1920 census, which they knew would skew redistricting in the cities' favor. San Francisco, notwithstanding its seventy-five days of quake-induced prohibition, was among the wettest and most cosmopolitan cities on the "Wet" Coast. As Oregon and Washington state began bending to Prohibitionist pressure to go dry, brewers and bottlers from the Pacific Northwest saw San Francisco as their last, best hope, a place where they could brew and bottle beer with relative impunity, either to sell locally or ship back to their home states.

Nationwide, Prohibitionists received a boost with ratification of the Sixteenth Amendment to the US Constitution on February 3, 1913 instituting a federal income tax and ending the nation's financial dependence on the taxing of alcohol. Drys also welcomed Congress's declaration of war against the Imperial German Government on April 6, 1917. But when President Wilson proclaimed that "all natives, citizens, denizens, or subjects of Germany, being males of the age of fourteen and upwards, who shall be in the United States and not naturalized . . . are termed alien enemies," he, by association, fueled sentiment against all Germans in America, citizens or not. Moreover, since most of the nation's brewers were of German heritage, supporters of Prohibition began targeting them and their products as unpatriotic if not treasonous.

Although anti-German propaganda wasn't as pervasive in the Bay Area as it was back East, local Prohibitionists were quick to turn wartime xenophobia to their advantage. The Anti-Saloon League denounced the German brewers of Vallejo, citing "suspicion that in addition to their subserviency to the booze interests they are altogether too friendly to the Kaiser."

The Food and Fuel Control Act, which Congress passed April 10, granted Wilson great power to

protect the food supply and promote national security. His wartime conservation measures included barley and fuel oil, both essential to the brewer, creating a form of prohibition based on scarcity rather than morality. In November 1917, a *Chronicle* reader argued for the escalation of wartime rationing of beer's raw materials to the prohibition of beer altogether, a shot across the brewers' bow:

We are having meatless days and wheatless days, and even ice-creamless days. Now, why not have beerless days? An expert who has computed the waste of grain in brewing of beer in the United States says: "About nine times as much grain is going into the beer-vat way as is being sent to the bottom of the ocean by submarines." We are told that conservation of food will win the war against Germany. Has the Kaiser any better ally than the German beer brewer in the United States?

As if in answer to these questions, President Wilson forbade, as of January 1, 1918, the production of all malt liquor, except ale and porter, exceeding 3.4% ABV (alcohol by volume). Brewers were also ordered to reduce their annual use of malt, corn, and rice—their "grain bill"—by 30%, creating a brewer's dilemma for 1918: should they reduce sales or reduce grain—hence, the

alcohol—in what they intended to sell? By successfully equating temperance with patriotism, both wartime rationing and Prohibition paved the way for Congress's passage of the Eighteenth Amendment in December 2017. Prohibiting the production, sale, and transportation of alcoholic beverages, it was immediately sent to the forty-eight states for ratification.

KRAUS PERSEVERES

On January 10, 1918, Joseph Kraus, seeing the writing on the brewhouse wall, made a bid for favorable treatment by literally wining and dining eighteen of his most influential, well-connected "friends," including the sheriff, district attorney, and ten judges, to a dinner at "Bergez-Frank's Old Poodle Dog" restaurant. The menu featured wild game, courtesy of "the marksmanship of Joe Kraus," cocktails, champagne, and California wine—but no beer.

Kraus's efforts to influence the power brokers of the city were to no avail. But at least, to address the hardships placed on brewers by wartime rationing, the federal government authorized cooperative beer manufacturing. That way, one brewery could offer its quota of raw materials for use by another brewery. On April Fools' Day, 1918,

Anchor entered into an agreement with the Pacific Brewing and Malting Company, at 675 Treat, to brew Anchor's beer quota for $8 per barrel. Anchor then planned to sell the beer to Pacific Brewing's bottler, Tacoma Bottling Company, at the same address, for $10 per barrel. It was a grand—and perfectly legal—scheme, foiled only by Pacific's failure to deliver the beer as agreed. Kraus sued Pacific Brewing & Malting in an attempt to recover $7,676 for the 960 missing barrels of beer. Fooled once, Kraus did not try this again.

INFLUENZA

Meanwhile, in September 1918, San Francisco faced a new crisis. The influenza that was already ravaging much of the nation arrived in the West. Unlike President Wilson, though, San Francisco Mayor "Sunny Jim" Rolph Jr. was determined to stop it and spoke to the challenges. Likening the lifesaving potential of gauze masks in the city to gasmasks on the front, he issued a mask order in October, to which "conscience, patriotism, and self-protection demand immediate and rigid compliance." Anyone "who will not wear a mask now," the city's leaders maintained, "is a dangerous slacker." Unfortunately for Rolph, he was photographed in violation of his own order and fined $50. But that order was so effective that it was rescinded in November—alas, too soon. Undeterred, he issued another mask order in December. During much of this time, the Presidio was closed, as were public gathering places like schools, churches, and theaters. Ironically, although liar's-dice games for drinks were prohibited and the "free lunch," thanks to rationing, was reduced to wheatless crackers, pickles, and olives, the city's saloons were not shuttered. Thanks to the Prohibitionists, 160 saloons had already closed in 1917, and more were closing every day. With all that loss of license and tax revenue, the city could not afford to shut down those that remained. By February 1919, over three thousand people would die from influenza in San Francisco, as many as the victims of the 1906 quake. Remarkably, Joe Kraus and his partners survived, though Anchor's days were numbered.

FINAL BREW, FINAL SALE

In September 1918, Wilson, reasserting his wartime powers under the Food and Fuel Control Act, issued an expansive proclamation, effective December 1, prohibiting the production of all "malt liquors, including near beer, for beverage purposes, whether or not such malt liquors contain alcohol." He later modified his order to exempt "nonintoxicating" beverages, although the definition of "nonintoxicating" would not be resolved until after the passage of the Eighteenth Amendment. With the armistice of November 11, 1918, came the end of war but not the end of wartime Prohibition. Ten days later, passage of the Wartime Prohibition Act—which remained in force until after demobilization of America's troops was complete (well into 1920)—virtually guaranteed that America would remain dry until thirty-six states ratified the Eighteenth Amendment. The dry was cast.

It is commonly believed that America's brewers made and sold beer until 1920. But thanks to Wilson, they were prohibited from brewing beer after November 30, 1918. Ten San Francisco breweries ceased production that night, including

Rainier Brewing Company, John Wieland Brewery, California Brewing Association, Enterprise Brewing, Eagle Brewing, Milwaukee Brewery of San Francisco, North Star Brewing, Jackson Brewing, Pacific Brewing and Malting, and Anchor. They had to sell their old stock before July 1, 1919, by which time 2.75% ABW (alcohol by weight) beer was legal. Anchor Steam didn't keep well and was about 3.6% ABW, so its time was up by early 1919.

On January 13, 1919, California ratified the Eighteenth Amendment to the US Constitution. Three days later, Nebraska, the thirty-sixth state to ratify, provided the two-thirds majority needed to make it the law of the land. At just 112 words, the Eighteenth Amendment would need the help of the Volstead Act, which, among other things, defined "nonintoxicating" liquor as any beverage containing less than 0.5% ABV, in other words, "near beer." On January 17, 1920, wartime Prohibition transitioned to peacetime Prohibition as America's—and San Francisco's—"noble experiment" of enforced temperance officially began. Fifteen minutes later, in the nation's second wettest city (New York was #1), the first local arrest under the new law occurred, when a San Francisco bartender sold two glasses of gin to a pair of undercover federal agents. Clearly, for San Francisco, as Will Rogers is said to have remarked, Prohibition was "better than no liquor at all."

Prior to January 17, 1920, San Francisco had a dozen breweries. By early June, six—Acme,

Joe Kraus's 1922 passport photo

Enterprise, Milwaukee, Rainier, Tacoma, and Wieland—were making "near beer." It was legal, but, as the *Chronicle* scoffed, "the man who named it near-beer was a poor judge of distance." Five breweries—Albany, Eagle, Hibernia, Jackson, and North Star—were shuttered. But whither Anchor?

August Meyer got a job clerking for a "dry goods" (no pun intended) company. Henry Tietjen went into the "legitimate refreshments" (no pun intended) business. Joseph Kraus, now a thirty-two-year veteran of Bay Area brewing, remained in San Francisco until 1922, when he went back to Germany for a well-deserved vacation.

And the brewery itself? In 1920, a rural California newspaper offered a tantalizing eleven-word clue—the only clue—as to what became of Anchor Brewery, reporting, "The latter's plant has been taken over by a chocolate concern." It's not hard to imagine Joe Kraus in 1920, stirring a brew kettle full of chocolate while daydreaming about Anchor Steam Beer. But it wasn't long before Olomel Manufacturing Company took over. Ironically, considering they were occupying a former brewery called Anchor, Olomel made waterproofing products for boats.

Mission District saloon ca. 1933–34, with an upside-down case of Anchor Steam bottles on the floor

REPEAL

(1933–1959)

Few retailers nowadays can afford to keep from a dozen to two dozen kegs of steam beer on tap simultaneously as was common in the old pre-Prohibition days, and the sight of fifty schooners, three quarters full, lined up along the bar waiting for the noon whistle to blow as a signal for the final "spritz" out of a new keg, now is only a memory. Steam beer, however, is irrevocably a part of our San Francisco tradition, and may well remain so.

—Longtime Anchor brewmaster Joe Kraus (1940)

By March 4, 1933, Americans needed a job, a bank, and a beer. In his inaugural address that day, President Franklin D. Roosevelt invoked the "American spirit of the pioneer" as the key to America's recovery from the Great Depression. Within three weeks, FDR initiated the Civilian Conservation Corps and signed the Emergency Banking Relief and Cullen-Harrison bills into law. The latter was a clever work-around, which fast-tracked the legalization of beer and wine while the states were still debating ratification of the Twenty-first Amendment.

The Cullen-Harrison Act rewrote the Volstead Act's definition of "nonintoxicating," changing it from any liquor containing less than 0.5% ABV to include beer and wine that was less than "3.2 per centum of alcohol by weight" (4% ABV). True repeal wouldn't go into effect until the ratification of the Twenty-first Amendment on December 5, 1933. But when beer came back at 12:01 a.m. on April 7, 1933 (in nineteen states and the District of Columbia), brewers, bottlers, bartenders, and beer drinkers—as well as malt and hop dealers; barrel, bung, bottle, and spigot makers; tax collectors; and pretzel benders—were singing "Happy Days Are Here Again." Local breweries Acme, Rainier, Milwaukee, and Golden West, which had last delivered their product by horse-drawn wagon, fired up sleek new trucks to get the beer out to a parched populace, who gathered at the first-chance saloon of their choice with foamy anticipation.

Remarkably but not surprisingly, Joseph Kraus, whose Bay Area brewing career had begun forty-five years earlier, came out of retirement to bring back Anchor Steam Beer. Kraus bridged a strait as wide as the Golden Gate, as perhaps the only person in America to own and operate the same brewery before and after Prohibition, ensuring the preservation and continuation of a small but important part of San Francisco's brewing

tradition. His Anchor Brewing Company was not the only brewery to take a flier on California common after Repeal. But it would be the only one whose gamble endured more than a couple of years.

By June 1933, as part of the second wave of Bay Area brewery reopenings, Kraus had reestablished Anchor Brewing Company at 1610 Harrison, between 12th and 13th Streets, in a homely building originally occupied by Standard Building Material Co. And he opened Anchor Bottling Company at 1107 Battery at Union. Built of brick for the Independent Wood Company in 1907, with lodging on its second story for sailors, the diminutive landmark building still stands near present-day Levi's Plaza. Beer was literally taxed by the barrel in those days, necessitating racking into barrels at one site before bottling at another—hence Anchor's two separate locations.

For the first time in its history, Anchor was in the bottling business, shipping cases of Anchor Steam Beer around the state. Known as "pints" (though only 11 ounces), they sold for 10¢ ($2.17 today) each, plus 2½¢ deposit for the returnable bottle. By law, as of April 7, 1933, each bottle's brand label had to display the brand name; name and address of the brewer/bottler; net contents; a statement that it was not more than 4% ABV (until

1934, after which Kraus could cross out the 4% and legally sell it at its pre-Prohibition 4.5% ABV); the brewery's U-type federal permit number (until 1937); and a statement indicating "Internal Revenue Tax Paid" (until early 1950).

San Francisco's Louis Roesch Co., whose union label is in the lower right-hand corner, printed the handsome face label. It features the graceful script *Anchor* from Anchor's 1909 Portolá Festival ad and the same anchor/rope design that graced the pre-Prohibition bottles of Kraus's former employer, the unrelated Anchor Brewery across the Bay. On the label's companion point-of-sale piece, Kraus staked his claim to being *Best in the West*, but best in the West for what? The paperboard sign originally said *LAGER BEER*, but *STEAM BEER* was later pasted over it. And he had two neck

labels printed: *LAGER STEAM* and *STEAM BEER*.
Does this does mean Kraus was making genuine
lager beer in those days? No. Without ice or refrig-
eration, how could he? Rather, it is an indication of
Kraus's apprehensions about the chances for
Steam Beer in a post-Prohibition lager world.

Ultimately, the forthright brewer chose the
STEAM BEER label, in which he took great pride.
In the Anchor archives is a rare 1940 clipping, likely
connected to the meeting in San Francisco of the
California Northern District of the Master Brewers'
Association of America (MBAA) that year. In it,
Kraus provides the earliest known description of
Steam Beer by an Anchor brewer:

Manufacture of steam beer differs from that of ales and lagers . . . yet borrows something from each. . . . The mash is similar to a lager mash, although usually leaving a higher extract in the beer than in the case of lager. With the use of the open "cool ship," the wort rarely gets below 60 degrees F. [15.5°C.], making the subsequent fermentation warm. The yeast is neither top fermenting nor bottom, but an evolved type which seems to be both at once, with the added ability to settle with great rapidity.

The tightly coopered six-hoop [15.5 gallon] kegs are filled with flat beer, leaving about a two-gallon space which, in turn, is filled with new fermenting beer [the kräusening process]. Then a little finings or isinglass [to help clarify the unfiltered beer]—and in goes the bung and in a few weeks the beer is ready for delivery.

The most striking difference of this beer is the short time between mash and keg, and the product is characterized by its rich, almost amber appearance, its clean, sharp tang, and the thick, creamy collar of foam, at once the envy and the despair of the lager brewers.

As steam beer conditions in the keg, the pressure rises to 75 to 80 pounds and a special faucet is needed for tapping. This takes the form of a pear valve, which necessarily draws a little slower than does lager. But a well-drawn glass of steam, with its full complement of gas and its brave array of ascending "Dutchmen," is surely ample repayment for the extra few seconds of waiting.

Kraus suffered a major setback on the night of February 19, 1934, when a four-alarm fire broke out in the second-floor malt and hops storeroom of his

brewery. Within two hours, flames gutted the structure. Kraus estimated his loss from the blaze at $25,000 ($525,000) for the building, plus $10,000 ($210,000) in raw materials and finished goods, including about three thousand gallons of beer to have been bottled across town.

Undiscouraged, Kraus bought a nearby building just ten days later, reopening in June 1934 at 398 Kansas (at 17th Street). Designed in 1912 by San Francisco architect Herbert Blount Maggs as a machine shop, repair facility, and lab for General Electric, the American Commercial–style brick building was not ideally suited for brewing, requiring the construction of a jungle-gym-like wooden structure to elevate and support the brewhouse. Today, 398 Kansas is home to a software company that operates on a very different platform.

After the move, Kraus gave up on bottling, rededicating his efforts to Anchor's draught-only roots. He offered Anchor Steam in pre-Prohibition-style wooden kegs and reintroduced Anchor Porter, which harkened to its Co-operative Brewery days (more about Porter later).

Anchor finished the year 1936 ranked thirty-third out of California's thirty-six breweries, with sales of just 3,847 barrels—17/100 of 1% of the state's total. Nationwide, there were 739 breweries, down 40% from 1917, a descending spiral of consolidation that would finally bottom out in 1978.

years, his hard work and dedication indispensable to Anchor's survival.

A gentle giant, Joe Allen was born on February 9, 1888 to Irish parents Mary and Joseph in Pine Island, Minnesota. He tried mining in Nevada and Montana, but by 1922 was working in San Francisco as—ironically—a steamfitter. With know-how that belied his sixth-grade education, the five-foot-eleven redhead easily outweighed the two-hundred-pound kegs he hoisted daily. On July 1, 1935, Anchor reincorporated, with three directors: Joseph Kraus, Joe Allen, and twenty-three-year-old bartender John J. O'Kane Jr., who lived with his parents and worked at his father's bar, Johnny O'Kane's, on 3rd Street. By the late 1930s, Anchor was the only remaining steam beer brewery in the world.

Chronicle columnist Robert O'Brien stopped by the brewery in 1947. He waxed philosophical over Anchor Steam, imagining the "thousands of men in the world who, when they think of San Francisco, think of the sharp tang of steam beer they drank here years ago. It had something about it: a certain time of the day came, a certain group of companions, and when it was like that there was no answer to it but a tall steam." O'Brien asked Joe if he drank steam beer. Allen "grinned. His blue eyes twinkled jovially. 'On the level, I never touch

Kraus persevered by making a conscious choice, just as he had with Schinkel in 1907, to remain an "old-tyme" local brewery, continuing to brew beer that was the very antithesis of the bland light lagers already flowing from the nation's mega-breweries. And he was an old-tyme brewer. Sixty-three when he reopened Anchor in 1933, Kraus relied on the able assistance of Anchor's manager, Maurice Phillip O'Dowd Jr., and Anchor's secretary-treasurer, Joseph Robert Allen. O'Dowd didn't stay long, but Joe Allen stayed twenty-six

anything else. Anything else is skimmed milk—and steam beer is cream.'"

Allen, like Anchor's brewers before him, was at the beck and call of his product day and night. "You got to live with it when you're making it," he told *San Francisco News* reporter Bill Steif. "We're no beer factory. This takes time." From the looks of the place, the Industrial Revolution wouldn't arrive for a few more centuries. But "we buy the best malt and the best hops," Allen reminds Bill. "It's got the groceries in it." And Anchor Steam is "not carbonated; it makes its own gases; no one goes around shooting gases in it . . . it's like champagne." Slowly Joe pours Bill a glass, bestowing it upon his inquisitive guest with the solemnity of a mayor presenting the key to the city. He beams with pride as he points to the dense foamy head. "Notice how the 'collar' remains around the inside of the glass with each sip. That's the test of a good brew."

By the late '40s, rumors had already begun to circulate that San Francisco's "wild and foaming form of suds," as a professor of physiology wrote in *The Ohio State Medical Journal* in 1948, was no more. "I weep the death of steam beer, which forty years ago comforted the laborers of our Western coast." But the report of its death was an exaggeration. The beer was not dying; its champion, Joe Kraus, was. In January 1952, as his mentor's heart was giving out, Allen stood vigil at 398 Kansas,

making the beer he shared with anyone who stopped by for a tale or a taste. After Kraus's death on February 1, Allen was the only steam beer brewer in the world. But at sixty-three, he couldn't do it alone. So he hired his stepson, US Marine/Korean War vet Clyde Robert Rowan, for a few years, after which a nephew, Jene LaRue, helped out. Joe's college-educated sister, Agnes Catharine Allen, became president and general manager. The pioneering female brewery executive applied her insurance underwriter skills toward maintaining profitability and made sure that Anchor's legacy benefited the family for generations to come.

THE ANCHOR TOUR: 1955

Bob Welch, son of 1906 earthquake survivors, first visited Anchor in 1955. While having an Anchor Steam with a friend downtown at the Crystal Palace Market, a longtime purveyor of Steam, the bartender suggested they go see where it was made. Here is what he told me about that wonder-filled day:

"In front of the building there was a beat-up old flatbed with a little trailer behind it and it had wooden beer kegs in the back, so we knew that had to be the place. A big, tall, Scandinavian-looking gentleman, Clyde, opened the door, and he was very friendly and good-natured. Unbeknownst to us, the owner and brewmaster, Mr. Allen, was upstairs. The atmosphere was old, rather decrepit, old bricks that were losing their paint, you know, and inside it looked very rustic, hand-hewn. You'd see old, big beams and two-by-fours all around, and the smell of the wood was there and the smell of the beer, too. But it was not modern or push-button things of any kind, and that suited me fine. Off to the left in a little room, still on the ground floor, were about 100 or 150 big-size barrels stacked up, and then to the right this big, old, oaken, tap box with a brass catch-tray where the spigots were. And there were a lot of old beer signs on the wall. Clyde said, 'You guys have to have a beer.' The beer was just delicious. We sat there about an hour and Clyde told us stories. And then he took us on a tour, and we saw the main kettle and it was all very rustic. I got a picture of Clyde and Mr. Allen, when the brewmaster was working on the hop jack under the kettle. It was a very exciting experience, a really great thing. I'll never forget it."

Since 2005, when Bob returned to Anchor for his fiftieth brew-versary, he has returned several times. In 2017, he and I re-created the 1955 picture of Bob pouring himself a Steam.

COMEBACK
(1959–1965)

It's making the product that means something to me. On an assembly line you might put a bolt on a right rear fender. Here, I'm responsible for the whole process. When I'm finished, I can say: "I did that. I made that beer."

—Lawrence Steese, brewmaster, Steam Beer Brewing Co. (early 1960s)

As the 1950s wound down, the proliferation of mass-produced, heavily marketed light lagers took an increasing toll on America's—and San Francisco's—small brewers. But a number of local establishments still proudly featured Anchor's signature product, in particular the Crystal Palace Market between Market and Mission at 8th Street. According to the *San Francisco Chronicle*, it was a "sprawling, pungent, cheap and exotic carnival of delicatessen and delicacy." During the '40s and '50s, Austrian Joseph Erdelatz served Anchor Steam and hot dogs at his bar in the southeast corner of this vast, colorful marketplace. Locals

called it the "Steam Beer Parlor," scarcely imagining its pivotal role in Anchor's or its beer's survival. For had it not been for the Crystal Palace, there might never have been an Old Spaghetti Factory, and without the Old Spaghetti Factory and its charismatic owner, Fred Kuh, there might be no Anchor Steam Beer today. Fritz Maytag, who tells the story better than anyone, shared it with me a few years ago:

Ah, Fred. A man of good taste. He had lived in Chicago and been to the Sieben's Brewery, where I later bought our bottling line. They were the last brewery in America to have a restaurant in the brewery, a little Bier Stube. And when he came to San Francisco for a visit, on the way into town from the airport, *the very first thing his friend did* was take him for a visit to the Crystal Palace Market, sort of the equivalent of today's farmers' market. He recognized it immediately as similar to the great traditions of good food in Europe. Then his friend took him to the taproom at the Crystal Palace Market, where they served Anchor Steam on draught. Fred told me that he vowed that day, in the bar, drinking Anchor Steam, that he would move to San Francisco, open a restaurant, and serve only Anchor Steam Beer on draught.

Fred Kuh at the OSF

ever. And it was a booming place with young people. It was a target for the brewers. Imagine all the salespeople from Budweiser, Coors, and Miller, who would call on Fred at the Old Spaghetti Factory and tell him that he couldn't *possibly* survive as a business if he didn't have their beer on draught. And he told them all to go jump in the lake.

Fred Kuh had made good on his vow.

Though Kuh's North Beach eatery was thriving, the Crystal Palace fell victim to changing tastes and times. On April 22, 1959, its landlord announced that the thirty-six-year-old market, with its legendary Steam Beer Parlor in the back, would close August 1 to make room for an $8 million, four-hundred-room "luxury motel." "Progress," scoffed one newspaper.

The impending obsolescence of one of his two best accounts got Joe Allen thinking. Business was good, and money, thanks to his sister Agnes's

Frederick Walter Kuh moved to San Francisco in 1954, where he became a waiter/bartender at the Purple Onion. Two years later, on October 19, 1956, Kuh and fellow "founding father" James B. Silverman opened the Old Spaghetti Factory Café & Excelsior Coffee House at 478 Green Street, in the former home of the Italian-American Paste [*sic*] Company. The OSF became San Francisco's "first camp-decor restaurant," Fred later told the *San Francisco Examiner*, "but it wasn't called camp then." Early on and counterintuitively, he advertised his bohemian North Beach watering hole and its "Steam Beer Underneath a Fig Tree" in the *New Yorker*. And the first person Kuh acknowledged on the OSF's offbeat menu, for his "material and spiritual help," was "Joe Allen of the Anchor Steam Brewery." Fritz continues:

And Fred Kuh served, on draught, Anchor Steam Beer *only*, all the years he was open. He had bottled beers, but no other beer on draught

management, was not a problem. And his brewery—the oldest in the West, the smallest in America, and *The Only Steam Beer Brewery in the World*—was still selling all the beer he could make, about a hundred half-barrels a week. It was more of a calling than a career, and Joe was Anchor Steam's unflappable high priest, deeply devoted to the joys of small brewing and the integrity of his product. But he was seventy-one. The robust brewer of the robust beer could no longer hoist kegs with the gusto of his younger days. Clyde and Jene had moved on, and there was no heir apparent. He hoped that someone would come along to take his place, but nobody did. So Joe and Agnes weighed their options and made a decision.

LAST BREW

On May 28, 1959, Joe wrote *Last* in his little brewbook, above the brew number (20) and date. On June 4, he made Brew #21, his last kräusen brew. He racked his last Steam Beer on June 15, his final entry simple but profound, almost like a benediction: *Very Good.* Anchor's last day was Saturday, June 28, 1959. "The taps are running dry today on a full-flavored souvenir of San Francisco's past," lamented the *Chronicle*. It was the end of an era. "Many a lover of malt beverage drank his tears with his beer in California last week," wept the *New York Times*. "The last surviving Steam brewery dating from the Forty-Niner era of San Francisco [has] closed its doors.... More than thirty taverns in California have been customers of the Anchor Brewery, which shipped out its final half barrel in late June. Some of these establishments had built their business largely on Steam beer. Their owners, as well as customers, are in mourning."

Mourning indeed, as if for a brother lost at sea. The *Chronicle* interviewed the dispirited California commoners. "This has broken our hearts," grieved Fred Kuh at the Old Spaghetti Factory. Across the Bay in Berkeley, Sam Wilkes

Jr.—whose restaurant, The Anchor, got its name from the beer he had served there since 1934—described his customers as "very perturbed." At the recently opened Old Town Coffee

House in Sausalito, owner Courtland Turner Mudge had been serving five hundred glasses of Anchor a day. Distraught regulars clamored for one more taste of Steam, including "one old fellow [who] got away from his nurse and came in for a last glass." The uproar was understandable. "The people are upset because they know they're losing an honest product, one that's 100 per cent malt and one nobody else has made."

LAWRENCE STEESE

Among the tearful at Mudge's place was Sausalito "ark-dweller" Lawrence Jackson Steese. A small-town Minnesotan like Joe Allen, Steese was born in Bibawik on April 30, 1912. By 1940, Steese was coopering for a Connecticut distillery. His sundry jobs would include road builder, carpenter, seaman, plumber, handyman, homebrewer, bartender, and Death Valley talc miner. The latter "makes the throat terribly dry," Steese told the *Chronicle*, "and beer is the only beverage that makes you feel better." But it wasn't until he arrived in San Francisco in the mid-1950s that the beer lover found Steam. "I liked it and went to see the old man who brewed it. I'll never forget the feeling that hit me as I entered the place. It was big, silent, and there was a smell of something alive, like when you bake bread. The whole place had the dignity of a cathedral. Where in our society can you find a place of work that has this dignity?" He was smitten.

Seeing the Bay Area's lugubrious response to the end of Steam, Steese offered to keep the kettle boiling. Although Allen had other suitors, he was impressed by Steese's sincerity. "I turned down all the Ivy-League briefcase boys," Joe told Marin County's *Independent Journal* (*IJ*), "because they didn't look like they would be the type to carry on the old Anchor steam beer tradition." But he had confidence that Steese would surely do it "as it should be done." So Allen said yes.

STEAM BEER BREWING COMPANY

On July 3, 1959, *Chronicle* columnist Herb Caen spilled the beans. "Courtland Turner Mudge, gorgeously named owner of Sausalito's Old Town Coffee House, and his ex-bartender, Larry Steese, have bought the equipment of the old Anchor Steam Brewery, and hope to revive the lost art before steam beer fans perish of frustration." With salvation at hand, the aging brewmaster gratefully offered his anointed successor "all the assistance that is in me."

As it turned out, Mudge's support would be more moral than monetary. But no matter; an angel with a much larger wingspan flew in to prevent the Gold Rush quencher—"as San Franciscan as cable cars and the Golden Gate," according to the *IJ*, "from going the way of the clipper ship, the buffalo, and the one-horse shay." Sanskrit scholar William Benson "Bill" Buck of Bolinas was the wealthy son of a US congressman and grandson of a Vacaville orchardist. His wife, Jane Hammer Buck, who had enjoyed Anchor Steam Beer at the Crystal Palace Market, was delighted when he became Anchor's secret savior. But the taps were still off, so the pressure was on.

Wasting no time, Lawrence Steese, Joe Allen, Bill Buck, and two attorneys signed the Articles of Incorporation for "Steam Beer Brewing Company" on December 18, 1959. The brewery's new name came about by necessity rather than desire. Agnes Allen had convinced her brother/partner of the prudence of retaining the company name, "Anchor Brewing Company," as well as the brand name, "Anchor Steam Beer." The former, they agreed, would not be for sale. The latter, however, would be for rent, by way of a royalty on every gallon of Anchor Steam Beer sold—*in perpetuity*. In a bind, Steese chose Steam Beer Brewing Company as the brewery's new name and agreed to the royalty payments for the brand.

The Anchor trio of Steese, Allen, and Buck found a suitable location at 541 8th Street—less than a mile away from the Kansas Street brewery— and Buck generously agreed to sign the ten-year lease and sublet to Steam Beer Brewing. The modest industrial building had been constructed in 1917 as an addition to a mammoth battery factory next door which, since 1937, had been occupied by wholesale paper company Blake Moffitt & Towne. The brewery's new home was shaped like Nevada, which accommodated the elevated highway that bisected its lot. But with its entrance set back from the street, the high-ceilinged taproom inside appeared all the grander.

It took nine months for Allen and Steese to re-create Anchor at its new home with the old equipment, from kettle to coolship to 8 by 10-foot hemlock tap box. Beer signs, mirrors, pictures, and other breweriana filled the wall space of the cozy taproom. San Francisco's fifteen-month-long

Joe Allen, Lawrence Steese, and Frances Steese

steam beer drought finally came to an end on October 7, 1960, when they anxiously drew the first glasses of Steam in the new taproom. Two days later, a tiny classified ad in the personals column of the *Chronicle* whispered, "AMELIA: Do you know that STEAM BEER is back at the Old Spaghetti Factory Café?—Geraldine."

MONEY TROUBLES

Publicity, as Steese discovered, would be a lot harder to attract on the way up than it had been on the way down. And it was a long climb up from "amber anachronism," as one reporter had dubbed Steam Beer in 1959. The '60s was an era of catchy slogans like "Schlitz, the great light beer with gusto." But Schlitz drinkers weren't steam drinkers. Steese considered those who favored steam beer "in a class by themselves," he told the *Oakland Tribune*. "They're quieter, obviously more discerning, and they are what you could call 'efficient drinkers.'" He likened his handmade beer to home-baked bread. And before long Steam Beer became known, without advertising or hyperbole, as "the beer for beer drinkers," "the brew with the natural bubbles," and "the sincere beer"—by implication, the antithesis of big beer's "insincere" light lagers.

By the end of its first ten months of operation, Steese and Allen had added twenty-seven accounts to their original nineteen and sold 1,385 barrels of beer, an impressive performance. But the books that Lawrence's wife, Frances Rafilson Steese, kept told another story. By late June 1961, the brewery had already lost $27,000, with just $877 in the bank to cover $4,200 in accounts payable. By that time, the munificent Bill Buck had already purchased $42,000 in stock. And they needed more money. The mash tun was worn and rusty, the brew kettle begged for smithing, and the hot water tank needed reinforcing. And they were cooling the wort with makeshift fans, which blew anything airborne right into the coolship. But the biggest bottleneck was the cooperage, which prevented them from taking on any more accounts. To stay ahead of demand, they needed three kegs for every one sold, since at any given moment there were kegs in the trade, kegs at the brewery, and kegs in transit. From the old brewery, Steese had only 350 wooden and 300 steel kegs, which had worn valves and bungs and were ill-suited to modern tapping systems. And the wooden ones required frequent pitching. All told, these new expenditures would add another $9,000 to their indebtedness. So while Joe and Lawrence brewed, entertained visitors, or called on customers, Frances, known affectionately as "Skeezix," sent out more pleas for loans and stock buys.

In March 1962, having completed his brewing apprenticeship with Joe Allen, Steese became the new steward of steam, echoing Allen's belief that it was a round-the-clock job. "Why, I even sleep down

here at night," Steese told the *Oakland Tribune*, "while the beer is fermenting, just to make sure nothing happens to it." But Steese's optimistic prediction that the rental of hundreds of aluminum kegs would increase business by about 50% misread the demand for his draught-only beer, which was dwindling in the stay-at-home, TV dinner 1960s. Instead, Steam Beer Brewing finished the year 1962 with sales of 1,720.5 barrels, a modest increase of just 5%. Joe now served as the unsalaried ambassador of steam, and brewery helper Frank Pesti moved on. So Steese, who had had back surgery in 1961, hired local Dave Lyon to do the heavy lifting. Lawrence, Frances, and Dave remained upbeat, amused by the outsized assumptions about the tiny brewery displayed in their fan mail. Whoever opened the mail would often shout, "Hey, who's vice president of public relations this week?"

As they learned, there were two affordable ways to get the public's attention: get the brewery out to the people or get the people into the brewery. On Labor Day weekend 1962, they served Anchor Steam at the Barbary Coast Fandango, to benefit the California Historical Society. In 1963, the brewery hosted Portfolio/63, a non-juried art

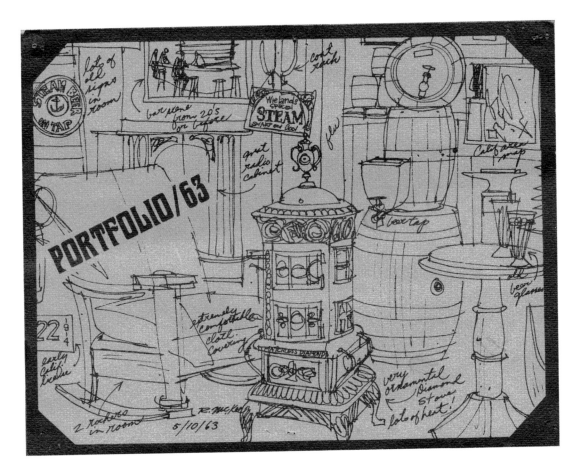

show featuring seven up-and-coming local artists, including Bill Hyde, who five years later would help design Anchor Steam's new label. In October 1964, Steese threw a "Steam Beer Benefit Bust" at the brewery—with folk singers and a jazz band—for the Potrero Hill Democratic Club and rising political stars John and Phil Burton. Herb Caen quipped that all the steam beer you can drink for $3 per person ($5 per couple) "sure beats those $1,000-a-plate banquets at which you'd like to get loaded but can't."

What Steese really needed was a fundraiser for Steam Beer Brewing Company. In late 1963, Bill Buck's frustrations with the brewery's inability to pay him $15,000 in accrued back rent boiled over, and he threatened Steese with eviction. As luck would have it, two new angels arrived on the scene, just in time to pay the bills and buy Buck's shares

of the Corporation. They were admen Bernard (Barney) Blake and Niels Mortensen, whose agency, Blake & Mortensen, Inc., would rise to prominence in 1965 with its ads soliciting investment in San Francisco's Golden Gateway Project on the Embarcadero. But despite Blake and Mortensen's bailout and creativity, as well as the ongoing support of the faithful—especially Fred Kuh, who loaned the brewery $17,000—Anchor Steam Beer remained undercapitalized and underappreciated in the city of its birth.

In 1963 and 1964, sales were as bad as any time since World War II. As money got tighter, Steese began to cut corners on raw materials—just as Allen had had to do on occasion—compromising the brewery's all-malt legacy by adding malt syrup, corn syrup, sugar, or Sweetose. Brewing had become too infrequent to maintain a viable yeast

STEAM BEER BARRELS ☞

An S.F. original of pre-prohibition era. Use as office water cooler or other things on picnics.

9⁹⁹

SPIGOT NOT INCLUDED

strain. And, since the brewery and equipment were not kept clean—one of the key secrets to making quality beer—the beer was often sour by the time the kegs hit the market. So, in an attempt to generate much-needed cash, Steese decided to raise the wholesale price of a half-barrel keg of Steam by 33%, from $15 to $20, effective August 3, 1964. But word of the price increase leaked out, so customers simply got their orders in early. As a result, sales spiked in June to 749 kegs, three times normal—but at the old, lower price—after which they declined precipitously. Inadvertently, Steese had created a more insidious problem. For years, kegs had been ordered, delivered, and tapped within days of being filled. Now, anticipating the price increase, customers were buying and holding kegs for months. The crudely filtered, unpasteurized beer soured in the trade before the kegs were even tapped, tarnishing the brewery's already spotty reputation for quality and consistency.

As 1964 drew to a close, Steese's brewery had just $128 in the bank and a sudsy sea of debt. In early 1965, he tried lowering the price of a keg of Steam from $20 to $17.50, but to no avail. So he began selling off the brewery's pre-Prohibition wooden barrels at the Sea Wall, opposite Pier 29, a warehouse full of "imports, historicana, and Americana." The price for a piece of Anchor history: $9.99—without spigot.

In July 1965, Steam Beer Brewing sold a total of 132 half-barrels of beer among its thirty-seven remaining accounts. The Old Spaghetti Factory bought the most—twenty-five—that month, and in addition to Kuh's loans, had been prepaying their keg orders to help Steese out. But the cash-flow situation remained dire, and Steese was at the point where the more beer he sold, the more money he lost. Six years earlier, the story "Last of Steam Beer—An Institution Dies" had been front-page news. Now, on July 28, Fred Kuh and his fellow readers of the *Chronicle* had to turn to page 46 to read "It Looks Bad for Steam Beer." Once again, the brewery was on the brink, only this time the brewmaster wasn't seventy-one and broken down; he was fifty-three and broke.

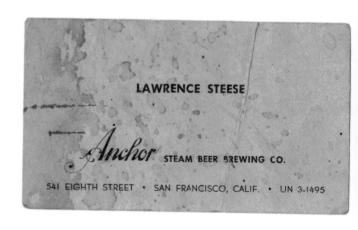

LAWRENCE STEESE

Anchor STEAM BEER BREWING CO.

541 EIGHTH STREET • SAN FRANCISCO, CALIF. • UN 3-1495

Skimming the starter fermentor

Teniers, pinxt.   Le fort, delt.   Pérée, Sculpt.

L'ALCHIMISTE.

PART THREE

FRITZ MAYTAG'S REVOLUTIONARY OLD BREWERY

RESCUE
(1965-1966)

I take a pleasure in inquiring into things. I've never been content to pass a stone without looking under it. And it is a black disappointment to me that I can never see the far side of the moon.

—Patriarch Samuel Hamilton in *East of Eden*, John Steinbeck

On Wednesday, July 28, 1965, the *San Francisco Chronicle*'s story "It Looks Bad for Steam Beer" gave Lawrence Steese an opportunity to explain Steam Beer Brewing's apparently imminent demise. "Finances," he told them. "We've been undercapitalized from the beginning, and, naturally, it's been downhill ever since." But despite the gravity of his predicament, Steese held onto his hope that a savior was out there—somewhere: "We're in a corner, kaput, that's it, unless a dedicated angel comes forth with about $15,000 to bail Steam Beer Brewing out and set it on the road to financial success."

That same day, buried deep in the *Oakland Tribune*, appeared a similar story: "Shed a Tear—No More Steam Beer," with an even bleaker prognosis: "One of the Bay Area's most hallowed and historical institutions seems doomed to extinction." Speaking to the *Trib*'s reporter, Steese chose to blame not undercapitalization, but rather increased competition from light lagers. "In the average English pub, you would find ten or fifteen different types of beer. Here, we drink lager-pilsner and that's all."

Indeed, since 1896, America had gone from 1,866 mostly small breweries, making many *styles* of beer, to just 163 mostly large breweries, making many *brands* of beer in *one style*: American light lager.

But now, in this moment, the competition Steese faced wasn't between steam and a profusion of lagers; it was between Steese and a profusion of creditors. And unlike 1959, there was no story in the *New York Times* and no angel on the wing. Steam Beer had apparently used up the last of its nine lives.

Or had it? On Thursday morning, Frances greeted "twenty people lined up wanting to put up $1000 apiece to save us, and at least seven more who wanted to go the whole amount." On Friday, an impassioned telegram arrived from the

1964 Christmas card from Kuh to Steese by Kaffe Fassett (Fritz on couch at bottom right)

Midwest. Ironically, it was from a man named Wager: "THIS IS SERIOUS. AM INTERESTED IN COMING TO YOUR RESCUE. IS IT TOO LATE TO SLAKE THE BLOODY CREDITORS? . . . WE WILL RISE PHOENIXLIKE FROM THE FLAME." Over the weekend, as the Steeses weighed the generosity, seriousness, and wherewithal of these would-be saviors, patrons of Bernstein's Fish Grotto on Powell, "up in arms about the new Steam Beer crisis," were "howling 'Save Steam Beer!'" Would anyone heed the cry?

FRITZ MAYTAG & THE OLD SPAGHETTI FACTORY

That summer of 1965, Fritz Maytag, twenty-seven-year-old great-grandson of the founder of the Maytag Washing Machine Company, was living on Russian Hill and hanging out in North Beach at the Old Spaghetti Factory, what urban sociologist Ray Oldenburg calls a "great good place." To Fritz, as he told me years later, it was simply "my place, my local. You didn't go for the spaghetti. You went for the camaraderie, the atmosphere, which had a kind of friendly, offbeat, bohemian feel. Fred Kuh had all those chairs on the ceiling—every one different. And there were paintings on the wall of local and hippie-world characters. The current dance poster was always up; those were hot. Chet Helms. The bands. Wes Wilson, who later worked at the brewery briefly, he did a lot of those posters." Draught beer was 35¢ a glass ($1.40 a pitcher), and there were just two on the menu: "Steam Beer, Light and Dark." Fritz preferred the former. The only difference, he later learned, was the caramel coloring in the dark.

But Fritz, who had dropped out of Stanford grad school in 1964, was adrift. "I didn't really have anything to do. I read books. I didn't have a goal in life. I was having a break; I needed a break—to find myself, as we say nowadays." As a boy, he'd played cello. All four Maytag kids took music lessons, which fostered Fritz's abiding love for music—especially chamber music. So on that providential Sunday, August 1, 1965, Fritz decided to attend an evening of French and Italian baroque chamber music at the OSF. As a friend of his likes to say, "there are no coincidences, only appointments."

As the button-down Maytag scion made his way up to the OSF's oaken bar, Fred Kuh nodded and began pouring Fritz's customary glass of Anchor Steam. The avuncular tapster knew that one of his favorite regulars was in the doldrums, without work, determination, or optimism to fill his sails. And he knew that Fritz was driven by curiosity, which English lexicographer Samuel Johnson calls "in great and generous minds, the first passion and the last." Fritz knew Kuh was the quintessential Anchor loyalist, a "true believer in the idea of a local beer." Yet despite Fred's support, San Francisco was about to lose its original beer—forever. So, as Fred handed Fritz his glass of Steam, he leaned over the bar to tell him that the historic little brewery that made their favorite beer would be closing "in the next few days. You should go

down and have a look around, because I know you'd be interested." For Fritz, it was the lighthouse in a fog—and the tip of a lifetime.

Fritz grabbed a menu on the way out, with its forty-seven-word description of the only Steam Beer in the world. Early the next morning, Monday, August 2, 1965, Fritz climbed into his Smyrna Green 1963 Porsche 356B cabriolet and headed south of Market. Brimming with curiosity, he was on his way to 541 8th Street, to see for himself where and how Anchor Steam Beer was made. Out front, he saw old wooden barrels for sale at 75¢ apiece, a last-ditch effort to raise toll money for the Golden Gate Bridge. Fritz knocked timidly and then slowly opened the front door, revealing a cathedral-like taproom within, its wainscoted walls covered with old beer signs and memorabilia. Brewmaster Lawrence Steese looked up from the bar, where he was shuffling stacks of paper, and greeted him with a broad, jack-tar smile. Steese caught Fritz staring at his incredibly curly, reddish brown hair. "Blame it on the Manx gene," Steese joshed.

Fritz introduced himself and asked if he might have a look around. Steese set down his pipe, said "Sure," and led him past a potbellied stove, through a heavy, large-windowed door, and into the warehouse. The very first thing that caught Fritz's attention was "a large, dusty, copper circular tube hanging on the wall, which intrigued me. I have never forgotten it. Today I know it must have been an attemperating coil for the 'first fermentor,' which was used before the wort was transferred to the shallow pan. The coil itself was not used in those days but must have been a relic." Clearly, Fritz wasn't in Iowa anymore. Wide-eyed, he took it all in: kegs on the floor, open-pan fermentor, the copper brew kettle. And the smells: fresh hops, wet barley, bready yeast. He was enthralled, as if the next turn might reveal some ancient alchemist, crouched over his workbench. And he felt the wonderment of being a boy again, in his basement lab with his microscope and experiments. "It was a

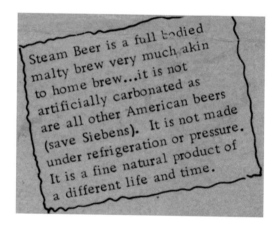

Steam Beer is a full bodied malty brew very much akin to home brew...it is not artificially carbonated as are all other American beers (save Siebens). It is not made under refrigeration or pressure. It is a fine natural product of a different life and time.

From Fritz's OSF menu that day

Steese welcomes guests to the taproom

Chan—my close friend, Chandler Flickinger, who had put himself through Stanford Law School delivering the *Palo Alto Times*—a route that I later took over during my Japanese days in graduate school—on the brewery phone and asked him if he had heard about the Anchor Steam Brewery. He said, 'Yes, sure,' and I said, 'Good; get up here, because I am going to buy it,' and he came. All on the same day."

Fritz, the latest dedicated angel of Steam, loaned Steese $9,200 and agreed to buy investors Blake and Mortensen's 51% stake in the company for $5,100. "They had lost something like 50K and wanted out, and the company was going into bankruptcy. They were eager to sell. They didn't want to have a bankruptcy on their record; that's why it was for sale." Steese kept the same 49% that he'd had all along. For Fritz, the day that had begun as an act of

marvelous sort of weird, funky place." He was home, spellbound, in "the last medieval brewery on earth."

As they talked, Fritz found Steese to be a charming guy, the pair of them like bookends on a very long shelf. Lawrence was a "creative rebel, willing to do something goofy just because he believed in it. He probably sensed that I resonated to that, that I understood his point of view, which I did. I think that he and I had a kind of eccentricity in common." In Fritz, Lawrence saw the same sincerity and enthusiasm that Joe had seen in Lawrence six years before. "And my name probably encouraged him in terms of being financially able; he had, after all, had a Buck as a partner."

Fritz sized up the situation. "They needed an angel. They were totally desperate. I don't think he'd had a serious offer. I remember Steese saying, 'They are going to come and take the kegs on Friday'—they were on lease—and that the malthouse would not sell him any more malt. The day after, my attorney and I hustled around taking care of *that* crisis." Innocently, Fritz thought that it wouldn't take much money to keep the brewery afloat, so the two men "agreed that same day, sitting at the bar in the taproom, and I called

L to R: "Boots," Matthew Steese, Courtland Mudge, Frances Steese, Lawrence Steese, Fritz, Unknown, Al Sebrian

curiosity ended with an act of generosity, a helping hand to save the sole survivor of San Francisco's golden age of brewing. If he'd toured the last cable car barn that day instead of the last steam beer brewery, he would have made a similar rescue.

Maytag and Steese, new partners in a long line of Anchor partners, shook hands. To this day, Anchor celebrates that momentous August 2, 1965 handshake as its brew-versary—the birth of craft beer, which ignited a revolution in brewing that would transform an entire industry. As he walked back to his car, Fritz looked back for a moment and shook his head. *Only in San Francisco*, he mused. *A kid from Iowa buys a brewery in California.*

THE MAYTAG WAY

Frederick Louis (Fritz) Maytag III, born in Des Moines on December 9, 1937, grew up with his three siblings in nearby Newton, the town that his great-grandfather, Frederick Louis (F. L.) Maytag put on the map with his eponymous washing

Fred Maytag, Fritz's father

machine. Upon F. L.'s retirement in 1921, he remained chairman of the board, but his son, Lewis Bergman (L. B. or Bud) Maytag became president, followed in 1926 by L. B.'s older brother, Elmer Henry (E. H.) Maytag. Despite a protracted union strike in 1938, during which the Iowa National Guard was called in to keep the peace, E. H., as described in *Holstein-Friesian World*, "helped to create ideal working and living conditions" for Maytag's two thousand employees, "which have made Newton a model industrial community" amid the cornfields and dairy farms. E. H. was "quiet and self-effacing"; loyalty was his watchword, and he had a knack for "surrounding himself with able lieutenants and inspiring them to do their best work." In addition to the Maytag Company, the great industrialist took special pride in his prizewinning purebred Holstein cattle, which churned out milk and blue ribbons for his beloved Maytag Dairy Farms, just a mile from the factory. As Fritz's mother was fond of saying, E. H. "loved cows because they didn't ask questions."

After E. H.'s death in 1940 at fifty-six, Fritz's father, Frederick Louis (Fred) Maytag II took the Maytag Company reins. "My father was in his twenties when his father got very ill and then boom, died. He never had a choice, nor did he want a choice. He was to the manner born. He was completely comfortable filling that role and being the head of the company, and the company, of course, basically was the town." Already a model of American enterprise, the Maytag Company made aircraft parts during World War II under Fred's watchful eye, with the same quality, consistency, and reliability that had made Maytag one of America's most trusted brand names. And he took over E. H.'s dairy farm and Holstein breeding program.

Fred had a penchant for cheese with character and soon took advantage of the practical know-how offered in Ames at land-grant-college Iowa State, transforming his father's dairy in 1941—with his brother Robert's help—into *the* pioneering artisanal

blue-cheese and mail-order food business. Fred's was the first domestic challenger to the great European "bleus." No one could have guessed that what Fred did for American blue cheese, his son would one day do for American beer.

Every Maytag, from F. L. to Fritz and beyond, has in their DNA "the Maytag Way": a compulsion "to challenge the impossible and to overcome the insurmountable" as F. L.'s biographer Abraham B. Funk put it. It is the modus vivendi for what F. L. Maytag himself called "the continual Trial-and-Error that we call Life." To follow the Maytag Way and achieve success in life and in business, F. L. believed in:

Work: Sheer work, plain plugging along, to get things done though they seemed actually impossible.

Determination: It is only the man of small caliber and puny performance that makes no mistakes. Venture is essential in large achievement and in its pathway is an occasional pitfall into which the aspiring may easily tumble. But ultimate failure is rarely the fate of those who do not yield to the fateful forces of defeat.

Optimism: Even in the face of dire discouragement I have found myself in the possession of hope and confidence as to ultimate results. It is not always easy to maintain this spirit, but it works. A man can think straighter, clearer, and faster; he can work more efficiently and with greater certainty and with more satisfaction if he is optimistic.

The beating heart of the Maytag Way is integrity. And where did this integrity come from as a theme for a company? Fritz says, "having grown up there and thought life through a bit, [I think] it came from Iowa, that is, the Middle West. You know this was taken for granted among the good people, not just the best people, but the good people. Normal people took it for granted that you *tried* to have integrity, but my family *had* integrity; I grew up with it."

But despite their shared values, Fritz and his father were never close. He was a "very impressive, serious, admirable figure in our lives, but he was not warm. He was very, very, very careful, very factual, very detailed, very organized, and I was not." As a result, Fritz had "a subtle feeling that I never quite measured up, like, you know, you're getting a B+ in algebra and the teacher obviously wishes you were an A+ student. You get that feeling." Nevertheless, Fred taught Fritz valuable lessons, including the difference between a debtor and a creditor. When he was just eleven, having squandered his $2 weekly allowance, Fritz needed a loan. To get it, Fred made Fritz sign his first promissory note: "For value received, I promise to pay to my father, on demand, 15¢ with interest at 1¢ per week."

Fritz's mother, Ellen Pray Maytag, was by far the most important influence on him; Fritz spoke of her tremendous empathy and depth of wisdom about people that he never forgot. "When I was a young boy," he reminisced while giving a talk at the 1988 National Microbrewers Conference, "I was watching my mother cleaning up after a cocktail party one day, and I asked her why people drank all those drinks. She said to me, 'Why, Fritz, alcohol is a gift from God. Your father is in business. People come from all around the world to meet with him. We don't know many of them, and they don't know each other. They are tired and busy, and they need to get to know each other and relax in a very short time. Alcohol is a gift that enables that.'"

Ellen Pray's mother had died in a car accident when she was just two, so her father's sister moved in to become "Mother's mother." Ellen's father, Dr. Kenneth Pray, was the first dean of the School of Social Work at the University of Pennsylvania, so she "grew up in a world where what mattered was the Quaker Home for Unwed Mothers or the Prison Reform Movement, in a home environment of caring for other people and thinking hard about how to do it." Dr. Pray and his colleagues "were all desperately trying to help people in terrible trouble and arguing in order to think through the question." Impressionable young Ellen, who ofttimes mistook these heated life-and-death discussions for bitter quarrels, grew up eschewing confrontation of any kind. Simply put, she hated arguments, which would profoundly influence the demeanor and management styles of both her husband and firstborn son.

Fred's credo, which hung in the lobby of Maytag headquarters, stressed the value of striking "a just balance among the interests of customers, employees, shareholders, and the public. Although these groups may apparently compete in their short-term goals, their long-range interests coincide, for none can long benefit unless the needs of all are served." Nevertheless, Fred "lived a kind of a constant nightmare shadow-world of competition with the United Auto Workers," a perennial struggle he'd inherited from E. H. Eventually, Fritz's "father hired a guy that I think must have been a genius at labor relations and worked out a working relationship with the Union

Fritz and his sister, Ellen

that actually turned out to be pretty good. But I grew up with that tension. It's in my bones. I dreaded the idea of ever being in an adversarial relationship with my employees."

It was only later in life that Fritz came to realize in business "that the model of the Maytag Company and my experience working there in the summers had a huge influence on me." The Maytag reputation for quality and reliability was built into every appliance that came off the assembly line. "You bought a Maytag because it was the best, and it cost you a premium."

As a young boy, Fritz spent almost as much time at his family's second home in Scottsdale, Arizona as he did in Newton. In the desert, he marveled at a night sky filled with stars and planets he'd never seen before, sparking a lifelong interest in astronomy. Back in Newton, in the basement of the Maytag family home, Fritz explored the world of science through his very own Gilbert Chemistry Outfit. When he was fifteen that hobby led to his first summer job, in the Maytag Company's chemistry department. There he happily performed daily quantitative analysis on the gray cast iron. But he was "shocked to discover that the employees in the lab, and there were only a few, didn't like coming to work, didn't like work, would rather be fishing or something. You know when you're a kid you see the grownups go to work, but you just assume that they love it."

The next summer he worked in industrial engineering, "in charge of the primary interview for the Idea Plan. If you had an idea at the company to save money or be more efficient, the industrial engineering department would study it and an employee could get a large piece of the savings. One guy eliminated a single board from every pallet, and he got the maximum award, I think it was $10,000." Fritz was all over the plant that summer, learning how hard it is to work, how long the day is, and how there can be ways of making work more satisfying and more rewarding. Fritz "got that from the company, and I tried very hard to do that at the

brewery." He wanted his employees to flourish and prosper in an environment of being helped, and he liked to half-joke: "You should give the employees so many benefits that they just can't even remember them!"

In 1949, Fritz's father told *Life* magazine that he wanted his children "to grow up normally, like any kids, in spite of the economic security they enjoyed. But the trouble is they think they are normal, and the other kids do not." Fritz credits his mother for seeing the Maytag children as big frogs in a small pond; whatever else was going to happen to them, they needed to be taught that they weren't so special. "She didn't approve of my great-grandfather's blustering, proud, self-congratulatory style," Fritz recalls. "He was apparently a brilliant salesman and pleased with himself, and she was terrified that I would be like that! And I think my mother realized her kids are not getting a great education and they think they're real smart and they are smart but they're not *that* smart. We've got to get them out of here and into a more rigorous, challenging environment."

When Fred was a boy, he wanted to quit Newton High School early to go to Indiana's Culver Military Academy, but his father said he could not do that; they were the Maytag family, this was their company, and the town depended on them, and his early departure would not look good. Fred would have been pleased if Fritz had gone to Culver, "but I was just horrified at the idea. Marching around in a uniform—that was not my style, which tells you right there, my dad and I were very different." Instead, in 1952, both Fritz and his sister headed east—Ellen, a junior, to the Ethel Walker School, and Fritz, a sophomore, to Deerfield Academy. Fritz instantly fell in love with his new pond. "The frog," he would soon learn from studying Thoreau, "had eyed the heavens from his marsh, until his mind was filled with visions, and he saw more than belongs to this fenny earth. He mistrusted that he was become a dreamer and visionary. Leaping across the swamp to his fellow, what was his joy and consolation to find that he too had seen the same sights in the heavens, he too had dreamed the same dreams!" At Deerfield, Fritz saw some boys "with books under their arms and coat and tie on, and I thought, *my God, they're seriously learning; I can't wait!* I was just thrilled at the idea of learning." And, just as his mother predicted, Fritz quickly learned at Deerfield that he was not the smartest boy in the class. (Nor was he the only future brewer. Fritz was class of '55; August "Augie" Pabst, grandson of Blue-Ribbon brewer Fred Pabst, was class of '52.)

Fritz vividly remembers "the very first morning, the very first teacher, the very first *instant* of my career there. It was English class—Mr. Merriam. There would have been about twelve or fourteen of us. He was a young guy, small, strong, and he came into the room, had a book in his hand, and he *slammed* the book down on his desk, the teacher's desk. *Wham!* And *God*, everybody in the room just jumped and *woke up*." Wide awake, enthusiastic, *engaged*. "You know there's that moment in the Episcopalian confirmation ceremony where the priest touches your forehead and that is symbolically to awaken the spiritual life in you. And that moment awakened the learning, the *ideas*."

When Fritz returned home for Christmas break, his father had a gift waiting for him: a 1938 Bausch & Lomb microscope, completely outfitted with electric light, full array of lenses, and heavy wooden case. Fritz, whose affinity for science was tempered only by his modest aptitude for math, was elated, and brought it to Deerfield with him in the fall of 1953. Fondly and with gratitude, he remembers Deerfield as a school designed to create integrity, honesty, and wholesome involvement in America. And he remembers the rules at Deerfield, the same rules Fritz invoked when he became "principal" at Anchor. Simple. "There were no rules. Just be punctual and behave yourself."

GO WEST, YOUNG MAN

Although they loved their respective boarding schools, Fritz and his sister "couldn't wait to get out of the East Coast, the whole elitism and status consciousness. We were egalitarian. We were Middle Westerners—Westerners I would say now." Ellen graduated first and chose Stanford. "I went out and visited her and realized right away that this was it." So, in 1955—microscope in tow—Fritz followed Ellen's westward footsteps to the school known as The Farm. "I was interested in ideas, but I thought I would be a chemist. I quickly realized I wasn't made for it, and I majored in American literature right away, with the idea that books are filled with ideas. I had read I don't know how many books at Deerfield in bed at night with the flashlight or when I should have been studying. And I read the Modern Library; I read 'em all. And I was deep into ideas, into caring about life, and so I thought if you read literature then you're interested in ideas." But he soon realized that really wasn't the case at all. Literature studies meant he didn't spend that much time on the kinds of ideas

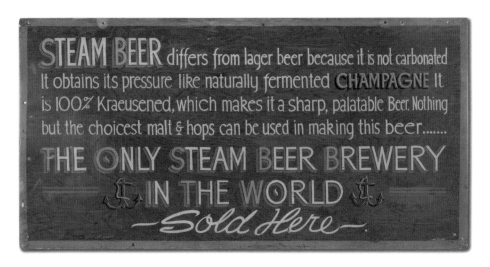

Original sign from the Oasis—a gift from the Tougas Family

that interested him. Disillusioned by the end of his first year at Stanford, Fritz "flunked out and [he] had three choices: either [he] could never come back, or take a year off and grow up, or go to summer school at Stanford and get straight A's and get back in." He chose the third. As a result, he got to experience California in the summer, "which was just a stunning experience for me. I just loved it, the smell of it, the long days."

During the summer of '57, his sister Ellen was living in San Francisco and invited him to the Old Spaghetti Factory—but not for a beer. Fred Kuh "used to have a champagne brunch on Sunday morning in the garden court: 'Steam Beer Underneath a Fig Tree.'" It wasn't until 1959 that Fritz had his first glass of Anchor Steam, and that was at the Oasis in Menlo Park. Opened in 1933, its name was inspired by the end of that very long American dry spell. Indeed, right after Repeal, it turned out that "The O" was just far enough from Stanford's still-dry campus to offer legal libations.

"Yessss, I can remember the first Steam I ever had," Fritz told the *Stanford Magazine* in 1996. "I don't remember the taste of it as much as the experience of it. It was at the Oasis. . . . I remember being told it was a funny local beer. I was told it was

special." Middle-Western manners prevented him from revealing the whole truth: that "it wasn't any good. It was sour. And I never drank it again down there, and then they took it out. When I bought the brewery, I had to beg them to put it back in." Unbeknownst to Fritz at the time, the reason the Oasis took it out in 1959 was that Anchor owner/brewmaster Joe Allen had closed the brewery and retired. It stayed out for more than six years.

Like Deerfield, "there were no rules" at Stanford, so in 1958 the American literature major took the fall quarter off. Inspired by fellow Stanfordian Paul Draper's Moto Guzzi exploits in Italy the year before, Fritz wanted to have an adventure. He toured Europe on a green BSA B31 motorcycle, falling in love with the Italy Byron describes as:

Thy wreck a glory, and thy ruin graced
With an immaculate charm which cannot be defaced.

Fritz did not graduate with his class in 1959 because of a course in American poetry taught by a man who was his bête noir. Fritz later came to understand his point of view, but at the time Fritz thought Yvor Winters was a "heartless, cold bastard." Professor Winters "began the class, either

Fritz and his BSA in 1958

the first or second one, by quoting from Walt Whitman's *Leaves of Grass*: 'I lean and loafe at my ease observing a spear of summer grass.' And he proceeded to *mock* him, mock *the very idea* of thinking like that or of talking like that. And mocked Thoreau for thinking like that. I don't know if he even bothered with Emerson. He mocked that whole point of view. And I was just absolutely thunderstruck." Fritz never went back. Unfortunately, according to his advisor, he needed that course to graduate. Since Winters's class was given only during winter quarter, Fritz would have to wait and re-enroll.

So Fritz, with almost a year off, leaned and loafed at his ease. By that time, he had become deeply interested in Oriental philosophy. He had fallen in love with Japanese poetry, and wondered if it could be even richer in the original. He saw "richness there just as I did with Whitman, with his blade of summer grass," so he enrolled in an intensive eight-week summer course in Japanese, after which he thought, *Here I've got some basic Japanese, I'll go to Japan and do the motorcycle thing again*. In the fall of 1959, Fritz rode his black and silver Yamaha 250 all over Japan. "In Hokkaido, I remember buying a big bottle of Sapporo—there were two sizes in those days—after a long day's ride. That was always my favorite beer. It tasted wonderful, as I sat there on the tatami, exhausted but happy."

When he got back to the States, Fritz learned that he had had enough credits to graduate all along. So, "a total novice, footloose and fancy free," Fritz applied to Stanford's MA program in Japanese. His father would have loved for him to choose Harvard Business School, but Fred didn't push him. Unlike Fred, Fritz was "raised with the knowledge that I should not even think about working at the Maytag Company, that there was no obligation, no expectation—even the opposite. There was the hope that I would move out and on and into my own life. It was a great gift, and it was, I think, partly due to the fact that both my mother *and* my father knew that *he* really had never had a choice."

In 1962, Fritz lived alone in a little house in La Honda, "sort of like a Japanese monk, and too deep in study." So he took up cycling, riding daily from La Honda up to Skyline on a derailleur bike with an alpine gear. It was built for him by Spence Wolf in Cupertino. His whole attitude and work at school quickly improved. That summer, he rode his bike from San Francisco to Quebec, with fellow Stanfordian Sam Armstrong along for part of the journey. In the fall of '62, Fritz went to Tokyo to continue his studies. There, he continued riding, especially on the unpaved country roads, where he saw closeup "the Japanese culture and life that first intrigued me into studying Japanese."

Fritz was in Tokyo when he heard that his father's long battle with cancer was coming to an end. He got to Newton in time to join his mother and three siblings at Fred Maytag's bedside. The Maytag patriarch died on November 4, 1962, just shy of his fifty-second birthday. The year before, *Time* magazine had lauded the Maytag Company for its "craftsman's passion" for quality and the "stubborn individualism of its management," a tribute to his father's values. True to the Maytag Way, Fred had remained determined and optimistic, valiantly "plugging along" at Maytag until just a few weeks before his death.

In 1963, Fritz returned to Stanford to continue his studies, moving into a little cabin in Sky Londa.

His favorite professor was Edward George Seidensticker, as patient as he was inspiring, whose love of knowledge for its own sake was devoid of pretension. "He was a *great* translator and mentor, who just thrilled me with his sense—you know when you talk about translations, you're always saying well, do you want to be accurate, or do you want to be poetic in the sense of conveying the same kind of tone that the original has?" And Seidensticker's "point of view was you do both. You gotta do both." He championed Nagai Kafū, one of modern Japan's finest writers. As translated by Seidensticker, Kafū laments the demise of "picture-like beauties of tradition in the interests of a new age," urging his countrymen to be "respectful of the past," the "mystical spring from which the future must always flow. It is the torch lighting the uncertain way of the present." Fritz was captivated and ultimately driven by these themes of balancing science and art and looking back to look forward.

At 10:30 a.m. on November 22, 1963, a little over a year after his father's untimely death, Fritz sat alone in his Sky Londa cabin. "I was translating from a short story by Nagai Kafū, a sentence about a girl stepping down off a bus, when I heard it on the radio." The assassination of President John F. Kennedy had a profound effect on Fritz, who was just twenty-five. It was as if he was back at Deerfield, when Mr. Merriam—*wham!*—slammed down his book. Suddenly, it "*woke me up*, to the fact that I'm not a Japanese scholar. I'm not going to be ambassador to Japan. I'm not going to be a professor. What am I doing? I've got to get on with *life*."

But before he could do that, Fritz would have to get on with living. That winter, "exhausted, mentally and physically," he was stricken with pneumonia. For weeks, he hovered between life and death. His girlfriend later told him the doctor had told her he didn't think Fritz would live. Fritz was terrified and almost gave up hope. "I can still remember the moment that I decided to live." He was in an oxygen tent, and the doctor, before he went home that night, counseled him: "'You *must* keep breathing.' I tell you, the tiny little breaths, God the pain. And I remember thinking *why would I want to live?* And then I thought about those trees up on Skyline, and I thought *well, I used to love those trees, maybe that's worth living for, because, although I don't love anything right now, I did love the trees.* Maybe it's worth trying to come back and live."

Fritz recovered, and he could even have earned his master's degree in 1964. But "I finally realized I just gotta quit." So he dropped out, rented a Green Street apartment on San Francisco's Russian Hill, and settled down to a life of ease. Ironically, that life—without work, determination, or optimism—made him increasingly uneasy. He remembers "getting on the cable car once, up on Hyde Street, heading toward town, and there was a young guy, my age roughly, with a coat and tie on, and he had a tube, like an architect would have, drawings, and I remember thinking *that guy has got something to do. I need something to do.*"

It was during this time that Fritz began to think deeply about the words John F. Kennedy had spoken in 1960 on the campaign trail: "How many of you who are going to be doctors, are willing to spend your days in Ghana? Technicians or engineers, how many of you are willing to work in the Foreign Service and spend your lives traveling around the world? On your willingness to do that . . . on your willingness to contribute part of your life to this country, I think will depend the answer whether a free society can compete." JFK's call to action became the Peace Corps, which Fritz's bicycling pal Sam Armstrong had joined in 1962, around the same time Fritz left for Tokyo.

So in 1964, inspired by Kennedy's challenge and Sam's service, Fritz formed an idea of trying to do something in the Third World, the underdeveloped world. He reached out to Sam, Lars Speyer (who would one day become Anchor's first master photographer), and Paul Draper (who would one day make Ridge wine from Fritz's grapes). He had first met Paul when Fritz was at Deerfield and Paul was

at rival Choate, and they were at Stanford together. Fritz proposed "that we try to do some good in the underdeveloped world somewhere, and that I would pay the bills and they would work for me at a reasonable salary." They agreed to the concept and were still debating what to do and where to do it when, on August 2, 1965, Fritz Maytag made his fortuitous visit to Steam Beer Brewing Company.

Fritz left the brewery that day exhilarated. But he was also anxious—not about the fate of Steam Beer, but rather about his upcoming exploratory trip to Mexico with Armstrong, Draper, and Speyer, where they saw "a whole bunch of community-development projects." Ultimately, for their private Peace Corps, they would choose the southern coast range of Chile. "My mother said, 'Why don't you just go to Mississippi, dear? They're struggling there.' I said, 'Because we don't want to go to Mississippi. We want to have an *adventure!*'" It was Paul Draper's idea to make wine—a non-irrigated, old-vine Cabernet—which they would do in 1966, '67, and '68, all the while helping Chileans improve their winemaking techniques, marketing skills, and self-sufficiency.

On September 24, 1965, after returning from Mexico, Fritz went back into brewery bankroller mode, meeting with Steese to sign more papers, which legally consummated their August 2 agreement. The next day, the *Chronicle*, reminding San Franciscans of the brewery's "historic dignity and infinite charm . . . not to mention its fine malty product," proclaimed, "Antiquarians, devotees of the-way-things-ought-to-turn-out and beer lovers: Rejoice! The Steam Beer Brewery is saved."

MARKETING WITHOUT MARKETING

Apparently, more creditors than customers read the paper that day, because "quite a few people came in with notes over the ensuing weeks." The

Steam Beer Brewing Company was still in deep trouble: brewing just once a month, $45,000 ($400,000 today) in debt, and hemorrhaging an additional $1,200 ($10,700) a month.

"Well, we were desperate to have the public know even that we existed when I started going out and trying to sell the beer. . . . But I quickly discovered that many people thought that the brewery had gone bankrupt, had disappeared, and that I was a fraud. 'Oh no,' they said, 'Anchor's gone.' And so we realized that any publicity that we could get of any kind that would just mention our name would remind people that indeed we existed. So we did all kinds of goofy stuff."

For weeks, Fritz drove around San Francisco with a suspicious-looking clear plastic bag of fresh hops on the passenger seat of his Porsche cabriolet, desperately hoping to get pulled over. It would have made a great headline, but, he remembers with a shake of his head, "Nobody could get arrested in San Francisco in the '60s."

In mid-October, curious about the brewing business, accidental brewer Fritz Maytag attended a convention of the Brewers' Association of America (BAA) at Chicago's Edgewater Beach Hotel. Fritz "was too shy and embarrassed to register, but I traveled there on the pretext of other business, and then snuck in the back door. I was scared to death, but I held onto the dream that someday I might become a member of the profession I had just gotten involved with. At that convention there were a lot of guys smoking cigars, and on the walls there were samples of stationery, business cards, and beer posters. It seemed to be a very practical, down-to-earth convention, and I was impressed."

Fritz returned to San Francisco and, riding on what Arthur Miller calls "a smile and a shoeshine," hoped to turn his newfound knowledge into a sale. Less than a week later, on October 25, 1965, he convinced the Oasis, a few blocks up El Camino Real from his alma mater, to take four kegs at $17 apiece. They had not served Anchor Steam since Joe Allen

closed down the brewery in 1959, which made the tenderfoot salesman's triumph all the sweeter.

Advertising was anathema to Fritz from the beginning—and he couldn't afford it anyway. So he tried "more goofy stuff," promoting the brewery's comeback with a tongue-in-cheek press release: "STEAM PUTS HOT AIR IN SPACE. ANCHOR STEAM BEER—the only steam beer brewery in the world—formally announces its entry into the space race." This took place on November 12, 1965, at the First International Aeroclassic in Palm Springs. The "spaceship," named Libra rather than Gemini, was actually a brand-new hot-air balloon, featuring a hastily designed company logo by Fritz's college/artist friend Richard Elmore and piloted by Fritz's balloonist friend "Fearless Deke" Sonnichsen. The balloon's ascension that day, though not victorious, was an uplifting metaphor for a revitalized Steam Beer Brewing. And it served as dress rehearsal for the "Grand Balloon Ascension" in San Francisco on December 15, which, as fate would have it, was a sobering metaphor for the challenges that lay ahead. By 7 p.m., Fisherman's Wharf was dark, cold, and windy. "Thank God it didn't ascend! There was too much wind, and Deke couldn't take off. God only *knows* where he was going. It was *night*. And he was going to go across the Bay, and land *where*? A hot air *balloon*. 1965. Insanity." Thankfully, the after-party at the brewery went great. And the next morning, Fritz's attempt at guerilla marketing made a successful journalistic ascent in the *Chronicle*, under the headline "A Valiant Fiasco."

Despite Fritz's efforts, sales were down 40%—from 1,455 barrels in 1964 to just 880 barrels in 1965. In November 1965, the brewery sold a paltry 136 half-barrel kegs, and in December 132—the brewery's worst months since January. The Old Spaghetti Factory was really their only good customer, responsible for 15% of the brewery's sales, and Kuh continued prepaying to help with cash flow. But Fritz had already advanced the brewery $24,000. If he were going to continue bailing out the brewery, he would need a bigger bucket.

Fritz's solution took advantage of Steam Beer Brewing Company's S corporation status, which means that it's taxed like a partnership. But "if I owned only 51%, then I could take only 51% of the losses. That didn't make sense, so we just made an arrangement that I would own 99% and Steese

could get it back if needed, 'cause he couldn't use the losses, and that allowed me to lose less—we lost money almost every week for years—and after tax it was less expensive for me than it looked." So on January 7, 1966, Steese sold him 2,400 shares,

bringing Fritz's total up to 4,950 shares (99%), and leaving Steese with 50 (1%). The deal closed January 13, 1966.

Still in angel mode and armed with a newly minted business card to prove that he and his brewery were for real, Fritz continued to pound the pavement, doughtily introducing himself at bar after bar, café after café: "I'm the president of Anchor Steam, and I'd like you to try my beer." He proudly added Menlo Park's Dutch Goose, known as the Busy Bee back in his Stanford days, and San Francisco's Tommy's Joynt to the list. "It was hard work, and it wasn't something I enjoyed, but I was determined."

But the goofy stuff—marketing without marketing—was Fritz's métier in those days. To make the brewery a destination, he sponsored evenings of harpsichord music and poetry, as well as rock 'n' roll shows by local bands like the San Andreas Faults and the Third Party. And although Hamm's had a giant lighted beer glass atop its brewery, Fritz chose a very different sort of beacon for his.

Coloradan Ron Boise was a sculptor of human figures and musical instruments in scrap metal—usually from old car bumpers and fenders. Ron and his art were the talk of the town in a widely publicized 1964 obscenity trial. On April 6, SFPD and a police photographer arrived at the Vorpal Gallery, located in North Beach near City Lights Bookstore. They were there to take pictures of the Boise sculptures on display. There was no question that the sculptures, inspired by the Kama Sutra, were

erotic. But were they art or were they obscene? The "dirty art" trial made headlines that summer, and the not-guilty verdict "freed" the Vorpal Gallery's owners and the sculptures that had been seized as evidence. It also vindicated a pioneering artist.

In April 1966, the brewery became the sculpture gallery for San Francisco's citywide "Spring Mobilization Art Show, protesting the war in Vietnam." On display was a provocative twelve-foot-tall Boise sculpture called "The Couple," which Fritz bought from Boise and mounted atop his 8th Street brewery, just a stone's throw from the James Lick Freeway. Prudish commuters complained, but Fritz's defense was eloquently matter of fact: "That freeway gets pretty monotonous," he told the *Chronicle*. "We thought we'd put up something to say hello." The story made all the papers and supported local art, enhancing Steam Beer Brewing's quirky notoriety. "We got *publicity*," and local columnists like the legendary Herb Caen "finally noticed us, and of course that made a huge difference."

But as Fritz began to spend more time selling, he started getting lots of negative reactions to the beer and the brewery. And it didn't take him long to grasp the reason: Nothing that grows in beer can harm you, but there's a lot that grows in beer that can harm sales. "It's hard to sell beer that's sour. The beer was not good." The *coup de disgrace* came one afternoon as Fritz was preparing to host a big party at the brewery. He tasted the beer. It was sour. He hooked up more kegs. All sour. Fritz got in his car and drove around the city, calling on every account he could think of. At each he ordered a glass of Steam Beer, until he finally found a couple of kegs that were OK. He immediately bought them back, brought them back, and hooked them up, just as his guests were arriving. It was a lesson he never forgot. "I didn't realize it at first. It was not good beer. And somewhere in there I began to get the idea that failure was a possibility, and absolutely I would not do it. I would not accept it. So then I focused on making better beer. It was only later that we worked hard again at selling."

TRANSFORMATION
(1966–1971)

A tradition is kept alive only by
something being added to it.

—Henry James, *Partial Portraits* (1888)

By spring 1966, Fritz Maytag was at a crossroads. The brewery was dirty, its equipment old and run-down, its processes haphazard, and the quality of its beer inconsistent at best. Jack London would have called Anchor—in his day or in Fritz's—a "magnificent atavism." Frozen in time, it had just

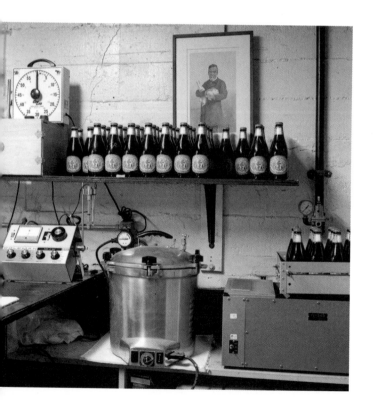

The Lab in 1971, with engraving of Pasteur

one pump. The boiler barely worked. The ancient malt mill resisted adjustment. There were no doors on the brew kettle. And other than the tap box, the only cooling was a decrepit refrigerator (not a Maytag). Within it, next to the cold cuts and cheese, sat a milk can full of yeast, which often foamed out of the fridge onto the floor.

For decades, they'd brewed too infrequently to maintain a viable yeast strain. So, like Gold Rush brewers, they improvised. "We used to get our yeast at all the breweries." In Joe Allen's day, that had meant breweries like Acme, Regal, and Burgermeister. Fritz got his "at Falstaff in San Jose, Hamm's, Lucky Lager, and Burgie, and then we got it in Santa Rosa at the Grace Brothers, so that was five different ones. We only brewed once a month and I would switch; I would get yeast from one brewery and then another and then another, so I was never pestering them more than twice a year. And they were very, very gracious."

But would Fritz remain in angel mode or roll up the sleeves of his crisply pressed white shirt and go all in, remaking Steam Beer Brewing Company and its unique beer to his own developing vision of what they could be? "I was insane for ten years," he recalls. What kept him going? "Well, among other things, the shame of failure. I was just determined. You know, I got some interesting lessons from a study at Harvard Business School. They

encouraged the students to have a business plan and start a business. And then they tried to buy the plans from them. Nobody would sell. They didn't want to make money. They wanted to be *proven right*. And I got that." The true entrepreneur? "I had that in me somehow, but I didn't realize it, I guess. And I was ashamed, you know, to think that we could—that I would—fail. It would have been very embarrassing—invest in this stupid brewery and spend a lot of money, and then fail?" That was not the Maytag Way. Nor was it the way of the West, "the genius of the West especially," as a *New York Times* correspondent had written about the transcontinental railroad a century before, "which welcomes obstacles and looks on impossibilities as incentives to greater exertion."

Like angels Buck, Blake, and Mortensen before him, Fritz Maytag eschewed the limelight. Steese had continued as the face, voice, and brewer of Anchor Steam Beer, while behind the scenes Fritz devoted himself to selling, marketing, and check-writing. Steese was quite content with—if not downright complacent about—the quality and consistency of the beer he made. Fritz, on the other hand, was becoming increasingly vexed by his company's unreliable, often sour product. His abiding curiosity, coupled with his fierce determination to succeed, compelled him to understand what was happening to the beer and why. His ambitious, almost quixotic quest: to take responsibility for Steam Beer and make it right. *Carpe cervisiam!*

THE SELF-TAUGHT BREWER

Supposing is good, but finding out is better, as Mark Twain liked to say. To scale the mountain of problems at Steam Beer Brewing, Fritz needed a

Sherpa, and there was none better for brewing than the 1957 translation of Belgian professor Jean De Clerck's two-volume 1948 treatise, *Cours de Brasserie (A Textbook on Brewing)*. "Volume I was how to brew, and Volume II was how to study what you'd done. De Clerck was our bible, and I read it just constantly. I used to fall asleep with it in my lap at home."

From Seidensticker, Fritz had learned that a great translator needs to be both accurate and poetic. Now, from De Clerck, Fritz learned that "a distinction is frequently drawn in the industry between the theoretical man who tries to explain everything from a scientific point of view and the practical man who relies on empirical knowledge and experience. A good brewer should be able to steer a middle course between these two extremes." Until Fritz came along, Anchor had relied—and survived—on Gold Rush traditions handed down from generation to generation of practical men. It was time to right the helm. Fritz thirsted for knowledge. "I used to go to breweries when they closed—and they were closing all the time in those days—to look for used equipment, and also I wanted brewing books and a complete run of the *Master Brewers Technical Quarterly* and *Wallerstein Laboratories Communications*. Those were the two journals in English that were useful, and I got a lot out of them." At Stanford, he'd learned Seidensticker's philosophy of translation, of striking a balance between accuracy and poetry. Now he was learning Wallerstein's philosophy of brewing: that it is both science and art, the former in service to the greater mastery of the other.

As his library grew, Fritz returned daily to his well-worn De Clerck, like a novitiate to scripture. Volume I became so stained and tattered that he soon had to replace it. Within its pages, De Clerck offers up a cautionary tale about the public, who "may be unable to distinguish purity of flavour, and sales may be good for a time, but without being able to give any definite reason, the customer will ultimately tire of it." So whatever the type of flavor, De Clerck warns, "it should always be pure, or clean, or clear cut." And the beer "should always be uniform. . . . The whole brewing process from beginning to end should be carefully watched and controlled if uniformity of quality is to be maintained." But watching, as Fritz was about to learn, was a lot easier than controlling.

Fritz recalls,

I was reading De Clerck of course, who said you should have a certain degree of evaporation from the kettle per hour, so I couldn't wait to measure our evaporation. That was when I first discovered how hard it is to do a real experiment in the real world, because the brew kettle stack was up against the Blake, Moffitt & Towne Building next door and, depending on the wind direction, we would have more or less evaporation, because the boil would take place in a very different way. But one of the things I realized is that the kettle had no doors and that we couldn't really boil the wort the way we wanted to—when I came, they were just kind of simmering the wort. So I had our coppersmith Fred Zaft put doors on the kettle, and that was a big deal.

With the rigor of De Clerck and the vigor of JFK, Fritz began nudging his little brewery into the twentieth century. He hung a shower curtain in a corner, behind which he had his original lab—Anchor's first. On the wall, he hung an old hand-colored engraving of Louis Pasteur, who still watches over Anchor's lab today. And he brought in his microscope—the one he'd had since he was fifteen—like a sextant to a wayward clipper ship. Fritz likes to joke, "The experts tell you never to look through the microscope, because if you see bacteria, it is already too late." And at the brewery, when he peered through its lens his jaw dropped like that of a modern-day Leeuwenhoek to behold a tiny universe, teeming with what the seventeenth-century Dutch microscopist called *diertgens* ("animalcules"). Fritz liked to call them "wee beasties" or just bugs. And there were more bugs at his brewery than a Volkswagen dealership, from wort-spoilage bacteria like *Obesumbacterium proteus* to beer-spoilage bacteria like *Lactobacillus pastorianus*.

Microbiological control, De Clerck stresses, is essential throughout the brewery, because the "risk of undesirable infection in beer starts from the moment the hot wort from the hop back begins to be cooled." So in April 1966, Fritz began an exhaustive scientific study of the yeast and bacteria in his brewery, from coolship to taproom, using his microscope, an autoclave, dozens of petri dishes, an incubator, and an ebulliometer (an instrument for determining alcoholic content). If his De Clerck had come with a holster, he would have worn it. He also relied on *Yeast Fermentation and Pure Culture Systems* ("To be a good 'beer brewer' one also must be a good 'yeast grower'"), the thousand-page *Basic Bacteriology* ("We have attempted to explain bacteriological phenomena rather than merely to state their occurrence"), and *Practical Points for Brewers: A Reference Book for all Interested in the Arts of Brewing and Malting.*

Fritz's bacteriological sleuthing began as soon as Steese pumped the hot wort out of the

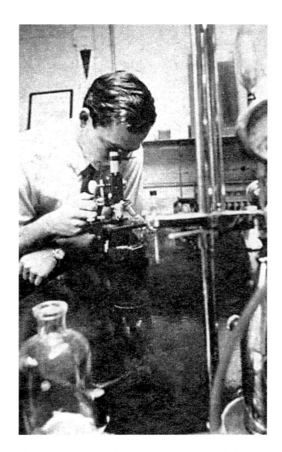

This Bausch & Lomb microscope traveled with Fritz Maytag from Newton to Deerfield to Stanford to Steam Beer Brewing Company, where it played a pivotal role in the birth of craft brewing.

brewhouse up to the coolship. Taking and testing samples all night was a lonely job, but Fritz kept himself company in his notebook: "Quite pleased with my sterile technique tonight," he scribbled, or "incubated at 3:15 AM Goodnight." Occasionally, Fritz's tests confirmed his fears: "I am very worried," he noted, after "micro observing" lactic acid bacteria in samples taken from the taproom taps. He also noted questions for future study: "How much oxidation does our beer have by the time it hits the keg?" and "What color would our beer be without the coloring?"

In the summer of 1966, Fritz initiated phase two of his De Clerckian study of the whole brewing process on the brew with Steese.

JANIS JOPLIN

In 1965, Big Brother & the Holding Company got its start, jamming in the basement of an old Haight-Ashbury mansion where Chester Leo "Chet" Helms and others made their bohemian home. In 1966, Chet invited his friend from Texas, Janis Joplin, to join the band. His Family Dog production company sponsored their first concert together, which took place at the Avalon Ballroom on June 10, 1966.

Chet hired photographer Bill Brach, hailed by rock 'n' roll historian Hank Harrison as "one of the most brilliant photographers to emerge from the Haight-Ashbury experience," to take pictures of Janis and Big Brother at the brewery in early June. Bill, who hadn't heard Janis sing with them, said, "Chet, you already have the best band in town—why do you want to add a new singer?"

Fritz was there that day. "I don't think I knew who they were. Chet had just told me that there was this person that he thought was a fabulous singer and that he had talked her into coming out to California and that he wanted publicity. He thought that the brewery might give it some attention because it was a San Francisco institution and that

way somebody might notice and print something about her." Ironically, after showing Chet the contact sheets, Bill remembers Chet saying, "Bill, I can't use any of the photos because there isn't one picture that doesn't have a glass of beer in it!'"

One of those pictures—of the band in the taproom—was pasted into an old Anchor scrapbook, without a clue as to who took it and when. Years later, a friend of Bill's called, asking me if I might be interested in meeting him. As it turned out, he had shot a whole roll of film that June day. Fritz and I selected our favorites, which Bill printed by hand and signed for Anchor. These rare images evoke a magical era in San Francisco rock—and brewing—history. The band members, relaxing by the potbellied stove in the old taproom, are (left to right) Janis, Dave Getz, Peter Albin, James Gurley, and Sam Andrew.

This required more than a modicum of diplomacy, but Fritz's notes show that it was all about "we," not "I," as in "we dropped mill down one notch and got much better grinding." Their time together was invaluable to his understanding of the old ways, as Fritz begin to feel like a fine art conservator, slowly removing the varnish from an ancient painting.

THE COBALT SCARE

In June, Fritz witnessed for the first time the skill and savvy of Henry Brazell King, president of the USBA, of which Steam Beer Brewing Company was the smallest member. King both represented and defended the industry, and, like Seidensticker before him, would become one of Fritz's greatest mentors.

A new disease had broken out—in Quebec in 1965 and Omaha and Minneapolis in 1966—that became known as "beer drinkers' heart disease." It had taken the lives of thirty-seven heavy beer drinkers, but no one knew why. When Henry King found out that cobalt chloride—an additive used to give beers made with adjuncts like corn or rice better foam stability and adhesion (lacing) in dishwasher-washed glassware—was the likely culprit, he leapt into action, calling every brewer in the USBA. He didn't care to know who was using cobalt and who was not (Fritz was not). And he didn't care that the use of cobalt was legal in beer, up to 1.5 parts per million. He just wanted a commitment from every brewer that they would sign an affidavit that said, effective June 14—seventy-two hours after Henry made his first call—they were not using cobalt at all. And he got that commitment, nearly two months before all "food containing any added cobaltous salts" was "deemed adulterated" and therefore illegal. Fritz was impressed.

In November 1966, Fritz attended the United States Brewer's Academy's two-week "Executive Seminar in Brewing" at Schwarz Laboratories in Mount Vernon, New York. He took notes on everything from Northern Brewer hops ("similar to Brewers Gold") to how many pounds per barrel of hops American breweries were using in 1966 (".278," which, he noted, "in the 1930s was .7") to methods of clarifying beer (centrifuges and diatomaceous earth filters) and bottling ("2% loss of beer pretty good for long runs but smaller runs even more"). It was the first of many seminars that he and his future employees would attend and eventually host.

During the winter of 1966–67, Fritz was back in Chile making wine. In March 1967, he returned to the brewery with renewed resolve, scribbling in his notebook: "Bought new ebulliometer, cleaned lab, re-caulked awning, + hung plastic sheet. Seems very good." He also approached State Senator John Burton (unaware of the campaign fundraiser the brewery had thrown for him and his brother Phillip in 1964) about the inequities of the state's regressive beer manufacturers' annual license fee, which, at $828, cost a brewery as small as Fritz's more than 75¢ a barrel, compared to 0.1¢ for the much bigger Hamm's Brewery down the street. Burton helped pass a measure that distinguished between beer manufacturers, at $828, and steam beer manufacturers, at $56, because of the local historical value of the latter. Fritz had hoped for a reduced fee for all small brewers below a certain size, not "steam beer brewers," but it didn't really matter, because there wouldn't be any other small brewers in California for years to come.

THE DECISION TO BOTTLE

Fritz knew all along that his brewery would have to bottle if it were to succeed. Without a bottled product, he recalled,

I cannot tell you what a struggle it was. There wasn't a beer distributor in America who had even the *slightest* interest in handling some

goofball small-brewery beer that tasted different, and looked different, and wasn't part of the standard world of brewing. Retailers didn't need it. We were draught only, and in those days, draught was not an in thing. American lager draught was fairly common, and there were a few imported beers on draught—Heineken, Guinness, Watney's maybe—but that was a rare thing. And of course that was our target, because their customers were already kind of in the mood for something different, but the last thing they wanted was a dumb American brewery with a funny beer. They wanted, you know, Guinness from Ireland, Heineken from Holland, whatever. So it was a very, very, very, very difficult sell. And it was very, very, very slow to get a retailer to take it, and later on to get a wholesaler to.

So in 1967 Fritz decided they should take the big step and begin bottling their beer. Serendipitously, that April, an opportunity interrupted Fritz's ongoing study of brewery processes and quality control. Chicago's Sieben's Brewery and Bier Stube was closing; its bottling line was for sale.

Fritz jumped at the chance to buy Sieben's twenty-four-valve Meyer filler and Meyer-Dumore eight-wide, three-compartment quart bottle cleaner.

I went ahead and bought the bottle washer, even though we didn't intend to reuse bottles, because I thought that it was very likely in those days that we would be forced to use a returnable bottle, which was a horrible thought, and which did not come about, because of the really sophisticated system for recycling that California put in place, which I still think is really clever. They couldn't sell us their labeler; they'd already sold that, so that was one of the biggest delays we ever had. We bought a secondhand World Rotary labeler through a machinery salesperson, somebody who knew the used market. We always thought he should have been put in prison for what he did. He found us a labeler that was just exhausted, and it was completely impossible to get it to work. But we were not in a big, big hurry, because we were still trying to perfect the beer and the filtration process.

Fritz's unhurried attitude in the run-up to bottling belies his Maytag determination. Throughout his career, when it came to such large-scale undertakings, he would follow Goethe's maxim *Ohne Hast, aber ohne Rast*, "without haste, but without rest." In May 1967, after a courtship that included several winemaking trips to Chile, Fritz married Lucy Diggs Jaleski, who had graduated from Brown University's Pembroke College in 1963. She had two young children from a previous marriage, Matthew and his younger sister Alexandra, who meant the world to them both. Almost overnight, Fritz had gone "from a hippie to a married man with two children and a house and a company of his own. It was like being jerked off the dock, like standing on the dock on your water skis and the speedboat has taken off and you're watching the rope get tighter and, at any moment now, the rope is gonna be tight, and you are going to go from standing on the dock to skiing, instantaneously—or dragged like a fool."

In the summer of 1967, after a restful honeymoon in England, Fritz was back at the brewery, still in pursuit of quality draught beer as the first signpost on his journey to quality bottled beer. He dreamed about his brewery every night, as he would for the next fifty-plus years, believing that one is not a full-fledged brewer 'til the nightmares start—what he half-jokingly calls his "weekend work." But to achieve his goals, it was time to get hands-on with every aspect of the brewing process: grinding malt, mashing, lautering, boiling and adding hops, cooling, fermentation, filtration, racking, and ultimately bottling, all with De Clerckian thoroughness, *proving*—as in its original meaning, *to make trial of*—everything that the brewery was

YORK CREEK

In 1968, Fritz bought a 320-acre ranch that runs up and over the crest of the mountains west of the Napa County town of St. Helena, a tranquil country place that would serve not as a winery, but rather as a retreat for him and his new family. Although the trees outnumbered the grapevines, he named it York Creek Vineyards (YCV), "in honor of the defining feature of the land, the wild and beautiful creek, which flows all year—undisturbed by the hand of man—for a mile and a half through thick forests and redwood groves. On hot summer days it has a pleasant, cool, trick-ling sound; and during winter rains it roars like a locomotive."

The old Petite Sirah vines there contributed to the complexity and varietal spice of the 1969 and 1971 Freemark Abbey Petite Sirahs, as well as those created for Ridge Vineyards, from 1971 on, by Fritz's "Vintners' Peace Corps" comrade Paul Draper. In March 1970, Fritz decided to do what his father had done at Ames years before: find the nearest land-grant college. He enrolled in a fermented beverage technology course at UC Davis on the "Composition and Quality of Wine and Beer as Related to Raw Materials." There were students from old-time breweries Burgermeister, Hamm, Lucky, Molson, Olympia, and Schlitz, as well as aspiring young vintners like Dick Erath, Mike Grgich, Louis Martini Jr., R. Michael Mondavi, Robert Stemmler, Bob Travers, and Fred Weibel Jr., with whom Fritz felt a special kinship. Since that time, Fritz has added thousands of grapevines and more than five hundred acres to his property, which offers stunning views of Napa Valley from Spring Mountain.

doing and might do. After a few more collaborative brews with Steese, Fritz felt that he was ready to take over the brewhouse, a decision easier to make than to implement. Steese was a good man, a salt-of-the-earth character who had saved the brewery and Steam Beer from extinction.

"At first, he and I saw things a lot alike," Fritz recalls. "It was just after I realized that the beer had to be improved, the brewery had to be cleaned up, and we had to learn all about brewing, and we had to be technical, and my whole childhood interest in chemistry and quality and all that sort of thing. And then we tangled, because he just couldn't stand the idea of being careful and besides—oh, he was just a rascal." But the only way the brewery would ever move into the twentieth century was if Fritz took over as brewmaster, bringing the science directly to the art.

GENTLEMAN BREWER

Fritz's first solo flight took place on September 28, 1967, with Brew #20 of just twenty-six that year. Lawrence didn't keep brewcharts, but rather just made quick notes—original Balling, final Balling only. Fritz recalls that, "Joe Allen had taught Steese to compute alcohol from that and would teach me. One day Joe, who occasionally stopped by the brewery for a beer and a chat, offered to walk me through the math, unaware that I already knew the formula. But then he surprised me. With a twinkle in his eye, he asked, 'But what do you do if the alcohol is too high?' I confessed I had no idea, upon which he turned his pencil around, erased the original Balling, wrote in a lower number, and laughed his hearty laugh!" Fritz, with increasing self-reliance, would be Steam Beer Brewing's only brewer for the next fifteen months. The entire brewery was now his ship, quality and consistency his lodestars, and brewcharts his captain's log.

Fritz was able to stay focused thanks to the protection of "Big Dave" Lyon. Hired by Steese in

1961, he had painted a portrait of St. Nicholas, patron saint of brewers, that hung in the brewhouse. Called *Brewers' Icon*, it graces Anchor's brewhouse to this day. Dave, very tall and strong as an ox, delivered the kegs. "Lifting a keg of beer for him," Fritz remembers, "was like lifting a case of beer for the rest of us." At dawn one day, as Fritz began mashing in, a retailer dropped by to say hello. Fritz nodded to Big Dave, who struck up a conversation with their uninvited guest. As he spoke, Dave gradually moved closer and closer to his prey, who had to keep backing up until, before he realized what had happened, he'd been backed right out the back door. "Great to see you! Thanks for stopping by. Come back anytime!"

Besides Big Dave, there was Bob Winnie, a handyman/carpenter who built malt carts for the flatbed to make it easier to get malt from Bauer-Schweitzer, who didn't deliver and didn't bag their malt. And there was Steese and his wife Frances. But it was Fritz, faced with a dizzying array of choices, who was making the hundreds of decisions that would accelerate the evolution of—and ultimately define—Steam Beer.

To cut corners, Lawrence had been adding sugar and/or malt syrup to the brews. But rather than immediately returning the recipe to its all-malt origins, Fritz opted to experiment with

FOR THE BREW-CURIOUS:
THE BALLING SCALE

The Balling scale was devised by Bohemian chemist Karl Balling in the 1840s, based on his observations that the total amount of dissolved materials (extract) in wort increases the density of wort in approximately the same proportion that saccharose (sucrose) increases the density of water. For his measurements, he used a weighted, floating instrument called a saccharometer, a special hydrometer calibrated to measure the density of sugar solutions at a specific temperature. For his scale, Balling defined a solution of 1° Balling as having the same density as a sucrose solution consisting of 1 gram of sucrose dissolved in enough water to make 100 total grams of solution. A Balling of 1, in other words, meant 1% by weight, 10 meant 10% by weight, etc. The Balling scale was later refined by Adolf Brix and Fritz Plato. Today, Anchor also uses refractometers for measurement and analysis.

The dissolved solids (primarily sugars) in wort make it heavier than water alone, so a saccharometer floats higher in wort than water and its Balling is higher than water. During fermentation, fermentable sugars are converted to alcohol (which is lighter than water) and CO_2, the density drops, the hydrometer sinks, and the Balling goes down. For any given beer's recipe then, the brewer will have a target and measured original Balling before fermentation and an expected and measured final Balling after fermentation. Armed with such measurements, it is possible to predict the alcohol content of the fully fermented beer.

So, if Anchor Steam, for example, has an original Balling when it leaves the brewhouse of 12.4° and a final Balling after fermentation of 3°, a quick prediction of the alcohol by weight can be made by multiplying the difference by .42: 12.4 − 3 = 9.4 x .42 = 3.948% ABW. To quickly convert ABW to ABV, multiply the ABW by 1.25: 3.948 x 1.25 = 4.935% ABV. Joe Allen had asked Fritz, "but what do you do if the alcohol is too high?" Joe's amusing solution: erase 12.4 and write in a lower number!

The brewhouse sink holds (L to R): the hydrometer, iodine for checking the starch-to-sugar conversion of the mash, and thermometer.

different amounts of sugar and malt syrup to fully understand their impact on the finished product. Given the plethora of light lagers made in San Francisco, it was no wonder Bauer-Schweitzer Malting Co., which had been malting for the brewery since Baruth & Schinkel's day, offered little variety. Their "Brewers Malt," a lightly roasted pale malt, had necessitated the addition of coloring to the kettle to give Steam Beer its traditional amber hue. In May 1970, to return the brewery to its all-malt origins and the beer to its original color, Fritz began adding caramel malt, which he called "dark malt," to the grain bill instead of coloring, varying the amount of dark malt until he felt the beer had achieved the proper color, as well as body and mouthfeel. And though there would be exceptions due to availability, he opted for 2-row over 6-row barley malt, so named because of the number of rows of kernels grouped around each stem. The former was more common in nineteenth-century California and hence more traditional. It has plumper, more consistently sized kernels and somewhat thinner husks, which had the added benefit of making it ideal for the brewery's small, primitive, pre-Prohibition, two-roll mill.

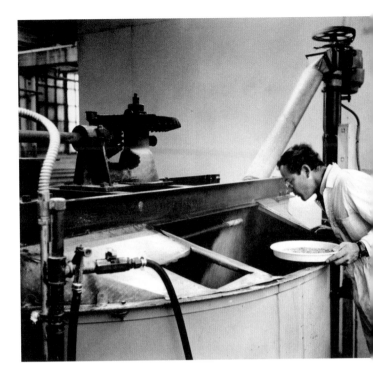

From De Clerck, Fritz learned of the acidifying action of calcium salts in improving the quality of beer, and he began experimenting with Burton salts, used by brewers to simulate the hard water used by the pale-ale brewers of Burton-on-Trent. He experimented with sodium chloride and calcium chloride, ultimately opting for calcium sulfate or gypsum.

Although he liked the whole-cone California Cluster hops the brewery was using, Fritz experimented with pellets ("pressed Calif. Hops for 50% approx. of hops") just to be sure he'd made the right call. And he tried the hops he'd planted at York Creek. After dumping that brew, he vowed never again to be "the entrepreneur that brings his home to work." But "*everybody* was using Cluster in those days," so Fritz wanted something unusual and distinctive. On March 7, 1968, he tried Northern Brewer hops for the first time, a dual-purpose (bittering and aroma) hop that immediately won him over with its subtle woody, peppery, herbal character. The longer one boils hops, the bitterer; the shorter, the more aromatic. So next he focused his hop experiments on the amounts, timing of additions, and number of additions—as many as four in the kettle plus a final addition to the hop jack. Eventually, he settled on three additions of Northern Brewer in the kettle.

Finally, since he was still getting yeast from a variety of sources, Fritz started noting whose yeast he used for each brew and how much. That way he could track its viability and effect, until, years later, he brewed often enough that he could successfully maintain the brewery's own yeast strains.

While refining the recipe for Steam Beer, Fritz confronted his nemesis: the cantankerous combination mash tun/lauter tun. Fritz had read that the French called the bottle filler *machine horrible*, because of all the damage that a bottling machine can do to beer, the difficulty of keeping it sterile, keeping the air out, and all the rest of it. "But the mash/lauter tun was the first horrible machine I encountered. It was a very common, simple compromise. It was not a great mash tun and not a great lauter tun, but certainly in England it was the norm. We had an unbelievable battle with that machine. The bed of grains in the mash/lauter tun was three, three-and-a-half feet thick. I spent, I swear, hundreds of hours struggling with that horrible machine, trying to get a decent runoff, a decent conversion. And I'd read De Clerck, and I thought you had to do it the way De Clerck says, but of course the problem was that it was just a very, very crude system. It was hopeless." But, according to English writer G. K. Chesterton, "it is only when everything is hopeless that hope begins to be a strength at all."

A HELPING HAND

As he acquired more knowledge from books and magazines—some from breweries that were closing, some from Foyles in London—brewing courses, and now hands-on brewing experience, Fritz started to ask more questions of his fellow brewers. Many of them saw him as a sort of Don Quixote, tilting at malt mills. Yet they were generous with their time and expertise, just as Fritz would be with future generations of small brewers.

In those days there was a tremendous sense of camaraderie and loyalty in the brewing industry among production people. You didn't go to Coors and ask them how to advertise, or how to print the 6-pack, or where they got their fancy neons. You didn't go for marketing, but for production, brewer to brewer, a brotherhood that was one of the thrills I found. And even at the very beginning when I took over the brewery, there were some people, some of whom are dear to my heart even to this day, who treated us as though we were a real brewery, which we were not. We were a *joke!*

Fritz adds, "The brewers at Lucky Lager were the biggest brewers locally that were helpful." One

brewer there was Otto Hans Wiesneth, who had come to America in 1957 from Eltmann, a small town in Bavaria where his family had had a lager beer brewery. In 1958, he enlisted in the US Marine Corps, becoming a US citizen four years later. He took a job in San Francisco with General Brewing, whose brewery in the Bayview district had been making Lucky Lager since Repeal. Fritz first met Otto in 1967, on a yeast run to Lucky's. Though Otto was a few months older, Fritz remembers the slender, six-foot assistant brewmaster as a young guy. Undoubtedly, Otto's gemütlichkeit belied his brewing acumen. "I asked him to come and take a look at my combination mash and lauter tun. 'Oh,' he said, 'you have a combination mash and lauter tun?' He knew right away what it was. He knew his stuff. He was a hands-on brewer—from his family."

The next day, Otto

came to the brewery, and we climbed up the ramp onto the back of the mash/lauter tun and I told him how horrible it was, and he could see the whole thing of course, immediately you know. To anyone who knew anything about brewing, it was immediately obvious what our problems were, which was that *everything* was wrong! But Otto Wiesneth climbed up and jumped into the mash/lauter tun, right there in front of my eyes. Now I'd been in that damn thing I don't know how many times. You had to get in it to shovel out the grain. But when he jumped into the lauter tun, I thought now there's a man who loves brewing. He did it with *enthusiasm!* I just loved it. Yeah, a lot of engineers, you know, they keep their hands clean, but he just jumped in. I couldn't believe it. I loved him.

Enthusiasm is a word that Fritz would use again and again throughout his life, as both guiding principle and high praise—cognizant, like Ralph Waldo Emerson, that "nothing great was ever achieved without enthusiasm." Right away, Otto saw that "the screens in the bottom were not real lauter tun screens; they were simply plate screens with holes drilled in them. Later we bought real [stainless steel] lauter tun screens with slots that are bigger on the bottom than they are on the top, that hold the grain back but allow the liquid to flow through."

And Otto offered to have the Lucky lab analyze the grist from Steam Beer Brewing's ancient two-roll mill with their sieve shaker, which Fritz had read about in De Clerck. It held a stack of five round sieves with different sized openings. When it shook the stack, the grist sample from the malt mill fell through the sieves, from coarse to fine, coming to rest in each at a measurable percentage of the sample. Fritz was concerned that he might be grinding his malt too fine, perhaps contributing to the bad conversions and poor runoffs. Otto recommended he go even finer.

I was just doing everything by the book and of course the book was De Clerck and of course our grind was completely horrible compared to what you were supposed to be doing. But I was unable to do any better with our mill. And then, at the new brewery in 1979, when we finally got a mill that could grind it exactly the way that we wanted it, we said let's don't change it. Even with our new mill, we tried to emulate the grind of the old mill at 8th Street. I frequently said if someone ever comes in and tries to change the grind, I hope everybody will fight it, because I think it's one of our secrets. And anybody who knows anything would prove right away how much money you could make by improving the grind and getting a higher yield, but the yield didn't matter a hoot to me. The price of barley was nothing compared to the price we were getting for our beer and the profitability of being a standout in the marketplace. So I was never sure, but I always thought that our original, pretty rough grind was actually not a bad idea.

In March, Fritz left for Chile. But he was back on the brew April 22, when he finally achieved a good conversion and runoff. With gratitude and optimism, Fritz invited Otto to observe the next brew on May 4. To Fritz's embarrassment, he had a poor conversion and bad runoff that day. Quality was improving, but consistency was still a crapshoot. Fritz had been so impressed by Otto that he "offered him a job to run my brewery." But by that time, Otto had already accepted a position at Schlitz in Tampa as corporate assistant brewmaster. (From there, he went on to manage Schlitz's Honolulu and Milwaukee plants, eventually returning to Tampa, where he managed the old Schlitz brewery again under four names: Stroh, Pabst, Stroh again, and finally Yuengling.) Fritz learned a lot from Otto, especially about *Freude am Brauen*—the joy of brewing. Soon, Fritz would have his own sieve shaker in the brewhouse. But more importantly, he realized how much he needed someone by his side with Otto's enthusiasm, can-do spirit, and moxie.

Gordon MacDermott remembers being interviewed on April 9, 1968, not by Fritz Maytag, but by Lawrence Steese.

Steese: We need to build this wall here to separate the fermenting room from the brewhouse. So when can you start?

Gordon: When do you want me?

Steese: Well, can you start tomorrow?

Gordon: Sure.

And that was that.

Fritz remembers Gordon as "my first employee in the sense that he had come to Steese's attention as a possibility to help in the brewery, and I was leaving for Chile, and I said, 'OK, you can hire him, but on a temporary basis, not full time, no commitment.' And when I came back from Chile, Steese had hired him full time. It was one of the things that Steese did that made me realize it just wasn't going to work."

By the time Lawrence hired Gordon, Bob Winnie had already left. Frances Steese took ill, so Carolyn Nadine Estes was hired in August 1968, to fill in as receptionist/secretary/bookkeeper. Carolyn, who grew up in Petaluma, learned the printing business from her stepfather, David (Jim) Makepeace, and was well-qualified to take care of the brewery's mounting paperwork—and bills. Always cheerful and efficient, Carolyn made sure her desk was adorned with fresh flowers every week. Sadly, Frances died that December, at just thirty-nine. She had brought hard work, dedication, and a loving spirit to the brewery.

Gordie, as he was then known, came to Steam Beer Brewing from a job at the post office, where he was criticized for completing his route ahead of schedule. He recalled when he first started working at the brewery:

One of the jobs was to pull the bungs and dump out the beer from the kegs. And then you'd wait 'til the next day to wash the kegs and put a bung back into them. And then another day would go by or two days and then maybe you'd fill the kegs. And when I first started doing it, I got all the bungs out and I got all the beer emptied out and I went and started washing all the kegs. [Dave Lyon] came over and said, "You know you won't have anything to do tomorrow if you do it all today!"

Even though we weren't brewing every week, within a very short time things were changing, things started happening; all of a sudden "Let's put this in, let's change this out, let's improve this, let's put a wall here so we can have a little

Gordon and Fritz

refrigeration for the three cellar tanks and for the kegs of beer."

It didn't take long for Fritz to realize that Gordie could turn anything he dreamed up into reality. Gordie soon became his right-hand man. Fritz's only proviso? If he was going to be managing people one day, Fritz said, he would need to be *Gordon*. And Gordie didn't mind a bit.

One of Gordon's first projects was the hot wort tank. Relatively new to the beer industry, its elegant simplicity made it a Fritz favorite:

We have several points in the brewing process where we're settling something out, because the ultimate product is a very clear kind of a clean liquid, and yet we start with something like oatmeal. In the lauter tun we're actually filtering by using the husks as a filter. After the brew kettle, we have the hop jack, a strainer that strains out the hops. Now the hot wort tank is interesting, because the wort, which contains fluffy little flakes of protein, is pumped into this circular settling tank at an angle, so that it swirls around in the tank. The protein quickly accumulates in the center of the tank. And that stuff at the bottom, including any little pieces of malt or hops that might still be in the wort, is called *trub*. It's like when you stir a cup of tea and you take the spoon out and all the tea leaves settle right down to the middle of the bottom. And it's so simple that it's marvelous.

For some time, Fritz had been concerned about the galvanized steel coolship, where the cooling wort remained vulnerable to bacteria for hours on end, until it was finally cool enough to drop to the starter fermentor below and pitch (add) the yeast. Any doubts he might have had about the coolship's obsolescence were dispelled the day he heard

The coolship

cooing in the cooling room. "I came in and there were pigeons everywhere." They came in through the dirty, broken windows. That was it. In no time, Fritz began investigating the *short time*, "one of the first serious things that Gordon did. That's what the dairy industry called the heat exchanger, our wort cooler. Dairy farmers used to cool the milk in cans in a bath, so when they started cooling it continuously in process, they called that the *short time*. We got it from the dairy industry, so we've always enjoyed calling it the *short time*, 'cause that's what the dairy guys called it. Nobody in the brewing business ever would have called it a *short time*." With characteristic alacrity, Gordon built a room and installed the short time himself, right next to the stainless steel hot wort tank.

Fritz championed the use of stainless steel in brewing, because once the hot wort exits the copper brewhouse and cooling begins, sanitation is critical. Surprisingly, though, he learned more about stainless steel from Bay Area dairy suppliers than from Maytag Dairy Farms:

My father died in '62, and I didn't realize I really had to be the family person in charge at the dairy farm until '65, '66. In those days, stainless steel was not being used in breweries to any great extent, and it was the dairy industry that helped us learn about it, that helped us make our equipment, that was making the kind of equipment we wanted—the sanitary fittings, the heat exchangers, the tanks, and all that stuff. But we learned about that not in Iowa, from the cheese making, so much as in San Francisco, from the dairy suppliers.

It was a bittersweet day when, on October 17, 1968, the last coolship in the West was demoted to hot wort holding tank, while Fritz sterilized the short time so *it* could do the cooling, quickly and cleanly. With the exception of the mild-steel combination mash tun/lauter tun and copper brewhouse, Fritz's brewery was well on its way to becoming the only all stainless steel, cleaned-in-place (CIP) brewery in the world.

A NEW LABEL SETS ANCHOR APART

In 1968, realizing that a labeler wasn't much good without a label, Fritz began sketching his ideas for one. Back in '59 in Japan, he'd enjoyed bottled Sapporo and liked the label's look and oval shape. Its verticality didn't work with the bottle he had in mind, but rotated 90 degrees, more like a Kirin label, it worked great, especially as his ideas for the label design began to gel. Fritz arced the words ANCHOR STEAM BEER above the illustrated anchor that the brewery had been using since the 1930s, adding hops and barley on either side of the anchor like parentheses. After verifying the year in an old city directory at the San Francisco Public

Library, he added the tagline "Made in San Francisco since 1896" along the bottom.

He was happy with the concept, but sensed that something was missing. So he called in Wilbur Rundles (Bill) Hyde, who had been the lettering man for the well-known San Francisco design agency Butte, Herrero, and Hyde, exhibited his work at the brewery in 1963, and even designed a US postage stamp depicting one of Fritz's heroes, Abraham Lincoln. Bill did exactly what Fritz thinks a great graphic designer should do: take a good idea and make it a great one. It was Hyde's idea to hand-letter the words ANCHOR STEAM BEER on a red banner, flapping cheerfully in the SF Bay breeze. And he came up with the label's mottled, yellow-ocher background, evocative of the brewery's Gold Rush heritage. However, Bill was more of a wine-label designer than a beer guy; that's why the hops on his original label look more like grapes. But that didn't bother Fritz at the time. He embraced the Japanese concept of *wabi-sabi* (侘び寂び), of the beauty to be found in imperfection. Plus, this was to be a handmade label for a handmade beer—the antithesis of most 1960s beer labels, with their glossy metallized paper and champagne aspirations. Instead, his label was quintessential '60s San Francisco: funky, offbeat, unconventional, and countercultural. No glitz, no glam.

This was long before labels came with government warnings, barcodes, or recycling information. So for the neck, Fritz wanted a wraparound label "filled with text. Even if you were nearsighted and couldn't read it, I wanted you to have the subliminal impression that there was a long story with our beer, a really good and wonderful story"—which there actually was—concluding with the self-assured truth: "This Anchor Beer is a hand-made beer, aesthetically pleasing and wholly superior in every respect."

On November 17, 1968, a newspaper article featured Lawrence Steese, who announced, much to Fritz's dismay, that Steam Beer Brewing would be bottling in early 1969. That wasn't going to happen, but on Thanksgiving Eve (November 27, 1968), Fritz and Ken Hepler (an old-school San Francisco lithographer) and their wives met in Ken's garage to print the four-color (black, yellow-ocher, blue, red) labels on his one-color Heidelberg press. This printing included the second of three iterations of the neck label, a result of ongoing efforts to get its design to center properly on the bottle.

With the printing of his new label, Fritz crossed the entrepreneurial Rubicon. On February 5, 1969, he bought out Steese's remaining 1% share. Lawrence "had an incredible task, moving and starting up again. Like Joe Allen, he ran the brewery almost single-handedly for years." Gordon, too, remembers Steese fondly: "To hear his life story—you name it, he'd done it. Like stepping back into the 1800s."

Fritz recalls,

When I told Lawrence that it was over, basically I went to Dave Lyon and told him that Steese was going to be leaving and no longer going to be involved, and that I hoped Dave would stay with the company, but I would understand if he didn't. And then I went to Gordon. And I told him the same thing. And Gordon said that he would like to stay, and what should he do? He was working on something way up high in the tap-room, a window into the shop or something. And I remember very clearly saying to him, "Well, finish what you're doing up there, and when you have finished that, come to me and tell me and I'll think of the next thing." And he did, and then another thing and another thing—a whole bunch of stuff, one by one—slowly trying to bring the brewery up. And he came to me again and again. And he was *something*. He was the rock on which I built the brewery.

MOVING FORWARD

By April 1, 1969, the Steam Beer Brewing Company was just Fritz and Gordon in the brewery and Carolyn in the office. Dave Lyon still helped with deliveries, but they were no longer made in the brewery's 1957 one-ton Dodge truck. In March, Fritz had bought a blue 1969 International Harvester flatbed, for $20 less than the brewery's purchase price three and a half years before. On April 1, Fritz was still on the brew. Gordon took the brewhouse reins with the next brew, April 10, one year to the day since his first day on the job, building a wall.

Having Gordon in the brewhouse gave Fritz time to study his options for the final step before beer is packaged. Known as finishing, it includes clarifying the beer and protecting it from spoiling.

L to R: Gordon, Fritz, and Phil

Two hundred years ago, the beer that's in the cellar would have been drunk just the way it was. It's perfectly fine and delicious; however, it's not clear, it's slightly hazy, there's a little bit of yeast left in suspension. Back then, they drank beer out of mugs and bowls and cups. They didn't know whether it was clear or not; it never occurred to them to worry about it. But nowadays we drink beer out of clear glasses, and modern aesthetics demands that beer, at least most styles of beer, be clear. The trick is to do as little harm as possible. The trouble with clarifying products is that you tend to strip beer of its flavor and aroma.

Since May 1969, he'd used diatomaceous earth (DE)—"marvelous sort of naturally occurring complex little crystals"—in a plate-and-frame filter. In it, a series of filter pads catch the DE and any solids remaining in the beer that might cause it to have a chill haze (that is, become hazy when cold), while allowing beer that's completely clear and ready to pass through.

"But if you don't pasteurize it or sterile filter it—which means literally filtering so tight that you

have removed the spoilage organisms—eventually it will turn sour. When we started bottling, I wanted to avoid pasteurizing." For filtering, Fritz had seen Sieben's

using the Millipore system. I may have heard about it at the Schwarz Laboratories Brewing Course, but I certainly saw it in place and decided we could do that. And that would allow us to avoid pasteurizing in the bottle. But we found that filtering so tightly in order to go through the Millipore was difficult, and I got the idea of flash pasteurizing. I had read about it in the *Master Brewers Technical Quarterly.* And Coors did really good, very interesting research articles on it, which really did inspire me. They said if anything, it might actually *improve* the flavor in the sense of blending flavors or rounding out flavors.

But the flash pasteurizer would need more study, so, like a Broadway director, Fritz decided to put it off until after opening night, continuing to rely on "sterile filtering using the Millipore filter, and frankly we never did get it to where we were sure. That's why we refrigerated it right from the beginning, and put KEEP REFRIGERATED on every case." In November 1970, a visit to Coors dispelled any lingering doubts Fritz had about bottling Steam Beer. He told Bill Coors that he "brought home a feeling of confidence in our ability to achieve our goals, which I owe to your staff and your enthusiasm."

1971

The bready, herbal aromas of the first brew of 1971 mixed with the frisson of excitement around the first bottling of Anchor Steam Beer in modern times. Although Fritz had hired a couple of part-timers in 1970, there was still plenty to do, so Fritz had Carolyn put the word out that the Brewery was looking for help. Philip Gabriel Canevari from Santa Rosa, fresh out of college, had been looking for a job as a high school English teacher, but his long hair and bushy beard—though certainly not unusual in San Francisco in the '70s—had been sabotaging his interviews. Phil recalls, "I got a call from an employment agency, and they said, 'Oh, we have a possible opening for you if you want to interview. It's at a brewery,' and I said, 'Oh God, I don't know anything about brewing.' 'Well, give it a try.' And I said, 'Sure.'"

So I go down on a Friday afternoon, and I met Gordon in the taproom. He was there by himself. It's a brewery, so I said, "Can I have a taste of the beer? If I'm getting in, I want to know what I'm getting into." So he pours me a beer. Pretty good! So he interviewed me—my military experience, mechanical training, helicopters—and he asked me a few questions. And he said, "Well, OK. I'll get back to you." And I said, "OK." And he said, "I'm coming in here tomorrow to rack beer." "Oh, what is that?" "Well, I'm gonna put beer in kegs, you know, fill kegs and get them ready for mar-

ket." "Kegs? Are you going to do this by yourself?" "Yeah." So I said, "Listen, I'm not doing anything tomorrow. Can I come in and possibly help you?" "OK." So I went in early Saturday morning and Gordon taught me all about washing kegs, racking beer, hammering the bungs in, rolling 'em down, and picking them up, and putting them on a pallet. And we racked a whole brew, about a hundred kegs. And then we put 'em in the cold box. We were done for the day. He said, "All right, you can start Monday."

Even with more hands on deck, "it took forever," Fritz recalls, "to get everything installed and working and then, the *labeler*. Gordon worked on the labeler literally for years, trying to get it to work. But we finally did the smart thing, which we could have—should have—done in many other areas in our work, but we wanted to do it ourselves and learn, and so there were some advantages in taking our time. But we just scrapped that old labeler and bought a new labeler, which came with all the proper measurements and no wear and tear, and suddenly our line came together."

Fritz and Gordon tell the story like best friends at a high school reunion:

FM: The labeler was so badly worn that we could never get it to do our job, which was a demanding job. An oval label and a wraparound neck label on a cold, wet bottle.

GM: That was a real struggle.

FM: We ended up finally buying a new World Rotary.

GM: And the washer was like a little locomotive.

FM: We had the filler bowl refinished with epoxy, but otherwise it was the same. And we were using the washer, the whole monstrous machine—

GM: *Only* to move the bottles from one end to the other—

FM: Only used at the very end, where we sprayed iodophor in the bottles."

Fritz was able to source amber, pry-off "NO DEPOSIT · NO RETURN / NOT TO BE REFILLED" bottles from Owens-Illinois in Portland. Amber glass protects the beer from sunlight, to which hops are very sensitive. To complement the blue

anchor on the label, Fritz chose a special blue for the crowns (bottle caps), which had a gold anchor and skirt. Before deciding on a suggested retail price, Fritz did a quick survey of the price of beer in San Francisco. He felt that his beer could command a price per bottle of 41¢ (about $2.64 today), comparable to the Mexican and Japanese imports, well below the European imports, and a clear cut above America's domestic beers. But he sensed that a six-pack of Anchor Steam at $2.46 would be a risky proposition. So he did the math that he hoped shoppers wouldn't do, and came up with the idea of a four-pack at $1.62 (about $11.23 today), which obfuscated the fact that by the bottle, his was America's highest-priced domestic beer.

On March 7, 1971, with just six weeks to go, Fritz Maytag and his brewery were the subject of an in-depth newspaper article, "Hometown Brew." Ever circumspect, Fritz Maytag made sure there was no mention of bottled beer. And, to his delight, he also managed to convince the reporter that his surname was *Magtay*. There would be no references to Maytag heirs or Maytag suds to jinx the upcoming bottling! Gordon remembers how "all the glass [brewer shorthand for bottles] came in loose in the trailer and you had to take it out one case at a time and restack it on pallets. The hand-stacking was to maximize all the cases in the semi, and we would spend the whole afternoon unloading them." With the glass in house, "Mr. Magtay" gave the go-ahead to test-bottle Brew #3 (even though its mash had not converted properly) on March 10, in order to fine-tune the line for the big day.

There were five stations on the line, as Gordon recalls: one, throwing glass (removing the bottles from their cases and sending them into the bottle washer); two, the filler (usually Phil, who remembers "tapping on the bottles to get the foam. The bottle has to foam, or you get too much airs"); three, the labeler (usually Gordon—the labeler was his baby); four, the rotating table (for casing off into the four-packs); and five, gluing and palletizing. Phil remembers using glue guns to seal the cases: "Talk about handcrafted beer—it was handcrafted packaging!" Although he wasn't there for the first bottling, everyone remembers a part-timer from Marin County for his exemplary skill on the bottling line. His nickname? "Four-pack Bill" Whidden.

On March 15, 1971, Gordon was on Brew #9 under Fritz's trusting but watchful eye. Its recipe called for 2,450 lb pale malt, 50 lb "dark" (caramel malt), 44 lb Northern Brewer hops (divided into four additions), and 8 lb Burton salts (divided into three additions). Before "going in with wort," Gordon used an acetylene torch on the fermentor's welds to kill any bacteria that might be growing in its nooks and crannies. Then he cleaned and rinsed the fermentor, started transferring the wort, and, at 3:05 p.m., pitched the yeast. This time it came not from Fritz's rotating lineup of local breweries. Instead, he wanted to try a pure culture yeast from Wallerstein Laboratories in New York. The wort was all in by 4 p.m. The beer was dropped into a sterile tank the morning of March 19, kräusened on March 23, and filtered April 22. Finally, on April 23, 1971, nearly a century after Gottlieb Brekle established Golden City Brewery, Fritz hung up a sign announcing that the brewery was preparing to bottle and asking visitors to postpone their visit. Then he locked the

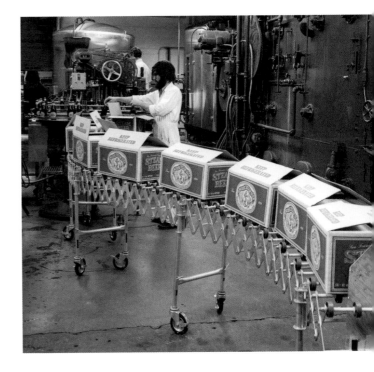

front door. Steam Beer Brewing Company bottled two hundred cases of Anchor Steam Beer that day. The sounds are etched in Fritz's memory. "We bottled at sixty bottles a minute. That was our standard, and I can still hear them coming off the filler: *Tsch . . . tsch . . . tsch . . . tsch.*"

Rejuvenating and elevating Anchor Steam Beer, from ingredients to recipe to equipment to process to bottling, was a Herculean and—at least with the combo mash/lauter tun and labeler—Sisyphean task. But in hindsight, Fritz and Gordon see it somewhat like Albert Camus: "The struggle itself toward the heights is enough to fill a man's heart. One must imagine Sisyphus happy." To Fritz, it was simple and logical: "Suddenly our line came together, and then our beer began to be good, and our process for filtering, so we started bottling." And Gordon concludes: "I don't think anything was tough. I mean everything was fun. That was the joy of being there. Every day, there you were, doing something you loved with people who cared."

Indeed, the bottle shop's maiden voyage was the work of a team. At the end of the day, Fritz asked Carolyn if she could break out a new receipt book and sell him some beer—at its retail price of $9.84 a case. Receipt #1: 1 case "for Freddie Kuh." Receipt #2 was for the bottling crew that day: 1 case each "for Gordie/Philip/Court/Norman/Carolyn/+Mr. Maytag." Court was Courtland T. Mudge, who had owned the Old Town Coffee House in Sausalito, backed Lawrence Steese early on, and worked as an electrician and carpenter at Fritz's brewery. Norman was Norman (Norm) D. Johnson, who'd worked at the brewery since the summer of 1970, delivered kegs, and collected COD and empties. Receipt #3: 1 case "for Joe Allen," who'd been at Anchor the last time the brewery bottled Steam Beer—in the 1930s!

After all the beer, toil, tears, and sweat, Fritz and his able staff were finally making Anchor Steam almost exactly the way he wanted to make it, using 2-row pale and caramel malt; fresh, whole-cone Northern Brewer hops; yeast—for the time being, wherever they could get it; and San Francisco tap water from Hetch Hetchy Reservoir in Yosemite National Park. No adjuncts, additives, flavoring, coloring, sugar, hop pellets, or extracts. Just great beer, made by hand in small batches in—paradoxically—the most modern traditional brewery in the world. In less than six years, Anchor Steam had become what Fritz likes to call the Platonic ideal of the perfect beer. It was the liquid manifestation of his radically traditional vision for Steam Beer Brewing Company. And that was just act one.

THE TRUE CRAFTSMAN
(1971–1975)

In all business, there is a factor which cannot be compensated for in dollars and cents or computed by any measure. It has no relation or connection with the mercenary and is represented only by the spirit of love which the true craftsman holds for his job and the things he is trying to accomplish.

—**Frederick Louis "F. L." Maytag** (**Fritz's great-grandfather**)

When Alice Waters opened Chez Panisse on August 28, 1971, no one could have known that she and her small Berkeley restaurant would change the way people cook, eat, and think about food in America. Nor, four months earlier, when Fritz Maytag started bottling on April 23, 1971, could anyone have known that he and his small San Francisco brewery would change the way people make beer, drink beer, and think about beer in America.

Monday, April 26 was just another day at the brewery for Norm Johnson, who loaded the flatbed with kegs and cases for the first time. By the end of the week, he would made forty-eight deliveries, up from twenty-five the week before. Before, he'd just delivered to bars and restaurants. Now he was delivering to liquor stores, neighborhood markets, and grocery stores, old accounts that wanted both kegs and bottles, and new accounts altogether, starting with Fritz's very first bottle account, Berkeley's Osaba Noodle Nook.

Local beer wholesalers began to take notice, including Don Saccani, who knew a good thing when he saw it. His father Al had started a wholesale beer business in Sacramento in 1936, distributing beers like Golden State, Pilsengold, and Burgermeister, and adding Hamm's to his lineup in 1951. Don, who got a job at Hamm's in 1954, opened his own distributorship, Anchor Distributing, in Marin County in 1962. Fritz: "It was a total coincidence that his company name was Anchor. He had been in the navy and so he had Anchor Distributing. That might have triggered his interest in us, just because of the coincidental symbiotic relationship of the names."

Don had been wholesaling Hamm's for years and, by 1971, Lucky Lager, Country Club Stout Malt

Liquor, Waldech (from Hamm's), Tuborg, and the only actual import in the bunch: Watney's.

There were 766 breweries in 1935, making a total 45.2 million barrels for per capita consumption of 10.3 gallons. Thirty-five years later, due to the gradual consolidation of the American brewing industry, there were just 154 breweries, making a total of 134.7 million barrels for per capita consumption of 18.7 gallons. And the ratio of bottled/canned versus draught beer flipped, from 30/70 percent in 1935 to 86/14 percent in 1970.

Don called Fritz as soon as he heard that Steam Beer was in bottles. But Fritz said no,

because financially he didn't see how he could make it work with a distributor. In mid-May, Fritz starting subbing for Norm whenever he was out or had too many routes to cover in one day. Fritz was becoming Anchor's "driver," much as Otto Schinkel Jr. had been in his day. He opened new accounts all over the Bay Area, like San Francisco's Buena Vista Café and Petrini's Market, Yountville's Chutney Kitchen, Menlo Park's Beltramo's Liquors, and Monterey's Capone's Warehouse. And it gave him the excuse to call on existing accounts such as the Oasis, Dutch Goose, The Anchor, Wine and the People, The Old Spaghetti Factory, Bernstein's, Alioto's, Tommy's Joynt, Perry's, and many more.

But by the end of May, Fritz and Norm were barely keeping up, so Fritz called Don: "OK, if you're really serious, I'll give you Santa Clara County." Fritz had learned that "this was about as far as you could go from the brewery and was the most difficult for me and, of course, for Don. But it was a proof of his sincerity and his energy that he said, 'Fine, I'll take it.'" Fritz likes to use the word *proof* in its original meaning as a test, as in *the exception proves the rule*. "And sure enough, Don started delivering to Santa Clara County and started developing new accounts. It was not part of his normal territory, but he could see it as an opportunity. Gradually and rather quickly I gave him everything except San Francisco, so he had the East Bay, Marin, and Santa Clara Counties, and I think he had San Mateo County." But Norm "decided to get married and so we were stuck, and I had to keep delivering." Forty-six deliveries in four days, after which Fritz, exhausted, turned the whole thing over to Don Saccani.

Despite the success of the first bottling of Anchor Steam in modern times, Fritz wasn't satisfied. A month later, he told a reporter, "We have not yet perfected bottling steam beer, although we're working on it." By that time, he'd already decreased the hops and doubled the amount of "dark" (caramel) malt in each brew, as he continued to tinker with the recipe. A year later, the recipe for Steam Beer was still evolving: 2,350 lb pale malt, 200 lb "dark," 45 lb Northern Brewer hops (divided into five additions), and 10 lb Burton salts (divided into two additions) per brew—the most noticeable difference being the beer's more distinctive amber color. True to form, Fritz wanted to explore the full range of possibilities, and bottled beer facilitated his brew-to-brew comparisons. And he had lingering reservations about sterile filtering.

HELP FROM A FELLOW BREWER

"John Segal, one of our hop suppliers and a wonderful man who loved brewing, was a delightful person, and became a very close personal friend,

knew that John Brzezinski at the Lone Star Brewery in San Antonio was using flash pasteurization for his bottled beers and recommended him to me." Brzezinski had joined Lone Star in December 1971, as vice president and technical director, following a twenty-three-year career at P. Ballantine & Sons in Newark, New Jersey. In 1972, Falstaff bought the Ballantine brands and closed its 132-year-old brewery. John Brzezinski never spoke with Fritz about Ballantine.

I went to see him on my own and again in early 1973 with Gordon [who had recently completed the same course in brewing at the United States Brewers' Academy that Fritz had taken back in 1966]. I don't know where John learned about flash pasteurization. I did not know then and still do not know of any other breweries using it on a commercial basis anywhere in the world at that time, but John swore by it, and I was terribly impressed. I knew about plate heat exchangers [the short time] because, of course, we were using that to cool our wort, and the beauty of flash pasteurization is that you heat the beer up to about 163°F and you hold it for about twelve seconds, and then you cool it immediately back down into the 30s, so the beer is hot only for a few seconds, and with no oxygen because it's a solid stream of beer. Whereas if you pasteurize in the bottle, you always have some oxygen in the bottle and then you have higher temperatures for a much, much longer time because you're heating the bottle up with warm water and then with hot water and then with very, very hot water, and if you're really good, you try to cool it back down with warm water and then with cool water and then with cold water. But many brewers would not cool it back down; they would just let the bottles come off of the tunnel pasteurizer and go into the case, which is even worse because it's insulated now, and then into the warehouse. So the beer would be warm for a long time and hot, even, for quite a while.

So the idea of having it go from very cold to hot to very cold in barely twelve seconds really appealed to me. And John was very encouraging, and I knew about plate heat exchangers, and so we set up our own flash pasteurizing system very soon after we started bottling. Meanwhile, I had gotten the idea of centrifuging rather than filtering, so in 1973 Gordon installed a Westfalia hermetic design automatic centrifuge, just a very accelerated gravity settling process, which takes out about 99% of the yeast and little else. So soon we began to centrifuge, rough filter [using DE], and flash pasteurize all of our beers, draught and bottle. We didn't shout the news from the rooftop, because in those days pasteurizing among true-blue beer lovers was assumed to be tunnel pasteurization in the bottle and was assumed to cause some harm to the beer because of the time it was hot in the presence of oxygen. But I thought it did a beautiful job, and I thought then and I still believe that Anchor Steam—especially Anchor Steam—was improved by it, along the line that Coors had hinted in their *Master Brewers* articles.

Fritz thanked John Brzezinski in 1973: "It makes me proud to be a member of the brewing profession when I see such traditional hospitality and good will as you showed us."

Gordon adjusting the centrifuge

HELP FROM A FUTURE BREWER

Mark Carpenter, who graduated from El Cerrito High School in 1961, remembers having his "first Anchor at LeRoy's Hooch House in Napa in 1962 or '63," where Steam and free salted-in-the-shell peanuts had been served since the Silverado Trail watering hole bought its first ten kegs from Lawrence Steese in 1960. Mark's first visit to the brewery was in 1971.

Yeah, I took a tour of the place. They had not started bottling but were just on the verge. And it was probably six months later that I went back and asked to see Fritz and asked him for a job. I'd quit my job at the telephone company like a year before. I was just having fun, traveling around, and figuring out what I was going to do. I'll betcha my interview was a week after I returned, 'cause as soon as I got back, I thought I'd better go find a job and I remembered the brewery, so I went down there and asked for a job. And Carolyn Estes, who was the secretary, remembered me from the tour and so she got me in to see Fritz. I had just returned from a trip to Europe where I'd gotten a motorcycle and gone all over, down through Yugoslavia and Greece. And he had done the same kind of trip probably ten years before or a little less, so we just talked about that more than anything, and I got hired.

On October 1, 1971, Mark's second day on the job,

I think I brewed with Gordon. It was really something 'cause it was real early in the morning you know, and just all the equipment. The mash tun had live steam injected in there to heat it up, and so when we changed temperature, you'd turn on these three live steam valves and it would inject steam into the mash tun and it made this really

Mark on the brew

circumstances." Bottled Steam should have garnered even more attention. Alas, there were no articles in the mainstream media in 1971 about Anchor Steam in bottles, one of the cyclic hazards of being dependent on free publicity. But that didn't mean there wasn't interest.

HELP FROM HOMEBREWERS

Homebrewers already knew about Anchor Steam. In March 1971, Fritz sold 750 lb of pale malted barley and 250 lb crystal malt "for malt vinegar" to Peter Brehm's home winemaking store in Berkeley, Wine and the People. In those days, there weren't so much homebrew shops as there were homebrewing corners in the back of home winemaking shops, like Peter's and nearby Oak Barrel Cellars. Peter, who had seen the article about "Mr. Magtay," told Fritz he hoped "it stimulates interest in 'The good brew.'" He noted how "interest has been gradually building for the all-grain beers. Some of this interest has radiated from your talks at our brewing classes, greatly appreciated by myself and the participants."

loud, rattling sound, which sounded exactly like at Tosca in North Beach, when they make their cappuccinos there and they steam the glasses with the spoon in it. It sounded like that exactly, but a lot louder. Anyway, it was a lot of fun. It was *really cool* making beer.

Sales had been flat in 1969 and 1970, at 1,254 and 1,264 barrels respectively. But in 1971, with about a third of the brewery's fifty-one brews going into bottles, Fritz got the boost in sales he'd hoped for, ending the year at 2,027 barrels. He observed, "This city is certainly one of the most unusual in the United States and has a history of supporting traces of its romantic past. It is also one of the drinkingest cities in the country, and the combination of these two facts means that free publicity for our beer is rather easy to come by. Honestly, I cannot imagine such a venture under any other

One homebrewer, Lee Coe, worked at the brewery off and on in the '70s as a tour guide. Fritz remembered Lee as "a true believer, really one of the very few people who gave me encouragement from the very beginning and who knew beer." And Lee was there bright and early April 26 to buy his first case of Steam. In November, Lee wrote Fritz about visiting The Anchor in Berkeley, "the saloon that used to be famous primarily because it had Steam beer. In 1936, when I first drank Steam there, it was located on San Pablo Ave. For many years now, it has been at 10th and University. The bartender told me proudly that he has Steam—in bottles." In his *The Beginner's Home Brew Book*, published in 1972, Coe admonishes his readers, "if you follow instructions, your home brew will be good, very good—your first batch and every batch. It will taste better than many US commercial beers, though not as good as the best, such as Ballantine Ale and Ballantine India Pale Ale in bottles, and San Francisco's famous and distinctive Steam beer in bottles and on draft."

Two years before, in April 1970, yet another brewer named Otto, Oregonian homebrewer Otto Frederick "Fred" Eckhardt, had offered a similar message in his groundbreaking *A Treatise on Lager Beers: An Analogy [sic] of American and Canadian Lager Beer*: "Beermaking began in the home long before it became commercial, and now we can take it back to the home. The commercial brewers in this country have tailored their product to the lowest common denominator. There are almost no quality beers made in this country, so if you want good old-country style beer you must make it yourself. Even the German beers imported into this country are being made to the so-called American taste. Pablum and pap for babies." Besides the fine instruction they offered, Fred's and Lee's unassuming books served as declarations of independence from the tyranny of mass-produced beer, fomenting a revolution that would eventually lead to the well-deserved recognition of quality home-brewed beers and the informed appreciation of revolutionary "work-brewed" beers like Anchor Steam.

In March 1971, a letter addressed to "Director, Anchor Steam Brewery" landed on Fritz's desk. It was from Fred Eckhardt, who had first sampled Anchor Steam Beer at the Old Spaghetti Factory in 1968 and was preparing an article on Steam Beer and its history for the *Purple Thumb*, a wine appreciation magazine. A professional photographer, Fred wanted to photograph the brewery, and he hoped to interview "the director" and the "brewmaster or technical director"—not realizing that at *this* brewery they were all the same person.

His visit led to the publication of several articles, the first of which declared, "Like many another person visiting San Francisco, I fell in love; not as you might imagine, with some frail petticoated

damsel, but rather with the one unique and distinct beer manufactured in all the United States—steam beer!" After a nod to Fritz's enthusiasm and dedication, Fred concluded, "Today Fritz Maytag makes an idealized beer, an infinitely more carefully controlled product than most of his lusty predecessors ever bothered to make."

To Mark Carpenter, Steam Beer Brewing was an idealized place to *work*:

I got a job at the brewery because I wanted to do something, a different job, and I wanted something kind of unusual. If I were looking for something unusual today, it wouldn't be brewing. Everybody and their brother's a frickin' brewer. But not then. If you told people you worked at Anchor Brewing, nobody knew what the F it was. You just didn't meet people who had ever heard of it, of Anchor Brewing Company, or steam beer. And that was fine. It was just a great job and looking back on it you can say, *oh yeah, I was part of this whole thing, this whole rise*, but at the time you weren't thinking about that. You were just going to work and having fun every day. And we had some great people we worked with, good personalities, funny and interesting.

Fritz had no worries about his happy handful of employees. But as 1971 drew to a close, he still had nightmares about the beer that—at least to him—was still far short of ideal, and a bottling line that had left him with a mountain of debt. So in late December, seeking recognition, he had the Thomas-Swan Sign Co. put up a new, 4 by 6-foot STEAM BEER BREWING CO. sign out front, with gold-leafed, prismatic letters on a black background. But it would take more than an expensive sign. He needed free press.

MEET THE PRESS

In January 1972, Don Wegars (UC Berkeley Class of 1963) wrote an article for the *San Francisco Chronicle* called "And Whatever Happened to Frisco Beer?" It lamented the ice-cold fact that there had been more than thirty San Francisco breweries in 1900 and now there were just three: Hamm's and Lucky Lager, with their million-barrel capacities, and the oldest and smallest, Steam Beer Brewing.

Beer sales in California in those days belonged to "imports" like Coors at 33% and Olympia at 12.4%, as well as Anheuser-Busch's Los Angeles brewery at 15.5% market share. It was a microcosm of what was happening nationwide: fewer and fewer breweries making more and more beer, nearly all of it so-called American lager. Fritz, Gordon, and later Mark were eyewitnesses to the death throes of many small-to-midsize family breweries. There was the historic Peter Bub Brewery in Winona, Minnesota, with its lagering caves carved right into Sugar Loaf Bluff, who sold Fritz a racking machine after they closed in 1969. And there was the Geo. Walter Brewing Company, a venerable fifty-thousand-barrel brewery in

Appleton, Wisconsin. After their closing in 1972, Fritz bought five empty kegs, their small library of old brewing books, and their *grant*, which is a copper trough with spigots through which wort flows on its journey from lauter tun to brew kettle. Each spigot is hooked up to a different drain in the bottom of the lauter tun. That way, the brewer can check the evenness of the runoff as well as the wort itself.

Yet Fritz was starting to get letters from people who had seen Anchor Steam in bottles and were "trying to organize a select few to build a small brewery" of their own. Fritz's advice:

The cost of producing a barrel of beer in this country is mostly labor, and this means that large, efficient breweries are able to undersell smaller, older breweries every time. And I would point out that many, many breweries in the two-hundred-thousand- to million-barrel range are going out of business regularly. They were all trying to produce a lager beer to compete with the national brands. I would say that $500,000 [$3.4 million today] would not be an inaccurate figure for the smallest commercial establishment. And a new brewery (although considerable publicity would be generated initially) could probably not sustain enough emotional enthusiasm to continue to convince any significant number of American beer drinkers to pay a very high price for its beer. Our particular operation has certain very special advantages, and I am well aware that even so, I am undertaking an enormous gamble.

After interviewing old-timers from Burgie, Hamm's, and Lucky Lager for his piece, Wegars snubbed Fritz, writing that "his beer, which he insists on making with barley malt and hops, is described by beer experts as 'bitter, bad tasting and heroic.' It is kind of small potatoes among the beer giants. He makes less than 2,000 31-gallon barrels a year, which puts Steam exactly last in the big California beer sweepstakes." Fritz, who had provided photos for the article, was crestfallen.

But instead of responding directly, he reached out to his new friend Fred Eckhardt, who came to the rescue with a letter to the editor. Published two weeks later, it was titled "A Heroic Beer":

In the one small paragraph concerning this brewery your reporter viciously put down the only one still brewing the last American common beer. This sophomoric malignment of what should be the pride of San Francisco must not go unanswered. Modern American beer has all sorts of junk added to it and almost constant filtration has reduced it to milksop. The so-called experts, who probably did as much to ruin American beer as anything else, have great nerve to refer sneeringly to San Francisco's finest product as "bitter, bad tasting, and heroic." Heroic it truly is. Maytag makes his great beer in the old tradition with pure filtered San Francisco water, San Francisco malt, and Washington [State] hops only. . . . The old low quality steam beer, invented in San Francisco and famous at the turn of the century chiefly for its harshness and low expense, has become a connoisseur's brew fit to take its place beside any of the world's great beers.

Here, in Fred Eckhardt, was one connoisseur who understood that Fritz Maytag had done more than rescue a brewery; he'd sought and found the beau ideal where the science and art of brewing meet, creating lightning in a beer bottle. But how many more beer connoisseurs were out there? The best way for Fritz to predict his future would be for him to create it.

Bolstered by Eckhardt, Fritz made himself readily available to all comers. Among the first was itinerant *Los Angeles Times* writer Charles Hillinger, whose "profiles of colorful California characters," wrote Otis Chandler (*Los Angeles Times* publisher), were "told with warmth and compassion. California, perhaps more than any other state, is home to a variety of amazing eccentrics who follow their unbelievable path." Entitled "Steam Beer: A Comeback Brewing," the February 1972 piece featured a photo of Fritz pouring a glass of Steam in the brewery's taproom, beneath a Tiffany-style lamp that had been Fritz and Don Saccani's first marketing collaboration.

On his visit to the brewery earlier that month, Hillinger asked the "tall, husky brewmaster" why he risked his inheritance on a brewery. "How often," Fritz replied, "does a person have an opportunity to buy a brewery? And for a relatively small amount of money? And the only one of its kind in the world? It's still a gamble. But I think it's going to make it. This year may be the first year in the black." Fritz the optimist would have to wait three more years for that. But the *Times* syndicated the article, and it soon appeared all over the US.

It inspired other reporters, like SF State grad/ UPI reporter James O. Clifford, to write their own pieces: "That first taste of steam beer is a real experience for someone used to the brew picked up at the corner store. It's as if you never had a beer before." When Gil Wisdom of LA County's Wisdom Import Sales Company, "Importers of Fine Beers," saw all this, he quickly added Steam Beer to his portfolio, proudly clipped articles for Fritz, and became instrumental in expanding Steam Beer

Brewing's distribution throughout the West. Thanks to bottled beer and Don and Gil's support, Steam Beer Brewing was in overdrive. From 1970 to 1972, sales in barrels were up 199 percent. It was a great number, but, as Fritz reminded an exuberant William M. O'Shea at the Brewers' Association of America in 1973, "It is true that in percentage points we are growing pretty well. I am proud of this, and hope for more this year. Nonetheless, I am always aware that statisticians have been drowned crossing streams whose average depth was five feet."

His eight-year "overnight success" notwithstanding, it dawned on Fritz that Anchor Steam Beer was a flagship without a fleet. So he looked back to look forward, reimagining a beer that—like Anchor Steam—was once in fashion but almost forgotten and had a fascinating but somewhat mysterious history, a connoisseur's working-class beer. And, like Anchor Stream, he wanted it to be handmade, distinctive, flavorful, traditional, all-malt, and naturally carbonated. That beer would be Anchor Porter.

ANCHOR PORTER

By 1802, porter (from the Latin *portare*, to carry) constituted, according to London resident and *Domestic Encyclopædia* author A. F. M. Willich, "the principal beverage of all ranks of this metropolis, particularly of the labouring classes." Among those, most notably, were London's porters. The origins of porter are as murky as the beer itself, so Fritz returned to his ever-expanding library of

antiquarian books. His 1850 copy of W. L. Tizard's *The Theory and Practice of Brewing* credits "an ingenious brewer" from East London, Ralph Harwood, with porter's contrivance (some believe today that another brewer, Humphrey Parsons, was first). But the pivotal innovation that propelled porter to prominence, Tizard maintains, was "Porter or Black Malt, commonly called Patent malt, from a patent granted for the invention and manufacture of it in 1817, to Daniel Wheeler, of the parish of St. George, Middlesex." It "is the legal colouring matter used in porter brewing, and is prepared by roasting inferior pale malt in cylinders, like coffee, at a heat of 360° F to 400° F." For the first time, brewers could now use black patent malt to color and flavor their porters, though some continued—in part because of high duties on malt—to use colorants and adulterants that would make *Macbeth*'s witches blush.

Fritz enjoyed reading Tizard's assertions that porter was a working-class beer, that its odd name had more than one origin story, that its method of production varied from brewery to brewery, that no two breweries' porters were "alike in flavour and quality," and that any "practised connoisseur" could tell them apart. But compared to porter, there is hardly any firsthand information at all about the myriad ways California common beer might actually have been made in its heyday. "From a brewer's point of view," Fritz suggests, "the details are scarce to say the least." The few period articles that survive invariably quote "an expert," he notes,

but having become the same, I realize how easy it is to appear authoritative when you are guessing. Also, there is another factor at work then and now. What one brewer says he does becomes magnified and celebrated as "fact" and "history." Believe me, I have had a firsthand lesson in how history is written since I've been with this brewery. I say, "We do . . ."; it is printed; it is reprinted as "Steam Beer is . . ."; then it is reprinted as fact and then it becomes history, even if I was misquoted or misunderstood the first time. All very interesting.

Which is why all Anchor can say definitively is what Anchor knows about how Anchor made and makes Anchor Steam Beer. *Caveat lector.* Reader beware.

The importation of porter to colonial America from King George's England had all but dried up by the time the first Continental Congress met in Philadelphia in 1774. The founding fathers' favorite was made by Robert Hare, son of an English brewer, who had arrived in Philadelphia the year before. In 1811, one Philly fan, James Mease, attributed its superiority to London-made porters to "no other ingredients entering into the composition other than malt, hops, and pure water."

San Franciscans were drinking London porter at least as early as 1847, shipped at great expense around the Horn. After the discovery of gold, in rushed ales and porters from far-flung bottlers like London's Robert Byass; London brewers like Abbott, Barclay and Perkins, Bass, and Hibbert; and brewers from Dublin, Glasgow, Philadelphia, and Albany, New York. And San Francisco had plenty of its own "Public Carriers or Porters" to drink it, who paid $5 ($150 today) a month for their license to carry and a badge marked City Porter Number XXX to show for it.

In 1852, they could partake of porter at any one of San Francisco's nine porter houses, its one porter saloon, or many of its 125 other drinking establishments. Or they could visit the new Eagle Brewery on Pine Street (between Montgomery and Kearny), which promoted its "Ale and Porter of the best quality constantly on hand," and "fully equal to any imported from England, Scotland, or elsewhere." Other ale brewers followed suit, making their porters in imitation of the great porters back East or across the pond. But what of California's so-called steam-beer brewers? Why couldn't they make porter like they made California common?

They could and they did. Indeed, Anchor has a history of making draught porter dating at least to its Co-operative Brewery days, and there is no reason to think that Golden City Brewery—which preceded it at the same location—would not have made it too. Baruth and Schinkel continued the brewery's porter tradition in 1896, and, even after Repeal, Joseph Kraus made Anchor Porter. But those porters were a far cry from the dark beer that Fritz inherited when he bought the brewery in 1965.

Beloved at the Old Spaghetti Factory, Sausalito's "no name bar," and a few others, the dark brew that Anchor was selling to these steadfast accounts when Fritz bought the brewery wasn't even pretending to be porter. By the mid-1950s, Anchor Porter had slowly devolved into Anchor Steam Dark or just Steam Dark, unapologetically colored with caramel syrup, which was the normal way to color beer in those days. It was "made" in the racking room by adding the syrup directly to a keg of Steam. And if Fred Kuh wanted it darker, they added more. It wasn't bad dark beer. It just wasn't real dark beer, and that bugged Fritz. Close your eyes and you couldn't taste the difference.

There weren't any real dark beers in America. The so-called dark beers were indistinguishable by taste; it was simply a matter of color, so the way to do it was to add caramel syrup, and they had done that at the brewery to try to stimulate sales. I put an end to that right away when I realized that it wasn't real and legitimate. So first we cancelled the dark beer, and that cancelled our sales, which were already minimal, and that cancelled them to 20 percent less than minimal, whatever that is, and it raised quite a fuss. But it was one of the first times that I took a stand for *integrity in brewing.* And then we got rid of all the funny things they were doing, additives and coloring and stuff—and some other things that I wouldn't want to mention. Oh yeah, and corn syrup. Nothing wrong with that, I mean that was the normal way to make English ales, even today, many of them, light beer basically.

But, like Robert Hare's Porter and Fritz's Anchor Steam, Anchor Porter would be all-malt.

For Fritz, the decision to make a porter was less about a replacement for Steam Dark and more about an extension of Steam.

It wasn't so difficult. It didn't really matter, you see, in those days, because first of all I owned the brewery, and I could do just whatever I wanted. And I had studied beer and brewing hard and read and knew the history, probably more than anybody with a brewery, and so for me to make a dark beer I knew right away what all the history and all that was. And when we made our porter, we were the only porter in the world—the only *real* porter. There were no porters in England; there was one in America I knew of, but it was, I'm quite sure, just colored with caramel. So our porter was a true porter, a true dark beer, the only one in America.

It wasn't going to be a London porter or a Philadelphia porter; it was going to be the San Francisco porter.

Fritz's recipe for Anchor Porter would take the Anchor Steam recipe, reduce the pale malt, beef up the caramel malt, and add black malt (short for black patent malt). The Northern Brewer hops and yeast would be the same as Anchor Steam. And, like Anchor Steam, Anchor Porter would be kräusened with Steam Beer, for historical reasons and, thinking practically, because he couldn't imagine ever brewing Porter often enough to be able to kräusen it with itself.

Fritz described Anchor Porter as

the traditional dark beer from San Francisco, a robust-flavored, dark beer brewed in the steam beer process. During the mid-1800s, steam beer was an extremely popular brew on the Pacific Coast. Neither a lager nor an ale, it borrowed from both brewing traditions. Porter was a special dark version of steam beer, brewed in an identical manner, but utilizing a special blend of malts—pale, crystal [caramel], and black patent malt—for its rich, dark color and full-bodied fla-

vor. The Anchor Steam Beer Brewery of San Francisco, the smallest brewery in the United States, is the only company in the world to continue this fine American tradition. We take special care to make it right, and making it right means by hand. There is no other dark beer like it in the world.

And because of that, Fritz had no idea where to get black malt. As far as he knew, no brewer in America was buying, let alone using it. Bakers, however, needed black malt flour for bread and cookies. So Fritz called around until he found the National Malting Corporation in Paterson, New Jersey, who had exactly what he needed. In mid-October 1972, they shipped him ten 100 lb bags of black malt.

At 5:30 a.m. on November 7, 1972, Steam Beer Brewing began mashing in its eighty-fifth brew of the year. But, for the first time in decades, it was not Steam. The recipe for the 54-barrel Steam brew the day before had called for 2,350 lb pale malt, 200 lb caramel malt, and 45 lb Northern Brewer

Jim Stitt and Fritz in 1979

hops. By comparison, Brew #85—Porter—used 1,100 lb pale malt, 670 lb caramel malt, 301 lb black malt, and 50 lb Northern Brewer hops, for a kettle volume of thirty-two barrels.

At 6:37 a.m. Fritz cut open the first bag of black malt and fed it down into the mill. "I could smell it, and I thought, *My god, they've sent us coffee.*" At 2:55 p.m., after a mercifully uneventful brew, it was all in Steam Beer fermentor #2, with Steam Beer yeast pitched. The brewery didn't have an ale fermentor, which traditionally would have been much deeper and with a smaller surface area. And Anchor Porter was kräusened in the cellar with Steam.

There were two more experimental porter brews in 1973, as Fritz continued to tweak the recipe. Mark Carpenter remembers his skepticism about introducing a new product.

Boy, I was against the porter. More shit to inventory! I said to Fritz, "Why do you want to do this porter? It's just more trouble, more stuff to inventory." He said, "Well, down the road, I don't want to be known for just making Anchor Steam Beer. I want to be known as the little brewery that makes Anchor Steam Beer, and Porter, and this ale, and that ale, and a number of things, because down the road you're going to see *hundreds* of small breweries around the US." That was in '73! There wasn't even one on the *horizon*.

GETTING READY TO BOTTLE

Immersed in the process of creating America's first craft-brewed porter, Fritz began to think about a label. In early 1973, by happy coincidence, he met James Stitt, who had attended Los Angeles's Art Center on the GI Bill, moved to San Francisco, and become a successful art director, illustrator, and graphic artist. Winner of the Art Directors Club of New York Gold Medal and a Clio, he decided to go into business for himself, sharing a studio on Stockton Street with a young copywriter with whom Fritz had an appointment.

On his way out, Fritz bumped into Jim, who boldly spread his portfolio out on the floor for him to see. It included Jim's iconic blue Matson logo from 1970, which featured an anchor in place of the letter "t." Fritz was impressed. A couple of weeks later, he told Jim about a new beer he was working on and showed him an old Anchor Steam label from 1933, which featured the word *Anchor* in florid script. Fritz the radical traditionalist and Jim the Luddite were aesthetically simpatico from the get-go, sharing the conviction that handmade beers deserve handmade labels.

For Anchor Porter, Fritz had Jim incorporate the graceful script "Anchor" from the brewery's 1933 Steam label and a rich color palette inspired

WINDWARD PASSAGE

In 1973, Fritz came up with an idea for a special Steam Beer label and bottling, the first of many to come. It was for Mark Johnson and the crew of the *Windward Passage*, a 73 ft ketch and the favorite to win the 2,225-mile Transpac Yacht Race from Los Angeles to Honolulu. The race, almost as old as Anchor, would have debuted in San Francisco but for the 1906 earthquake and fire. Fritz gave Mark two cases of *Windward Passage* Steam, which he brought aboard so they could toast their hoped-for victory when they got to Hawaii. Although the race took more than nine days, *Windward Passage* lost to *Ragtime* by just 4½ minutes. Afterward, Skipper Mark, with a twinkle in his eye, thanked Fritz for the beer, telling him that without its weight slowing them down, they most assuredly would have won!

clay-coated, bright-white surface for printing—
would give the carrier a slick, sleek look that
clashed with the old-fashioned look of his label
and the rich, dark color of the beer. *Why not just
turn the 6-pack inside out*, he mused, *and print on the
kraft-colored side of the board?*

To help them visualize the way the 6-packs
might look if run through the press upside down
(kraft-side up, clay-coated side down), Fritz asked
Jim to provide comps. Short for comprehensives,
comps are usually quite formal presentations to
show a client the look and feel of a new design. But
this was '70s San Francisco. So Jim grabbed an
empty box of Big John's Hamburger Fixin's Spanish
Rice Dinner and comped the label right on the box.
It was perfect—craft beer on kraft board.

After just three trial porter brews—plus one
trial bottling (six cases) January 29, 1974—the next
Porter, Brew #40, was April 23, 1974, snugly
squeezed into a tight fermentor schedule, followed
by another Porter, Brew #44, on April 30. In 1972,
Fritz had bought five 200 lb bales of Oregon
Bullion hops from hop dealer Len Richardson to
try, so from Brew #44 until May 1975, he experimented with Bullion in the Porter, before deciding
to go back to Northern Brewer. In July, Brew #40
and Brew #44 were combined in the cellar in preparation for bottling.

In the spring of 1974, in anticipation of a strike
at Owens-Illinois (OI), Fritz had begun hoarding
glass—the distinctive amber bottles that were by
then familiar to Anchor Steam Beer drinkers. By
the time the two-month strike began, the brewery
was overflowing with glass, from loading dock to
bottle shop. Not knowing when the strike would
end or how long it would take OI to get his bottle
back into production, Fritz didn't want to risk raid-
ing his Anchor Steam glass cache for Porter. So he
improvised. Hamm's had an East Bay warehouse
full of green 11 oz glass, which they had been using
for their apple-flavored Right Time brand. So,
thanks to Hamm's, it would be a green bottle for
the first few bottlings of Anchor Porter. He also

by the beer itself. The label's design went more
smoothly than its printing. Fritz remembered
"going over to Stecher-Traung-Schmidt, the clock
tower building near the Bay Bridge, with Ken
Hepler. The press check went on and on into the
wee hours. Finally, it came together and was beautiful. I looked at our one pallet of Porter labels and
then slowly up and all around to the endless pallets
of shiny, red-white-and-blue Budweiser labels.
Quite a sight."

By this time, Fritz had realized that the 4-pack
was too far ahead of its time and too confusing for
the consumer. Plus, six 4-pack carriers were cost-
ing cost him more per case than four 6-pack
carriers would. So, going forward, he ordered
6-pack carriers for both Porter and Steam from
Standard Paper Box. But he was concerned that the
paperboard for the Porter 6-pack—with its

THE ANCHOR BREWING STORY

ally hand-made, with exceptional attention to the smallest details of the traditional brewing art. We use 100% Barley Malt, whole hops and entirely natural carbonation.

The word *connoisseur* was Fritz's secret thank-you to Fred Eckhardt. The beer, according to Phil Canevari's lab report: "Well-received and up to expectations."

LINDA ROWE JOINS THE ANCHOR TEAM

On July 22, 1974, eight days after the first Porter bottling, another new hire showed up for work at Steam Beer Brewing. "I was twenty-four when I started at the brewery, and not the youngest!" remembers Linda Rowe. Fritz hired her to replace Carolyn Estes, who married one of Fritz's good friends, Sonoma Vineyards president and wine-by-mail entrepreneur Peter S. Friedman. Linda, who grew up in Connecticut, had been an American Studies major at nearby Wheaton College and headed west to San Francisco in 1973. She'd been doing temp work and heard about an opening for a bookkeeper. Carolyn didn't need to teach her much. After two days on the job, Linda was already doing payroll and accounts payable with élan. As Fritz tells it,

Linda has a theory that there are only two kinds of people: those who can do numbers and those who can't. And that came from the fact that I think, to her own surprise, she was just a genius with numbers. John Clow [father of future Anchor employee Bayley Moynihan] was my accountant in those days and took on the task of teaching Linda, first bookkeeping and then accounting, and she was just a star pupil. She just loved it. And it was completely beyond me. I did the books at one time, and did all the billing and everything, and I got a book—*So You're*

reached out to his friend Bobby Schmidt, president of Olympia Brewing. Bobby had encouraged Fritz on his 1971 visit to Tumwater, where, Fritz wrote to him, "it was a very real pleasure for me to find that a large brewery like yours would be able to combine such a friendly and personal touch with such high standards of excellence." Now, in 1974, during this great crisis—and going forward—Bobby allowed Fritz to use Olympia's bottle mold at Northwestern Glass for his amber bottles. The look was similar, but the glass was much rounder, more even, and much stronger.

Anchor Porter, at 5.5% ABV, was bottled July 17, 1974. Fritz's neck label, brimming with text, conveyed his goals for this trailblazing dark brew:

Anchor Porter derives its name and formula from an old San Francisco tradition. Many years ago most Steam Beer breweries brewed a Porter such as this. The formula follows the traditional Steam Beer recipe but includes Dark Malt and Black Malt in addition to the usual Pale Malt. Relatively larger amounts of hops are also used. It is stronger in flavor. We hope the beer connoisseur will recognize it as a worthwhile revival of a West Coast tradition. Anchor Porter is virtu-

Going to Have a Company, or something like that—and learned about the balance sheet and all, credits and debits. Linda just took to it. I knew that her father had been a very successful businessman, and that she had grown up in a household where business was respected and normal. And she admired her father. And John Clow was a brilliant, charming man and a great teacher, and he just taught her and the next thing we knew we had real financial records and order in the office.

And thanks to Fritz's support and encouragement, Linda earned her MA in legal studies in 1978, setting a precedent for Fritz's standing offer to help with any of his employee's educations—from financial assistance to time off.

Steam Beer Brewing, thanks in part to 21 Porter brews (plus 139 Steam), finished 1974 at 6,186 barrels, up 40% from 1973 and 430% from 1967, when the *Los Angeles Times*'s Thomas W. Bush had written, "There's one way, at least, to remain a small brewer and stay alive. That's to be unique. And that's the case with Steam Brewing in San Francisco." In December 1974 the *Wall Street Journal* picked up that theme. Fritz remembers consenting to an interview because the interviewer was a homebrewer. A. Richard Immel emphasized the plus side of Fritz Maytag's unorthodox methods, which fly

in the face of the national trend toward lightness in looks and taste by making a beer that is a rich, amber color, full-bodied and highly hopped—in short, the kind of brew the big beer makers say can't be sold in the American market anymore. . . . Not only has the tiny operation . . . climbed back into the black, but also it is outgrowing its premises as demand outpaces capacity. That just isn't supposed to happen to a small, independent brewer in a cutthroat industry dominated by the mammoth beer factories of Schlitz, Pabst, and Anheuser-Busch.

Actually, it hadn't quite happened yet. Fritz's brewery wouldn't become profitable until 1975.

THE ANCHOR BREWING STORY

REVOLUTION
(1975–1976)

Now in history there is no Revolution that is not a Restoration. Among the many things that leave me doubtful about the modern habit of fixing the eyes on the future, none is stronger than this; that all men in history who have really done anything with the future have had their eyes fixed on the past.

—G. K. Chesterton, *What's Wrong with the World* (1910)

By his thirty-seventh birthday—December 9, 1974—Fritz was already an essayist of beer, in the old sense of the word, meaning one who tries, experiments, explores. He had a lot in common with another essayist, Ralph Waldo Emerson, who published his essay "Self-Reliance" when he was about the same age: "Trust thyself: every heart vibrates to that iron string. . . . But do your work, and I shall know you. Do your work, and you shall reinforce yourself. A man must consider what a blindman's-buff is this game of conformity."

To conform to Anchor's legacy would mean confining himself to steam beer and porter. So Fritz decided to try his hand at making a genuine lager beer. His lager essay began with a trip to San Bernardino, where, on December 28, 1973, he procured a 378 lb bale of Hallertau hops at an ice and cold storage company. He had bought it from Anheuser-Busch (AB), who used this hop, along with other noble hops, in Budweiser.

Fast-forward to December 10, 1974, Brew Day for a one-off single-hop (34 lb Hallertau), single-malt (2,100 lb pale) lager. The yeast was pitched into the shallow, open-pan fermentor as usual, but rather than fermenting it there, the brew was then transferred directly to holding tank #7, where it remained at approximately 50°F for five days.

Then the experimental cooling was turned on, dropping the temperature of the lager in the tank to the mid-30s. There it sat, lagering until this lager was filtered and bottled at 4.1% ABV on April 7, 1975, the forty-second anniversary of legalized beer. But this brew was not sold in stores. Fritz made this lone lager to prove a point, not pour a pint—the point being the joy of making beer for its own sake.

Fritz shares his vision with brewer Paul Michaels.

In January 1975, the eponymous creator of *Robert Finigan's Private Guide to Wines* published an article in *San Francisco* magazine entitled "The Best Beer in America." In it, he became one of the first—if not *the* first—to proclaim that Anchor Steam "is quite simply the finest beer made in America." And Steam Beer had coattails. "To call Anchor Porter dark beer," Finigan continues, "is like calling Château Lafite red wine. It's not quite as powerful as Guinness, . . . but it does expose American dark beers for the artificially colored bores they are."

In February, Fritz was elated to see that J. E. Siebel Sons' Company, the lab in Chicago to whom he'd just started sending his beers for analysis, confirmed Finigan's bold testimonial about Anchor Porter. Siebel gave it an A rating, an improvement over its A- rating in '74. Their evaluation: "Perfectly fresh in aroma and taste. The aroma is pleasantly caramel-like. Very full-bodied and flavorful. Smooth palate. Distinctive hop character, which is robust and possesses pleasant afterbitter. The flavor is aromatic, very malty and caramel-like, moderately tart, estery, and sweet. Overt defects are not noted. All our panelists ranked this beer highly. Excellent overall appeal. . . . Rating: A."

But Fritz didn't need a lab or a respected wine critic to tell him that Porter was a great beer. Rather, he embraced their kudos as recognition of the eleven great people he now had working for him, including his part-time bottling crew. And he

saw it as an endorsement of their continuous improvement of the processes by which Steam Beer Brewing made and packaged its beer.

LIBERTY ALE'S MIDNIGHT RIDE

Anchor Porter was all about the malt. Now, Fritz had an idea for a new brew that was all about the hops. US hop growers, including John Segal, were becoming concerned about the US brewing industry's increasing reliance on European-grown varieties. An experimental hybrid—known simply by its USDA accession number, 56013—was first selected in 1956 at the Oregon Agricultural Experiment Station in Corvallis. Its pedigree: English Fuggle crossed with a male hop, which was itself a cross of the Russian hop Serebrianka and a Fuggle seedling.

On January 3, 1972, the Oregon and Washington Agricultural Experiment Stations and the USDA—with a nod to the USBA—proudly announced the release of this first new American hop variety from their research program. This hop, named for the mountain range east of Washington State's Willamette Valley, where Segal had his hop fields, was Cascade. Its comparatively high yields, resistance to downy mildew, and similarity to European varieties got Coors interested, but they ultimately found it too assertively pungent to use in their light lagers in any significant quantity. Fritz, however, liked what Coors didn't like about the Cascade hop. This distinctive, dual-purpose hybrid, useful as both a bittering and an aromatic hop, had *character* and a uniquely citrusy, piney aroma.

Fritz recalls fondly,

John Segal told us about Cascade hops. He was a hop grower in Yakima and took a great pride in that business. He was on a committee of the Hop Growers of America that was in the process of regularly trying new varieties, hybrids, and stuff, and at the University of Oregon they would grow small amounts and then brew small brews, taste them, and see want they thought. And John told me, "Fritz, I think this hop that they're calling Cascade has an English Ale characteristic and I think you ought to try it. And I'll grow some for you, in quantity sufficient for you to try it." And I said, "Great, let's try it. We want to brew an ale."

Fritz wasn't sure yet what sort of ale or when, but managed to procure one 241 lb bale of Yakima Cascade in October 1973, with the help of George Segal Company (John's company), Yakima Valley Grape and Hop Company, and his old friends at Wine and the People. That was the good news.

For the brew-curious, the Brewing Value of this bale of Cascade was 7.7% [5.1% alpha acids, 5.1% beta acids], compared to a bale of Silverton, OR Northern Brewer he'd just received, which was 11.75% [9.6% alpha acids, 4.3% beta acids].

However, as it turned out, the debut of Cascade hops in craft beer wouldn't be in an ale at all. It would be in Brew #22 on March 8, 1974, followed by brews on March 11, 12, and 15, of *Anchor Steam Beer!* Brew #22 was kräusened with #24, also brewed with Cascade, and bottled on April 11. And there was draught Steam with Cascade, too. Phil Canevari, a glass-is-half-full kind of a guy, documented the mix-up in his April 1974 lab report: "Cascades. The single bale was mistakenly used in brewing, but not with adverse effects."

Ironically, his next entry was "Tasting Program. Has lacked priority time-wise, but in the next couple of weeks should be well-developed." Fritz took it in stride and blamed no one. It was as if his great-grandfather was whispering, "It is only the man of small caliber and puny performance that makes no mistakes." But this mistake was a sensory wake-up call. Of all the QC tests and analysis performed at a brewery, the top three are taste, taste, taste.

There was no Cascade left in the brewery for Fritz's new ale, but Hallertau hops had performed well in the lager. And he had plenty left over. *It's a great hop*, Fritz thought, *a noble hop, earthy, spicy, and herbal. Why not use Hallertau for my new ale?*

Steam and Porter—as improved, perfected, and successful as they'd become under Fritz's leadership—remained deeply rooted in Anchor's history. But by this time Fritz felt that Steam Beer Brewing, history notwithstanding, was paradoxically both old and brand new. The possibilities were endless—boundless. "It was quite simple. In those days we didn't have to justify anything to anybody. We could just try something . . . "

The brewery was running at capacity; there was no time or space to make an ale on a regular basis. But it occurred to Fritz that "we didn't want someone else to make the first ale around the Bay Area, so I got thinking." Linda Rowe remembers that "Fritz wanted to do something for the American bicentennial, but in his own unique way, and he certainly didn't want to wait to celebrate with everyone else." Fritz thought of Longfellow's "Paul Revere's Ride" from his school days: "Listen, my children, and you shall hear . . ." First published in 1861, the epic poem is as much a product of antebellum America in the nineteenth century as of the antebellum colonies of the eighteenth.

From this poem Fritz had his brew date for a revolutionary ale: April 18, 1975. "We took great care," Fritz wrote that year, "to brew this Ale in as traditional manner as possible. We believe it is very similar to what Paul and his friends might have been drinking that night in 1775." It would be Brew #48 that year. He called it Liberty Ale, and it would become the first single-malt (the first brew was not all-malt; subsequent brews would be), single-hop, dry-hopped ale in modern times, and the forerunner of all craft-brewed IPAs to follow.

Fritz brought back Jim Stitt, who is to hops and barley what Monet is to water lilies, to help him design the label. The eagle came from a nineteenth-century job printer's book of designs for banknotes and stock certificates. Jim removed the olive branch from its talons and replaced it with "the vegetables," as his drawings of hops and barley would come to be known at the brewery. Every single word on the label is hand-lettered, most of them in Jim's rough-hewn take on the eighteenth-century typeface of English typographer John Baskerville, evocative of revolutionary proclamations and broadsides. The label's colors evoke Old Glory.

BREWING THE REVOLUTION

About the beer, Fritz remembers,

We wanted a real top-fermenting yeast from an ale brewer, and there was only one brewer in America who was doing that. And they were a million-plus-barrel brewery way up north in Rochester: Genesee. They were a regional brewer and made lager and ale and then they mixed the two and called that Genesee Cream Ale.... I went there myself and got the yeast, which they put in a yeast press for me.

Fritz wanted 1¾ lb of hops per barrel in the kettle, which in 1975 he described as "very, very high hopping rates by today's standards, but proper for this type of brewing." And the main fermentation went well, though not in a typical ale fermentor, which would have been much deeper with less surface area, but in the only fermentors Fritz had, the same shallow, open pans used for the primary fermentation of Steam and Porter. In a letter to Genesee master brewer Clarence C. Geminn, Fritz shared his brewing play-by-play:

We pitched at 60°F and allowed the temperature to rise to approximately 75°F. At this point we were quite optimistic, but made the mistake—I think?—of trying to prime with sugar in order to achieve carbonation by a second fermentation. Apparently, the yeast was a little tired, for this fermentation never took off, and finally we withdrew a small amount, and with tender loving care we got a small batch of fresh wort fermenting with the original yeast and worked this up to a size to enable us to kräusen the whole. This achieved a satisfactory CO_2 level, but there is no question that a residual sweetness indicated that a fermentation once "stuck" is hard to "unstick"? We had quite an adventure with the brew, and certainly your courtesy and willingness to help were one of the most pleasant aspects of the whole affair. I will always remember the spirit in which you pitched in to help me.

Liberty Ale was dry-hopped at ⅜ lb of hops per barrel for two months in a 52°F cellar. The low carbonation, while providing a distinctively traditional note to the ale, was, as Fritz confessed to Geminn, "not intentional; we goofed and lost almost all our CO_2 prior to bottling. The Ale was a stubborn baby, and it seemed never to be quite

ready to bottle." But bottle they did. According to the bottling book, 527 cases came off the line June 26, 1975, plus two cases for the lab and one for Fritz to take home, always the best place to evaluate the fruit of one's labors. They would go on sale the next day at $16.80 per case ($87 today). Bottling day was exactly two hundred years after George Washington, about to take command of the Continental Army, wrote of "the Establishment of American Liberty on the most firm, and solid Foundations . . . in the bosom of a free, peaceful, & happy Country."

Fritz is a traditionalist ahead of his time. Liberty Ale, Mark Carpenter remembers, "was just so hoppy. It's unfair to say we didn't like it. But it was just so different. It was so hoppy. It was so far out there. And you look back at it now, it was so mild compared to so many beers that are out there." Linda said it was "incredibly different." But her brother bought the first case. Indeed, at 6.3% ABV and as hoppy as it turned out, Liberty Ale was quite a shock to 1970s taste buds. But Fritz went ahead with his plan to send samples to Genesee. "Now that the Ale is out," Fritz wrote Geminn, "I confess that in my opinion it is far from delicious! As you can see, the great Ale adventure was a series of misadventures. I think the moral is that few things go exactly right the first time. I hope as you sample this rather unique brew your laughter will be tempered with compassion for a beginner in the art of ale brewing."

In his lab report, Phil Canevari mused, "the Ale was a one-shot effort; it may or may not be heard around the world." But, if not around the world, it was certainly heard, appropriately, in Washington, DC, at Maurice Coja's Brickskeller Dining House & Down Home Saloon. There, "you can buy a bottle for $5, and they are going fast!" wrote William Rice for the *Washington Post* in August 1975, by which time Liberty Ale had mellowed a bit, like fine wine. "Anchor is responsible for the current Lafite Rothschild of the beer world." The revolution had begun.

ROAD TRIP

High praise indeed, but by the time Fritz read it, he had already gotten more Cascade from John Segal to experiment—on purpose this time—with Anchor Steam Beer, starting on July 23, 1975, often using Northern Brewer for bittering and Cascade for the rest. Steam Beer was never dry-hopped, but, as Phil's lab report reveals, "after tastings on 8/20 [which by then were de rigueur for every bottling], it was decided to continue with the steam brews using Cascades." It was a curious departure from the "final" recipe for Steam, but Fritz wanted to give Cascade a thorough tryout.

There was a reason. Liberty Ale was not going to be a one-off after all. There would be a "2nd L.A.," as Fritz called it, and it would feature Cascade hops. But before making it, he wanted to go to England and see how they brewed ale. So he reached out to Henry King, president of the USBA.

And Henry got in touch with The Brewers' Society. He knew them well, of course, and he wrote a very, very gracious letter to the head of the Brewers' Society [Rear-Admiral C. D. Madden], introducing me and asking them to take care of me on my trip. Well, you know how it is in England, a letter like that was just a magic carpet. It was of course absurd considering our size, but again it was one of those situations where they treated us like real brewers because technically, we were a brewery. The Brewers' Society gave me a list of brewers and they had all agreed to see me. And so we went around and visited all these breweries. It was quite something.

Fritz, Gordon, and photographer Lars Speyer's excellent October 1975 adventure was like a backstage pass—or a TARDIS time machine—to the ancient art of English Ale brewing. Fritz wrote thank you letters to everyone they visited, which provide insight into the takeaways from their trip. It began in Wandsworth, London, with John Young and his head brewer at Young and Company's The

Ram Brewery. Fritz wrote John "I will never forget those hours that you spent with us, sharing your brewing experience and most especially your unique enthusiasm for your profession. . . . The finest glass of Ale that I had in England was from the barrel in your tasting room." But for a man like Fritz, who owned Standardbreds, "the most memorable experience for me was holding Henry Cooper," the brewery's star Shire, "and watching him being trotted out." Then it was on to meet Head Brewer Wilson at Wadworth & Company's Northgate Brewery, where equine tradition also reigned, setting "the tone of tradition and enthusiasm for brewing."

Next, they visited Mr. and Mrs. Claude Arkell at Donnington, "a beautiful brewery, well maintained and infused with a sense of pride and tradition. At all of the breweries we visited we felt welcome . . . but in my own mind, there is only one brewery in England." Mr. Alpin, head brewer at Marston, was next, where Fritz was especially grateful to see their Burton Union system in operation, a traditional fermentation system using an array of huge wooden barrels. Upon returning to San Francisco, he wrote Alpin that their first trial ale would probably be "somewhat similar to the Pale Ale that you condition in the small pressure vessels. If we are successful . . . Gordon and I will certainly know that we owe you a debt of gratitude for your time and patience and especially your enthusiasm for brewing."

At Samuel Smith's in Tadcaster, Managing Director Wilson showed the intrepid California trio their unique method of open fermentation, the Yorkshire Squares. "I can still see us sticking our fingers into the yeast heads and bombarding you with a never-ending series of questions." And finally, before returning to Donnington's, they had a delightful visit with Mr. Hey, head brewer at Knowle Spring Brewery (Timothy Taylor's). "Your bottled Ale," wrote Fritz, "was the finest we tasted in England, but as I look back on our trip I am also reminded of the cleanliness and order in your brewery, and especially your obvious pride in the brewing art. . . . In our mind Timothy Taylor stands out as the very model of a perfect small brewery."

As the whirlwind English Ale tour wound down, the three anglophiles came away inspired by the universal enthusiasm of the brewers they'd met and humbled by their openness and hospitality. But they could hardly wait to get back to San Francisco to brew a new Ale.

By then, Fritz's radically traditional philosophy of brewing had become as well-developed as it was simple: *traditional* in the sense of something passed down from generation to generation, but *radically* so, in the sense of looking not to the result of the tradition but rather to the root of it. "What is traditional?" Fritz asked himself. "And I realized it's all barley malt and whole hops and nothing else, and that's *extreme*. In those days most brewers thought traditional brewing was impossible because you needed this and you needed that and those things and adjuncts and additives and on and on. I mean it was *spooky* what was being done." True to the spirit of '60s and '70s San Francisco, Fritz's beers would represent a radical departure from the beers of the day, which had become mere shadows of their former selves and their rich traditions. "We at this brewery," Fritz replied to a letter from *Esquire Magazine* in 1974, "are proud to say that we use only malted barley, whole hops, yeast, and water in our beer. There are no additives, preservatives, or other '-ives' in Anchor. We are the smallest brewery in the United States, committed to brewing in the most traditional manner, for beer drinkers who really care about what they drink."

So it was no wonder that Fritz and Gordon returned to America at once elated and

very disappointed, because we learned quickly that English brewing was not traditional at all, in the sense that they were all made with sugar. I never found out how they got that bitterness, but I'm quite sure they didn't get it from using a lot of hops. But we knew a lot about brewing by then

and English ales were kind of a joke to us, just the way the English used to make fun of American beers. There's nothing wrong with either one of them. That's the way that people like their beer in those countries. But to us it was disappointing because they were not all-malt. Mind you, we saw some very traditional things. We saw the Burton-Union system at Bass, which was unique and wonderful. We saw the Yorkshire Squares at Samuel Smith. We saw some very traditional things, and one of the things we loved was the sign shops; the fact that these breweries were able to own their own pubs was astonishing to us because that was illegal in the States in those days. But the signs, the whole tradition, there was lots of tradition *around* the beers and the brewing; for example, the so-called Real Ale campaign, which was not anything to do with ale. It had to do with their love for the pubs and the funky, old-fashioned kind of smelly, dirty pub tradition and the way the beers were brought from the brewery in the cask and finished their coming into condition, as the British would say. They would finish coming into condition in the pub and then be pulled up to the bar with what they called a beer engine. So that was very traditional, it was just that the *ales* were not very traditional.

Gordon flew back to San Francisco to attend to the yeast, shipping two empty 115-gallon yeast containers and some zero-freeze cooling cans to Genesee, who had graciously agreed to help out again. Meanwhile, Fritz headed to Iowa for meetings at Maytag Dairy Farms, where he'd become chairman of the board in 1973, and nearby Grinnell College, where, following a longtime, unradical family tradition, he had become a member of its board of trustees. "And then Fritz came back," as Mark recalls, "and he had an evening at his house where he did a big slide show, talked about the whole trip, got everybody excited."

"We came home," Fritz reminisces, "determined to do something really traditional and real

and true." But, as with all of Fritz's brews over the years, "2nd L.A." (still its working title) needed not only a name but a theme.

I had read lots of books about beer and ale in those days and was very aware of the "Christmas ale" tradition, but mostly the English "Whitsun" or "Whitsuntide ales" as I remember. For some reason Whit Sunday (Pentecost) was apparently the most important Christian day in England, and those Whitsun ales and bride ales also referred to the celebration itself. A friend had been making a special Christmas label for some of his regular beer—John Koch at his brewery in Dunkirk, New York—it said something like "Holiday Beer." And I also knew about the Christmas Ale that Ballantine had once brewed for the Fin, Fur, and Feather Club. I had been given three ancient bottles by Len Richardson, a hop broker who was one of the very few real gentlemen in the industry that I knew in my early days. I was

stunned by the ale. It was not dry-hopped, but they had a process of extracting hop oil in the lab, he said, and so it was sort of a shortcut for dry-hopping style.

In 1978, with memories of having tasted such marvelously "aley" ales, and plans to brew some distinctive ales on a regular basis, Fritz, with John Segal's help, reached out to Bob Wright, the man at Ballantine in charge of the still and fractionating apparatus, for advice. They had a wonderful chat, but Fritz decided that rather than emulating Ballantine, it would be best to forge ahead with the dry-hopping technique Fritz had pioneered.

I knew about dry-hopping, of course, from our Liberty Ale, although with the exception of a very few draught ales in England it was no longer done, and those very lightly. And until the early '70s, there had been a dark brew from Mexico called Noche Buena, hard to find but actually a nice, rich, dark beer. Our first Liberty Ale was not all-malt, so our Christmas Ale would be the only all-malt and dry-hopped ale in the world, I think. And as far as I could discover, the only real Christmas brew in the world. The tradition had recently disappeared, I think, even in Scandinavia, where it had lingered. The Christmas Ale and Old Foghorn were the product of the trip we took to England in 1975, which stunned us with the *lack* of traditional brewing— charming advertising sign at pubs, and charming "cask conditioning" process by some brewers, but sugar and color and thin products.

OUR SPECIAL ALE IS BORN

By Brew Day, November 17, 1975, Fritz had his radically traditional concept for Brew #151 ("2nd L. A."), which would not be anything at all like Ballantine's Burton Ale, Koch's Holiday Ale, or Noche Buena. Instead, it would be an all-malt,

dry-hopped ale, with a novel, distinctly American twist. Instead of 100% Hallertau hops, he would use 100% Cascade, which was already proving itself in Anchor Steam Beer. He didn't have a name and bristled at the thought of calling this brew a holiday beer or wishing his customers "Season's Greetings" or "Happy Holidays" on the label. The Ale wouldn't be watered down, and neither would its Christmas message. Instead, he came up with the brand name Our Special Ale, vintage dated it like wine, and wished his customers a sincere "Merry Christmas and a Happy New Year" on the label. It would be sold only at the brewery. And, until 1987, rather than a neck label on the bottle, there would be die-cut blank neck labels, so his friends and customers could write their own personal greetings and glue the labels on by hand.

Linda remembers the first Christmas Ale like it was last Christmas. "That was so hand-done. And quick too, like six hundred cases? Loose-packed in 24-packs. And with the label that Fritz drew, the tree." To save time, Fritz had drawn a simple tree on a vertical oval and showed it to Jim, who took it to the graphic design finish line. And just in the St. Nick of time. Linda submitted the finished label to the Bureau of Alcohol, Tobacco, and Firearms (ATF) for federal label approval on December 12. It was approved in three days, and the first Our Special Ale from Steam Beer Brewing Company, at 6.5% ABV, was bottled December 16, 1975.

Unlike Liberty Ale, it was slightly hazy, possibly due to dry-hopping with Cascade instead of Hallertau hops, but it was wonderfully aromatic— unlike any other beer in the world. Ron Siebel at J. E. Siebel Sons' Company "thoroughly enjoyed this product. To sum up my impression in one word: beautiful. I personally didn't feel on visual examination of your ale that the product was all that hazy," and he went on to point out how Guinness, as far back as the 1930s, accentuated the positive about such things with phrases like "none of its natural goodness is filtered away," a concept that Fritz would remember years later in describing his gin. Siebel continued, "I myself would almost consider this a positive aspect for a higher gravity, all-malt product such as you are making. All eight members of Siebel's tasting panel described Our Special Ale as "robust and hoppy, with above average bitterness and afterbitter." And though they also called it different, they saw that too as a positive, giving Fritz his first A+. His father would have been pleased.

OLD FOGHORN

On November 24, 1975, one week to the day after the first brew of Our Special Ale, a very different ale was in the brew kettle. This time it was to be a radically traditional barley wine. "A most unexpected result of my travels," wrote Fritz to Rear-Admiral Madden at the Brewers' Society, "was that I fell in love with the wonderful Barley Wines . . . which we found to be a wonderful after-dinner drink and/or a 'nightcap.'"

In England, Fritz had taken notes on the brewing of barley wines, so named because they are made with barley but similar in alcohol content to wine, at several breweries, especially at Marston's, where they made a dry-hopped barley wine called Owd Rodger. But Fritz's barley wine, like Our Special Ale, would not be brewed in imitation of anything. Mark recalls, "When Fritz and Gordon came back from Europe, they told us about barley

wine, that it was really just little old ladies in pubs who were drinking it. It was not a popular drink. It was really on the outs. And that's right down Fritz's alley."

There were no barley wines in America, nor had there ever been any as far as Fritz knew. Nor were there more than a handful left in England. Fritz loved their quaint names, which, because barley wines aged for months in the cellar, were often called Old This or Old That. And he loved that fact that in the US the descriptor *Old* was not regulated for alcoholic beverages, regardless of their age. Phil Canevari recounts one of his proudest moments working for Fritz:

I'm sitting in the roundtable meeting in the tap-room with Fritz and the gang and Fritz says, "I want to make barley wine." Nobody'd heard of barley wine, except Gordon, and Fritz said, "And I want to get a name for it, something that's like a San Francisco tradition. I want to connect with the city with this brew, with this barley wine." I'd just seen *The Honeymoon Machine* with Steve McQueen and Dean Jagger, where Dean plays an admiral they call Old Foghorn behind his back. It only took me half a second. I thought, *Well, foghorn's San Francisco*, so I said, "How 'bout Old Foghorn?" And Fritz just lit up. A light-bulb went off in his head. He slapped the table. "That's it!"

Fritz, who always embraced a great idea that was also a good idea, even if it wasn't his, thanked Phil and offered him a royalty. Fortunately for Fritz, Phil turned it down.

"Old Foghorn is my baby," crows Fritz. "It's brewed from an unusually strong 'first wort,' just the rich extract of a thick, all-malt mash. We pour on the fresh Cascade hops, and dry-hop it in the cellar too. The result is a rich, thick, sweet, hoppy elixir. This is liquid gold, the richest brew imaginable. It's perfect for a nightcap or sipping after dinner like a liqueur. This is to beer what Sauterne is to wine."

Although the very first Foghorn, Brew #155, was not dry-hopped as later brews would be, it was made from first wort, requiring two mashes (Foghorns today need three) and almost twenty-seven hours of brewing to net enough wort for a single brew. The debut recipe called for a total of 5,200 lb 2-row barley malt, 500 lb caramel malt, and 42 lb of Cascade hops—about 1.5 lb per barrel. The yeast had been collected from Our Special Ale the week before. The first Foghorn's original gravity was 24.4° Balling, almost double Anchor

Steam's. All the fermentable malt sugars accounted for its high ABV (8.8%); all the unfermentable malt sugars its sweetness. But only time in the cellar would tell how it would taste.

Steam Beer Brewing finished 1975 with sales of 7,402 barrels, over eight times its 1965 number. In 1979, Fritz reflected on the difference between his business strategy and that of other American brewers. "My emphasis has been upon the quality of the product, the reputation of my brewery and product, and obtaining a premium price for a premium quality beer. Notwithstanding my most energetic efforts and investment of large sums of money, the business was touch and go and accumulated losses over $500,000 before operations turned the corner to profit in 1975."

It had taken more than a decade, but at long last, thanks to the inspiration and perspiration of Fritz and his loyal, enthusiastic staff, Steam Beer Brewing had become an unqualified success. It wasn't technically a family-owned brewery, but it sure felt like a family-*run* brewery. And Fritz didn't just pour his profits back into the company; he poured them into the futures of his employees, establishing the Steam Beer Brewing Co. Pension Trust, to which he, as owner, appreciatively and generously contributed a match of 8.5% of their wages. "Fritz," Linda recalls, "said that would be the amount necessary over time to be able to retire comfortably." Mark takes special pride in having worked for "the company during its golden era, and it had a leader who really respected labor. I think of all he did for us. As soon as the brewery made a profit, he started a pension plan. And he put in 8.5%! When other companies weren't even coming *close* to that. I mean he just ran an unbelievable company."

WORLD BY THE TAIL
(1976–1977)

On Groundhog Day 1976, Steam Beer Brewing made its seventh Ale brew. All but Liberty Ale had showcased Cascade hops, and all but the very first Old Foghorn had been dry-hopped. So Fritz was thrilled to receive a letter from John Segal informing him that three hop research men from the Prosser, Washington Experiment Station, along with Yakima hop grower Francis Patode, would be in town and appreciate a brewery tour. The three were Chuck Zimmerman, USDA agronomist, one

of the four scientists who registered Cascade ("Reg. No. 1") with the Crop Science Society of America; Cal Skotland, WSU plant pathologist, who studied Prunus necrotic ringspot virus (PNRSV) in Cascade hops early on; and Wyatt Cone, WSU entomologist.

February 25 was "proof of the pudding" day, and Fritz rolled out the Cascade carpet for his good friend Segal and the four VIPs, who got to experience 100% Cascade in bottled Our Special Ale (OSA), as well as the two OSAs and Old Foghorn in the cellar. Plus, they got to try one-day-old Anchor Steam from fermentor #2, Anchor Steam in the cellar, and some finished Anchor Steam that Fritz was still brewing with Northern Brewer and Cascade. And they also got to see Porter being brewed, but to a very special recipe just for that day and the next. Instead of 38 lb of Northern Brewer, Fritz decided to use 28 lb of Northern Brewer and then have his guests add 5 lb Cascade to the kettle plus 5 lb to the hop jack. The Cascade Porter from that day was later kräusened with a Steam made with a combination of Northern Brewer and Cascade and bottled March 23, so Fritz could send them custom-hopped souvenirs of their trip.

On April 23, 1976, Phil organized an in-house tasting of the Old Foghorn and Our Special Ale that was still in the cellar. The former, he noted, was continuing to improve, with a "sweet, winey

aroma—very pleasant—and extraordinary flavor." Our Special Ale—which would be blended with new brews of Our Special Ale in the fall—had "a fruity, flowery bouquet, with good afterbitter and no rough edges." Fritz felt good enough about both to discontinue Cascade in Anchor Steam, reverting to 100% Northern Brewer with the next brew on April 27. OSA and Foghorn would be joining Steam and Porter in his expanding lineup, and they needed to be completely different from each other.

Sadly, the day after the tasting, April 24, Joe Allen died in Petaluma at the age of eighty-eight. "I had a very great affection for your late brother, Joe," Fritz wrote Agnes, "and respect for your family's ties to that brewing tradition which has passed into my hands." The funeral took place April 28, 1976, in San Francisco, exactly one mile west of the 17th Street brewery where Joe had once been brewmaster. In Joe's memory, Fritz closed the brewery that day.

FRITZ ON BEER AND BREWING

In the fall of 1976, with Lilliputian irony, Fritz was invited to give a talk to the St. Louis chapter of the Master Brewers' Association of America (MBAA). There, in Anheuser-Busch's hometown, he enjoyed "sharing with your members some of the adventure and misadventures that will occur to anyone rash enough to become president and master brewer of a brewery, with no experience at either position." It was the first of many such talks over the years. Before he left for Missouri, Fritz replied to a request from a young beer writer across the pond named Michael Jackson for more information about his beers and brewery. He included tasting notes, rare for Fritz because he eschewed pigeonholing, preferring to let his customers draw their own conclusions.

- » Steam Beer: "Amber, malty, and hoppy."

- » Porter: "A darker, richer stronger version of Steam Beer, very similar to a fine British or Irish stout, but not so bitter as Guinness. Nearly black with a slight hint of sweetness."

- » Christmas Ale: "Similar to a fine Pale Ale in England, it is not so bitter as British 'best bitter,' but is similar. Amber in color, it has a very hoppy nose and considerable body."

- » Barley Wine: "Aged over six months before bottling. It is sweet, of course, slightly vinous, and very rich and perfumey, typical of the very best English Barley Wines."

Fritz also summed up some of the philosophy and methods by which he had transformed the failing Steam Beer Brewing into America's first craft brewery, long before the phrase "craft beer" came into vogue:

Our beers and ales are all brewed only with barley malt, no other grains or sugars. They are also carbonated only by natural means, by bunging in the case of the Ale and by kräusening the Steam and Steam Porter. Our hopping rates are high. We try to do every aspect of brewing in as pure and traditional a manner as possible, using no preservatives or additives of any kind.

All our bottled beers are now pasteurized in the so-called "flash pasteurization" method, which we think is inherently superior to "tunnel pasteurization" or to "sterile filtration." The latter method was used successfully for over three years after we began bottling in 1971, but we greatly prefer "flash pasteurization" now, as it seems to allow a fuller and richer flavor and aroma.

As Fritz reminded me years later, "All of our beers were utterly true, and utterly traditional, and utterly honest, and utterly real, and historically valid, and absolutely different—each one. There was no blending of two beers to make a third or anything like that, which was so common. We were blazing a trail. We knew it. I used to say, 'We have the world by the tail. The world doesn't know it yet, but we do!'"

NAME CHANGE

As far back as 1969, after Fritz became sole owner of Steam Beer Brewing Company, his trusted attorney and friend Chan Flickinger advised him, "if you do get into a good production with steam beer, it might be advisable to buy the 'Anchor Brewing Company' name." Under an agreement shrewdly made with Lawrence Steese in 1960, Joe and Agnes Allen retained the name "Anchor Brewing Company" and had been charging a royalty of 2¢ on every gallon of "Anchor Steam Beer" sold (62¢ per barrel). After Joe's death, Fritz called Agnes to offer his condolences and, after an appropriate time, wrote her to suggest a path forward that would be mutually agreeable and beneficial. Fritz's opinion was that

the best future for this brewery will be to produce several other beers and ales besides the current Anchor Steam and Anchor Porter. I believe that this basic "Steam Beer" product has a good, although limited, potential. However, the healthiest long-range goal for my brewery, I believe, is to produce several other types of beer. As you know, we have already sold several Ales, which were variously called "Liberty Ale" and "Christmas Ale." My problem is that calling my brewery "Steam Beer Brewing Company," although it has a fine appeal, does limit the degree to which I can associate other beers with a central brand.

Fritz proposed that the existing royalty agreement continue, but that he purchase from her "the right to call my company Anchor Brewing Company, and, of course, the exclusive use of the name Anchor in brewing, offering her $20,000 [$99,000 today] plus expenses and taxes. . . . I can foresee the day when Steam Beer is not necessarily the main product of this brewery. Thus, my real goal is to have Anchor as a central name for my brewing *company*, so that other beer *brands* could reside under a single umbrella."

Agnes saw the wisdom of Fritz's offer and in February 1977 her Anchor Brewing Company changed its name to Neslen Corporation (from *Agnes Allen*) so that Fritz's Steam Beer Brewing Company could once again go by its historical name, Anchor Brewing Company. On April 4, 1977, Fritz signed the amended Articles of Incorporation. Other than the notary's, all six signatures on the document were Fritz's. Thanks to Chan Flickinger, the new articles were filed April 19, 1977; this was important, because Fritz expected to bottle his barley wine soon, and it would need the name of his brewery on the label. After Agnes's death on May 30, 1983, and over the ensuing years, Fritz made several very generous offers to buy out the royalty agreement, but the family declined.

LENDING A HELPING HAND

Earlier in 1976, Fritz had given a brewery tour to US Navy vet Jack McAuliffe. A longtime homebrewer, Jack was thinking about starting a brewery in Sonoma, to be called New Albion, which would ultimately begin selling its beer in the summer of 1977. "Well, he was gruff," Fritz recalls. "I just can't think of a better word for it." But Fritz made a point of extending the same courtesy to Jack that other brewers had shown him more than a decade before.

As soon as Jack left that day, Fritz began to lay the groundwork for a meeting with one of the state's most influential lawmakers, State Senator Albert S. Rodda, which took place on March 12, 1976, to discuss "the possibility of changing the law so that small brewers would pay a more equitable cost for a state brewery license." In 1967, Fritz had gone to his state senator, John Burton, and told him:

I thought the $828 fee for a brewery of our size was very unfair. Mr. Burton agreed with me, and at that time, and even today [1976], there was only one small brewery in California, which is mine. Why Mr. Burton chose to have the law read as it does, I do not know. The fact is that the only breweries allowed to pay reasonable fees for licenses are "Steam Beer exclusively" breweries. Perhaps at the time that seemed like a reasonable way to do this, but today, if it seems right that small breweries should pay fees somewhat comparable to small wineries, then there is no doubt that the law should be changed so that a small brewery can produce any kind of beer that it likes.

Fritz never took credit for initiating the conversation about the inequities of this law. He is a firm believer that credit is something to be given, not taken. And Jack had a strong case. While AB's brand-new brewery in Fairfield, CA, making 3.4 million barrels, would pay $0.00024 per barrel (bbl). Jack's brewery, which would open in summer 1977, making 150 barrels, would pay $5.52 per bbl.

Then, as Fritz had hoped, Jack and New Albion cofounder Suzanne Stern took the lead (with Fritz's ongoing support), getting a bill passed in 1978, which retained the $828 fee for large breweries but reduced the fee to just $100 for breweries making fewer than sixty thousand barrels of beer a year. It was a win-win. Jack would never pay more than $100, and Fritz would not have to do so until 1990! And it initiated a spirit of advocacy for small brewers that continued long after New Albion closed in 1982.

CONTINUED GROWTH

In 1972, Fritz had estimated the capacity of his brewery at 5,000 barrels. Two years later, it sold 6,186 barrels. In 1973, he revised his estimate to 7,500 barrels. Two years later, it sold 7,402 barrels.

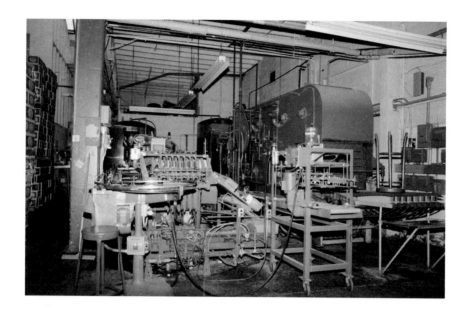

Although he was thinking seriously about moving as early as 1975, by 1976 the 9,136-square-foot brewery building was feeling more like paddock than pasture. They'd already expanded into the circa 1907 two-story building adjacent to the brewery, using the first floor to create Cellar B. And in 1977, Fritz leased a building across Decatur Street as a warehouse. It was time to brew smarter.

In summer '76, Fritz had attended the Executive Program for Smaller Companies at Stanford's Graduate School of Business. And in winter '77, both Fritz and Gordon returned to the United States Brewers' Academy, planning not to refurbish an old brewery but to create a new brewery inside an old building. Meanwhile, Mark Carpenter, who had taken the USBA's Course in Brewing and Malting Science at the University of Wisconsin in 1974, attended the USBA's Course in Packaging Technology at Michigan State, along with San Francisco native, USF grad, and relatively new hire Chris Solomon, who had started in 1974.

By June 24, 1976, after exactly seven months in the cellar, Old Foghorn was ready to bottle—and occupying increasingly precious cellar space. But since Fritz didn't have federal label approval, he opted to bottle what are called *shiners*: filled and

crowned, but unlabeled, bottles. Even without labels, it took two days, June 24 and 25, to fill and crown the traditional 6.3- to 6.4-ounce green bottles (called *nipperkins* in England, one-third of a British pint) which resisted virtually every machine on the line, getting hung up in the washer, filler, and crowner. But thanks to what Mark lauded as the "exceptional efforts by all employees, including Linda, who helped with the bottle washer," all were satisfied with a job well done and this one-of-a-kind brew.

No brewery had made—let alone bottled—a barley wine in the United States before. And that led to the sort of challenge Fritz faced again and again throughout his career. In September, Fritz again reached out to the Brewers' Society for advice: "The potential problem I see is with obtaining US government approval for the term 'Barley Wine' to appear on our label. There is no evidence that such a phrase has ever been used on a US Beer or Ale label, and I expect some questions as to its validity, especially since the word 'Wine' might possibly seem to conflict with the wine people here. I want very much to use the term nonetheless, because we believe in traditions here and in traditional beers and brewing." Fritz hoped that a descriptor on the label like "Barleywine Style ALE" would mollify the authorities, and he hoped to establish the validity of barley wine as a legitimate and traditional product.

The Brewers' Society sent a packet of barley wine labels as well photocopies of *An Essay on Brewing, with a View of Establishing the Principles of the Art* (London, 1758), which defines wine as "a brisk, agreeable, spirituous and cordial liquor, drawn from vegetable bodies, and fermented. In this sense beers and ales may be called, and really are, barley wines." They also included evidence from Bickerdyke's *The Curiosities of Ale & Beer: An Entertaining History* (London, 1889): "Since the dawn of our history Barley-wine has been the 'naturall drinke' for an 'Englysshe man,' and has had no unimportant influence on English life and manners." And they sent an extract from their Monopolies Commission Report on the Supply of Beer (1969), which notes that "virtually every brewer offers in bottle a similar selection of beers, including a pale or light ale, a brown ale, a strong ale, sometimes called 'export,' a stout, a barley wine, and a lager."

All jolly good—in England. The USBA, though willing to deliver Fritz's application for label approval personally to the director of the ATF, was not sanguine about its prospects: "I do not believe the ATF will approve your application for label approval despite your careful use of type size and style to indicate that 'Barley Wine' is ale. I base this firm opinion on the Bureau's traditional vigorous opposition to permitting the use of the word 'wine' in conjunction with 'beer' or 'ale' on malt beverage labels."

It was a case of one tradition besting the other. Some things just need to wait for the world to catch up to them. "It is quite a new thing here in the States," Fritz wrote to John Young at the Ram Brewery, "and we don't view it as much more than a satisfying sideline." So Fritz opted to sit tight for a while and not push his luck. "This has been an experiment," Fritz wrote Claude Arkell at Donnington Brewery, "and not too businesslike I am afraid. The Barley Wine is delicious however, and we plan to sell it only at the brewery," a plan which, like barley wine, would be slow to develop.

1976 CHRISTMAS ALE

Meanwhile, it was time for Fritz to brew his "3rd L.A.," aka "Our Special Ale 1976," aka "1976 Christmas Ale." Three new traditions began with the release of the 1976 Christmas Ale: changing the recipe from year to year, changing the label, and changing the tree. Fritz loved creating a sense of anticipation around the Ale's release and the comparison of a new "vintage" to its predecessors. There were two bottlings of 1976 Christmas Ale. The first, on November 19, was a blend of the two ales that Fritz's guests from Prosser had sampled in the cellar in February, the cellar time being what set it apart from 1975 Christmas Ale. It was sold in Northern California. The second bottling, November 22, was a blend two ales that had been brewed five to six weeks before. Here, besides the lower ABV (6.1%), the key change was the yeast, which Fritz had obtained from Pabst for these brews. To avoid confusion, this bottling shipped to Southern California.

As usual, Fritz was embracing another opportunity for what Peter F. Drucker calls *purposeful innovation*, in this case on his quest for the perfect yeast for his ales, whether it would be Genesee, Pabst, Molson, or baker's yeast from Red Star across the Bay. "George Goerl, the retired brewmaster from Acme, gave me some practical advice: 'Just go over to Red Star and get the baker's yeast, and tell them to give it to you before they put the starch in it. It's great yeast. It's *Saccharomyces cerevisiae*.' It was a brilliant idea. It was also important to me in my arguments about whether steam beer was top fermented or bottom fermented." In other words, California common beer could technically have been an ale one day and a lager the next, given the day-to-day realities of brewing under primitive conditions and changing circumstances.

The year 1976 was not just America's bicentennial. It was also the fiftieth anniversary of President Coolidge proclaiming the General Grant Tree, a giant sequoia in California's Mariposa Grove, to be "Our Nation's Christmas Tree." And it was the twentieth anniversary of President Eisenhower declaring that same tree to be the nation's only living National Shrine. For his 1976 Christmas Ale

label, Fritz engaged Richard Elmore, who had been helping him with design projects since the 1965 Balloon Ascension. He was also an accomplished architect, and Fritz knew that he would be a trusted partner to assist him with the design and layout of his new brewery. Richard's illustration of "Our Nation's Christmas Tree," with a handful of admirers at its base for scale, would become the perfect metaphor for Fritz and his brewery's strength, endurance, resilience, and perseverance, all of which would be tested in the years to come.

On January 3, 1977, *New West Magazine* ran a small piece entitled "A Winter's Ale." Beneath a black-and-white Christmas Ale label, they wrote: "Move over, wine country—at Christmas time San Francisco becomes the home of the finest ale around. The folks at Anchor, who ordinarily bring you their extraordinarily flavorful, all-natural beer, one-up themselves this time of year and produce a limited edition of a truly superlative ale. Six hundred cases are all the Anchor Ale there is; a single case ($18) would bring ecstasy to ale amateurs of your acquaintance." With such hoopla over Christmas Ale, it's hard to imagine why the brewery's overall production was so limited that year, up by just 459 barrels. But there was a reason. "Since late 1976," wrote Fritz two years later, "we have been rationing our production among wholesalers because even with special efforts our production has fallen well behind demand. Wholesalers have been instructed to be very selective in opening new accounts, and unfortunately we have had to forgo some very excellent and enthusiastic prospects."

BEST BEER IN THE WEST

So, on January 17, 1977, it was with a mixture of anticipation and apprehension that Fritz read *New West Magazine*'s main cover line: "Tops of the Hops: Best Beer in the West." The First New West Beer Test was a blind tasting organized to determine the Best Beer in the West. It was similar to

1976's Judgment of Paris, a competition that pitted up-and-coming California wines against more established French ones. That competition didn't start a Trojan War, but it surprised the judges and shook up the wine world. For the beer world, thirty brands of commercially available suds from Colorado to the Pacific Coast and eight foreign countries—plus six homebrews from Byron Burch, Bay Area author of *Quality Brewing* in 1974—were "subjected to scrupulous testing. Judging was on appearance, aroma, and taste, on a scale of 1 (lowest) to 6. By the end of the day's tasting, many of the judges were having trouble seeing well enough to rate appearance." But they reached a collective conclusion. Anchor Steam Beer, at 67¢ per bottle, was "Grand Winner" and "Best of Show," with a total of 128 points, 17 points ahead of its closest competitor. The only beer more expensive than Anchor Steam was Anchor Porter at 70¢ per bottle,

which placed twelfth with 87 points. "Everyone at our brewery was very proud," wrote Fritz to "Fellow Beer Lovers" in an open letter. "Winning the competition was especially satisfying, but we are also encouraged to see further evidence that the concept of serious beer tasting and judging is growing in popularity. It is our ambition to brew the very finest glass of beer in the world. We can't win them all, of course, but the growing interest in what makes for an excellent beer is heartening to us." Today, of course, beer tastings, ratings, rankings, contests, and competitions are ubiquitous. In those days, such events were unheard of, which gave the New West Beer Test a Judgment of Paris–like gravitas. Almost overnight, Anchor vaulted into the national consciousness.

To some *New West* readers, 67¢ for a bottle of beer seemed exorbitant, even for a grand winner. But not to Fritz.

Around 1975, somebody made a joke about how expensive the beer was. They said, "You won't believe this, but I paid 75¢ [about $3.91 today] the other day for a bottle of Steam Beer." It just irritated the hell out of me. And I said, "Well, what was on the floor?" And he said, "What do you mean?" And I said, "Was it peanut shells or carpet?" "Oh, it was carpet," he replied. "I was at the Bankers Club, at the top of the Bank of America Building." Give me a *break*. And I said something like, "Well, of course, you're on the ninety-ninth floor or something, so it costs more." So then he said, "Well, what does a bottle *actually* cost?" And I said, "Well, it depends on which bottle. The first bottle cost me about a million dollars."

Following the publication of his *The English Pub* in 1975, Michael Jackson—who deserved a free pint for every time he had to say "No, not *that* Michael Jackson"—decided to go global, literally, "in pursuit of exceptional beer." Jackson, who first visited Anchor in 1976, possessed a perceptive palate, keen wit, and great flair for writing and public speaking. Although they never discussed it, he and Fritz shared an ability to connect with an audience—any audience. Inspired by Hugh Johnson's 1971 *The World Atlas of Wine: A Complete Guide to the Wines & Spirits of the World*, Michael's 1977 *The World Guide to Beer*, a self-described book for the beer-drinker, was a masterpiece. Of its first edition's 255 pages, fourteen were devoted to US beer, of which three were about California beer. That meant that three pages were devoted to Fritz Maytag and his "great little brewery," as Michael called it when he signed Fritz's copy. Inside, Michael declares, "No beers in the United States are more idiosyncratic than those produced by the Anchor Steam Brewing Company, of San Francisco. The smallest brewery in the United States has added a whole new dimension to American brewing."

Not all the attention that Anchor Brewing received in 1977 was serious. In 1976, a location scout for ABC TV asked Fritz about filming an episode of *The Streets of San Francisco* at the brewery. Called *Dead Lift*, it aired on May 5, 1977. The episode opens with the murder of a young woman by a sensitive bodybuilder named Joe, played by an aspiring young Austrian actor named Arnold Schwarzenegger. It turns out that Joe works at a local brewery—Anchor. The brewery scene opens with a cameo by Fritz Maytag, as he inspects bottles on the line. Joe walks briskly past him, carrying on one shoulder what TV viewers are supposed to believe is a full keg of beer. Joe works too hard and fast for his fellow employees. When the foreman fires him for his buffness and enthusiasm, Arnold's character goes ballistic, hurling what appear to be full, 15.5-gallon Golden Gate kegs around the warehouse. He will kill again, but fortunately for his coworkers, it will be on his day off. The episode became a cult classic. In the well-publicized words of Oscar Wilde, "there is only one thing in the world worse than being talked about, and that is not being talked about."

Since 1969, when Fritz bought out Lawrence Steese, being talked about had been the direct consequence of Fritz's business strategy, which he

created to set Anchor apart. Its three pillars of quality, reputation, and premium price were supported by upgrades to the brewery's essential equipment, coupled with carefully controlled production standards. The result was a brewery that was uniquely very modern and also one of the most traditional breweries in the world. Years later, Fritz told me,

It was quite something. Pete Coors was one of the early people—business professionals—who came and toured the brewery. With his eyes just bulging out of his head, and to my great delight, he was very laudatory. He said he could see what I had done, he was astonished by what we were doing, and that "I would just give my right arm to be doing what you are doing here." Well, you know, I knew Coors as a brewery that was the most impressive in the world to me in terms of quality control, and so that was a thrilling experience.

Fritz's Anchor was no accident. Nor was his radically traditional credo. In 1978, in his loan proposal for a new brewery, Fritz wrote that this combination

of the modern and the traditional results in beers which score very well on any objective

L to R: Mark Carpenter, Sue Anders, Chris Solomon, Aaron Donald, Greg Kimball, and Mike Lee

product analysis. It also has resulted in a high degree of interest from customers and beer historians as well as writers and media. This has favored us with very advantageous "word of mouth" advertising and many very fruitful mentions in newspapers and magazines, and on TV and radio. The company has limited its advertising dollars to point-of-purchase displays, informational brochures, and distinctive, high-quality packaging, but has benefited from "media" publicity far beyond the financial reach of a small company. We believe that by purposely maintaining a very quiet and low-key position in the marketplace, we can attract more goodwill and interest than if we were to follow the more usual beer marketing practices.

Not unlike the Maytag Company, the brewery has sought "to entrench itself in the marketplace as an unusually reliable and old-fashioned company, with a proud tradition of quality. Many imported specialty beers have come and gone over the years, often with huge advertising and marketing budgets, which seek to accomplish rapidly what we believe to be best accomplished quietly and gradually."

Anchor's products, Fritz noted, were positioned in

the import or "specialty beer" segment of the market, which in recent years has grown much faster than the general beer market. This rapid growth of "specialty beers" is a new factor in the US beer market. The "specialty beers" have generally been imports because the US brewers tend to be either very large companies in fierce mutual competition, unwilling to allocate resources to such a relatively small total business, or smaller companies in remote locations who are unable to enter the market for management and geographical reasons. We have been able to establish a relatively high price for our beer, and this is a very important element in our business strategy. Many smaller- and medium-sized brewers [often

family owned] have been having difficulty in recent years, but without exception they have positioned their products at the bottom of the price scale. We have taken the opposite course. By establishing a reputation for uniqueness and high quality, we have been able to position our beers well above any domestic products and in the upper range of imported beers. This combination of reputation, higher price, and smaller volume is the essence of our strategy.

[Since 1969,] Anchor has been carefully placing itself in a leadership position as *the* US specialty brewery, and it has developed a national reputation for the integrity and tradition of its products. Now, in 1978, the company has a unique opportunity to develop a niche in the beer market, that of very flavorful and unusual products, designed to appeal to tradition and to the growing interest in purity and naturalness in food products. The unusually small size of the brewery, its location in San Francisco, and the fact that its products have a unique validity in American brewing history, all combine to place the company in a strong market position.

And to take advantage of that position, Fritz would need a new brewery.

AIMING HIGH

(1977–1979)

In the long run men hit only what they aim at. Therefore, though they should fail immediately, they had better aim at something high.

—Henry David Thoreau, *Walden*

Fritz had big plans for his small brewery. So his first trip in 1977 was to a family-owned brewery ten times Anchor's size, which also happened to be America's oldest brewery. It was Yuengling ("The Beer Everybody Likes") in Pottsville, Pennsylvania. "For many years I have known about your company," he wrote Richard L. Yuengling Sr., "and I have always looked forward to the possibility of visiting and seeing how you do things." Fritz, with Richard as his tour guide, had a backstage pass to a well-run regional brewery. Yuengling had become the sole surviving brewery in Schuylkill County following

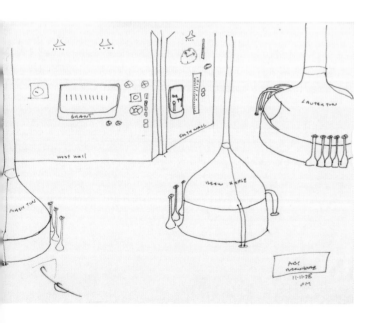

the closing of nearby Mount Carbon Brewery—after Yuengling purchased its Bavarian Premium Beer brand and recipe. Though Yuengling was feeling the squeeze from America's megabreweries, Fritz found Richard to be optimistic and determined to succeed. "I was especially pleased with your obvious sense of pride and enthusiasm in your company." Fritz's game plan for success, though, was as different from Yuengling's as East and West.

Fritz's next trip, to Germany and England in September 1977, was emblematic of his radically traditional strategy, as well as the incredible power of imagination when allied with judgment. He began in Munich at Interbrau (now known as drinktec), the world's leading trade show for the beverage industry. There, under one roof, he could see, touch, and discuss state-of-the-art brewing equipment from all over the world. Then he and his wife, Lucy, revisited two of England's oldest, most traditional breweries, The Ram Brewery and Donnington's. In advance of his trip, he wrote to John Young at Ram: "Since our visit in the fall of 1975, our Ale brewing plans have developed even further, but we have been so busy with our regular brewing that we still have not been able to launch Liberty Ale as a regular feature. Our facilities are at capacity in this building, so a full time Ale is still in the future." And he wrote to Donnington's Claude Arkell: "We have been having a very busy year. So busy that we have not had time to begin brewing Ale as planned. Perhaps we will move soon to a larger building and will have the time and space." Fritz and Lucy also visited R. Peach & Co. Ltd., a maltster in Burton-on-Trent (from whom he would buy malt for the 1978 Christmas Ale). Fritz thanked them, writing: "After more than ten years in brewing, I have had many satisfying experiences, but visiting your maltings and stepping out onto the growing barley on the malt floor was one of the highlights. Perhaps the experience of growing wine grapes and making wine has colored my attitudes, because there is something essentially right about working with the whole process. In any event, I don't think I'll rest easy until we are making our own malt." Little did Fritz know that a scant two years later he would regret not having his own maltings.

Next, Fritz headed to Karlsruhe, Germany, where he visited the former Schrempp Brewery. In 1871 (the same year Gottlieb Brekle purchased a beer-and-billiards saloon), Karl Schrempp purchased a brewery with roots extending to the

early eighteenth century. By 1889, the Schrempp Brewery, with its distinctive griffin logo, was producing more than fifty-two-thousand US beer barrels a year. After WW I it merged with the A. Printz Brewery. In 1967, the brewery succumbed to the same sort of consolidation that was gobbling up small to midsize breweries in the United States, when Binding-Brauerei AG, Frankfurt, and the Bank für Brau-Industrie took it over and ended the Schrempp Brewery's entrepreneurial independence. Ten years later, Binding closed the brewery forever, creating an opportunity for Fritz, who wrote Claude Arkell:

I think I found a brewhouse that would be ideal. It was built in 1955 [the mash tun in '56], but the lauter tun has not been used since 1961. It is a three-vessel copper brewhouse, with mash cooker, lauter tun, and kettle. The brew size, about 110 US beer barrels, is just twice ours, so it would permit us to make one or two brews in a comfortable day, each twice our size. That would be ideal. We hope to do 10,000 barrels this year [they would finish 1977 with 10,251], and are hoping to grow to between 20,000 and 30,000 in the next five years or so. I hope we can do it.

Fritz had done his homework. Anchor would reach 21,454 barrels in 1980 and 33,356 in 1983. The solid-copper vessels were made by A. Ziemann G.m.b.H, established in 1852 in Ludwigsburg, less than 4 km from Gottlieb Brekle's birthplace. Mr. Brecke [no relation], Binding's brewmaster, was stoic as he gave Fritz what must have been an emotional tour of his brewery. After the tour, Fritz headed home for the October grape harvest, "but in my mind's eye, we are already making imaginary brews in our Ziemann brewhouse."

Fritz relied in part on the expertise of Peter Kollnberger, a German brewing engineer who worked for Ziemann as well as Heinrich Huppmann G.m.b.H, a reputable German company engaged to dismantle, ship, and reassemble the Schrempp brewhouse in San Francisco. Peter's involvement

gave Fritz added confidence to pull the trigger in February 1978 so dismantling could begin in March. His financial strategy for his "expansion project"—painstakingly worked out in consultation with his accountant, his tax attorney, his bank, and his wife—was for him personally to buy the equipment and pay for the building and its remodel out of his own pocket and then lease everything back to the company. "The bank wouldn't loan money to a *brewery*. They were terrified of the uncertainty. They would only loan to me. Now of course, later, Wells Fargo loaned money to Sierra Nevada, oh sure, because Anchor proved you could make a lot of money!" The all-copper brewhouse, with its three vessels, grant, and sink, was just one piece of an incredibly gutsy puzzle. Installed, it

alone would set Fritz back over $325,000 [about $1.5 million]. And yet, for years to come, it would be the sparkling jewel in the crown of Anchor's magnificent new home.

Fritz returned from Germany in fall 1977 with a clear idea of how his brewhouse would look, which gave him a good sense of what sort of building he needed to find. And there was no question that it would be in San Francisco. "We think that it is important for the company to maintain its location in San Francisco because of the very positive marketing image involved. San Francisco is perceived as a romantic and exciting city. Our history is associated with San Francisco. And more and more our beer is known as a famous San Francisco product and a part of the city's heritage." Fritz was referring to Anchor as *meibutsu* (名物), a Japanese word that literally means the "fame-thing" for which a particular city or region is known. "I really learned it in Japan. It became a major inspiration to me, and I applied it in my thinking that we've got to have Anchor Steam become meibutsu for San Francisco"—like the loaf of sourdough visitors to San Francisco brought home for friends or family as a special memory of their trip.

For years, Fritz had been secretly prowling the streets of San Francisco for a new home for his brewery. By 1977, there were quite a few industrially zoned buildings for sale in the City, and he'd

toured every one of them. But when he heard that an old coffee roastery on Potrero Hill would soon be on the market, he and Gordon went right over to have a look. It was big, but it was perfect, so Fritz went all in. Knowing that he would be competing for the building and property with speculators rather than manufacturers, Fritz flew to New York to appeal to the owners, Standard Brands, Inc., face to face. There, he told them that he would be willing to pay *any fair price* they asked *and* that he would be the *best next owner*, bringing jobs back to their old building in their old neighborhood. After waiting in their Manhattan lobby all day for an answer, he got it and the building for $850,000— worth every penny.

Built in 1937, the art deco building was designed by Harvard-educated San Francisco architect Edward Alonzo Eames in the Streamline Moderne style for Standard Brands' Chase & Sanborn division. Eames's claims to architectural fame included St. Brendan's Catholic Church and a 1929 addition to Old St. Mary's. But his art deco work, first at

Francis Scott Key Elementary School and then Standard Brands, created some of the city's finest examples of the style, and Fritz felt the latter's construction, location, and appearance would be ideally suited for Anchor's future. Its architecture, to paraphrase Goethe, was frozen music. And within its walls Fritz hoped to brew liquid architecture.

Located at 501 De Haro Street, it was two buildings in one, with a total square footage of 83,000—about nine times the size of 541 8th Street. The main building totaled 51,000 sq ft, including three floors at 15,000 sq ft, a tower, and a 6,000 sq ft cellar built right into Potrero Hill. Chase & Sanborn's loading dock and warehouse had been housed in an adjacent 32,000 sq ft, one-story building with cellar, designed by an unknown architect in a utilitarian style and built in the winter of 1950/51.

A siding track behind the brewery on Carolina Street had allowed Standard Brands to ship in and out by rail, even after the railroad tunnel that once ran beneath Potrero Hill was destroyed by fire in

1962. Fritz's new neighbors would include the old Pioneer Soap Factory building to the south, the coffee roastery for Safeway Stores to the east, and US Enterprise Corp., makers of Wing Nien Longevity Brand soy sauce, to the north. Coincidentally, that meant that fermentation would soon be happening on both sides of Mariposa Street.

Anchor had always been a neighborhood brewery, and returning to Potrero Hill felt like coming home. The old brewery building at 17th and Kansas was just a few blocks away, and "Pot Hill" or "Goat Hill," as its residents often called it, was unique. "Potrero Hill is the reverse of Nob Hill," wrote Edwin Rosskam in *San Francisco: West Coast Metropolis* in 1939. "With a view of the city second only to the panorama from Twin Peaks, it is unfamiliar to San Francisco's upper crust. It is the hill of little people, not a boarding house district like the Mission, but rather the location where small homeowners—shipyard workers, waterfront workers, and factory workers—raise chickens and hang up their laundry against a magnificent backdrop." As Fritz told his neighborhood newspaper, *The Potrero View*, in 1978, he liked the location because it has "one foot in the industrial section and the other in the residential." Famous residents of the sunniest neighborhood in the city included Lawrence Ferlinghetti and Wayne Thiebaud, and catercorner from the brewery was Jackson Park, where employees could play softball or jog after work. It was perfect—with one exception. Although Francisco de Haro had been Yerba Buena's first *alcalde* (chief magistrate), Fritz felt that compared to "De Haro Street," "Mariposa Street" more vividly evoked California and the Mariposa Grove. So even though the main entrance was on De Haro Street, he opted to use the side entrance to the brewery, 1705 Mariposa Street, as its main address. Long before he could begin installing his Ziemann brewhouse, fermentors, cellar tanks, bottling line, racking room, offices, and taproom, the inside of the old roastery would have to be completely gutted and sandblasted, removing the remnants of its equipment and the redolence of its coffee. Ever the optimist, Fritz expected to be in operation in early 1979.

But it was time to get back to business, and that meant the 1977 Christmas Ale. Having had Jim Stitt help him with the 1975 label and Richard Elmore the 1976, Fritz's idea was to engage a new artist for each succeeding Christmas Ale vintage. It was a *great* idea, inspired by Baron Philippe de Rothschild's choice, for each of his Château Mouton Rothschild Bordeaux vintages, of a renowned artist for the new label. These included Cocteau, Braque, Dalí, Moore, Miró, Chagall, Kandinsky, and, in 1975, Andy Warhol. But Fritz soon realized that it was not a *good* idea. The concept for each of Fritz's labels was Fritz's, and what he needed was someone he trusted to breathe life into that concept. So Fritz went back to Jim Stitt, for whom Fritz had only to "paint a word picture," as Jim likes to describe their process. Often, Jim would sketch the label in real time as Fritz described his concept for it.

By 1977, anticipation of the annual release of Our Special Ale had created quite a following. "It took a few years," Linda Rowe remembers, "but there would be a steady stream of people coming to the brewery, from pretty far away, lined up to buy the Christmas Ale." There were those who couldn't wait to find out what tree was on the label each year. And there was one group Linda called "the tree people, because they would come in and ask, 'Hey, got that tree beer?' They were from Mendocino, and they all had wads of cash, and all of the cash really smelled like marijuana. I mean it reeked."

As 1977 drew to a close, Fritz was gratified if not relieved that Anchor sold 10,251 barrels that year, a number comparable to Baruth & Schinkel's fin de siècle heyday. And, for the first time in its 106-year history, the brewery's gross sales exceeded $1 million (about $4.6 million today). The search for a brewhouse and a building to house it was over. But Fritz still had a sense of foreboding, that the road less traveled by, on which he'd been traveling for eleven and a half years, was about to get a lot bumpier.

Roasting equipment at 501 De Haro (1977)

COPYCAT

In January 1978, Fritz was pleased to learn that Richard Dye of San Rafael had been brewing experimental batches of beer using traditional methods, but dismayed that Mr. Dye proposed to call his product "Steam Beer" or "California Steam Beer." Fritz had always been protective of his brands. Six months earlier, on seeing a G. Heileman Brewing Company ad claiming, "Old Style is the only premium beer in America today that is fully Kraeusened," he had written to Heileman's VP of marketing: "Although I want to make my point clearly and firmly, I also sincerely hope that you will understand that I wish to make it in a friendly and reasonable spirit. Our Anchor Steam Beer and Anchor Porter are both 'fully Kraeusened' in the true and traditional manner, and therefore I object to the claim in your ad. Please can you reassure me that your company will no longer use or encourage others to use such phrases as appear in this ad?" And they did.

But as important as it was to call out Heileman ("Pure Brewed from God's Country")—for what turned out to be an inadvertent error, quickly and apologetically remedied—Dye's apparent plans to appropriate Fritz's brand name was another thing altogether.

> I called upon Mr. Dye at his brewery in San Rafael. . . . I wished him every success in his new venture and explained that I had invested years of my time and all of my money in developing the reputation of my Anchor Steam Beer as—I believe—one of the finest beers available . . . I believed the public understood "Steam Beer" to refer to my beer, and asked Mr. Dye to use any name other than my tradename "Steam Beer." I also had my attorney write a letter to Mr. Dye explaining that "Steam Beer" was my tradename and trademark.

Fritz was gobsmacked. He thought about Lawrence Steese, Joe Allen, and all those who had worked so hard to preserve and protect Anchor Steam Beer. And he looked back on his dozen years as brewmaster, building up the brewery and fighting the good fight to turn an anachronistic beer with a goofy, archaic nickname, which had been Anchor's alone for decades, into a unique beer with an internationally recognized brand name.

Anchor had been the only brewery to use the brand name "Steam Beer" in commerce, key to protecting one's trademark, since the 1930s. And no one had taken any interest in it at all until Fritz put it on the map. Inspired by the special "Steam Beer" label he'd created for the *Windward Passage* in 1973, Fritz doubled down on his "Steam Beer" trademark by creating and selling three new brands: California Steam Beer, Golden Gate Steam Beer, and San Francisco Steam Beer. And Fritz worked fast. The labels were submitted for federal label approval on Friday, January 20, 1978, approved the next Monday, bottled Tuesday, and sold to his Nevada distributor (so as not to confuse the Bay Area market) on Wednesday, long before Dye had *anything* on the market. And Fritz followed that up in February with another shipment.

He would hear nothing further of Dye and his enterprise until January 1979, so Fritz did his best to compartmentalize the aspiring interloper's existential threat to his brand.

MAYTAG THE MULTITASKER

While Fritz was circling the trademark wagons around his Steam Beer, he again found himself between the rock of sales orders and the hard place of rationing, under which wholesalers were getting just half the beer they ordered. Anchor's advertising and promotion expenditures in 1977 were $20,221—compared to AB's $79,171,000 on advertising alone that year. In an effort to curb demand, Fritz slashed Anchor's advertising and promotion budget in 1978 to $433. That aligned well with his long-held belief in the folly of dipping his toe into the quicksand of beer advertising. But with Fritzian irony, by eschewing advertising he ended getting more than his share of publicity from mainstream media like *Newsweek* and *People*, who came to him because he had a story to tell that was both interesting and true.

> Well, you know the story about *Advertising Age*, don't you? They did the story on brewery advertising? Oh, it was one of the triumphs of my life. *Advertising Age*, 1978, story about advertising in the brewing industry. And there was a little box that said, "There's a little brewery in San Francisco called Anchor Brewing and they don't do any advertising at all." In *Advertising Age!* Free ad—I got the diploma! You know, "They don't do advertising as a matter of principle, because they want to be small and special." It wasn't a joke. It was factual. But to me that was an absolute triumph. Written up, in *Advertising Age*, for not doing any advertising.

On March 31, 1978, San Francisco's General Brewing Co. crowned its last bottle of Lucky Lager. The closing was part of a grand scheme by its owner,

sold six cases of 6.4-oz (later labeled 6.3-oz to allow for more *ullage*, or headspace) bottles at $20.40, compared to $18 for a case of 12-ounce Christmas Ale, $15.80 for Porter, and $14.88 for Steam. Foghorn, at the equivalent of $1.59 per 12-ounce bottle, was now America's most expensive beer—with or without peanut shells. Linda also wrote off eleven cases of Old Foghorn to the drinkingest customer that day—and most days—at Anchor: "Consumed." The glasses lifted at Anchor that day were to their unlucky fellow brewers across town.

Memorial Day weekend 1978, the San Francisco Bay Area was swarming with brewers—homebrewers attending the Home Wine Merchants Association's annual convention/trade show in the East Bay, which had a special session for them. Lee Coe, who had become the Association's legislative representative, offered to arrange a tour of Anchor for his fellow homebrewers that weekend. He was very busy at the time working with State Assemblyman Tom Bates and US Senator Alan Cranston on separate bills, the idea of each to provide the same legal rights for homebrewers that home winemakers already enjoyed, as long as the fruits of their labor would not be sold.

Fritz personally hosted the homebrewers on Saturday, May 27, 1978, as a gesture of friendship to Lee and support to the homebrewers, their passion, and their cause. Fritz gave them his "brewer's tour," with all the beer bells and whistles. Knowing they were coming, he made sure that there was beer in each of the now three open fermentors—two Steams and a Porter—and, since Anchor was now brewing six days a week most weeks, there would be a Steam Beer in the brewhouse too. His guests included another old friend of the brewery, Fred Eckhardt; and the Maltose Falcons homebrew club was in attendance, including founder Merlin Elhardt, John Daume, John Rountree, Jim Brenneman, Brent Wilson, and two young Falcons named Ken Grossman and Paul Camusi, who in 1980 would open their own brewery in Chico. Had they all come the following week, they would have

beer magnate Paul Kalmanovitz, who bought and sold breweries like used cars. The upshot for Anchor was that, by default and literally overnight, it became San Francisco's sole surviving brewery, with Fritz and his thirteen full- and part-time employees the last professional brewers in the city. Anchor was now one of just eighty-nine breweries in America, the lowest recorded number before or after Prohibition. And Anchor was definitely the only one making barley wine, which finally went on sale at Anchor that same day, March 31. Fritz had decided to take advantage of the fact that in its home state Anchor did not need federal approval for the Foghorn label that he had created with Jim Stitt. Ironically, limited availability created a cult following for this ancient ale, so ahead of its time. Linda met Anchor's new hire, Douglas Odell. Doug, who worked at Anchor June through August, 1978, would open his eponymous Odell Brewing Co. eleven years later. For the homebrewers, meeting Fritz at his brewery must have been akin to young runners meeting Roger Bannister at Oxford University's Iffley Road Track, where he became the first to run a mile in under four minutes in 1954. After this they could say, like Emily Dickinson, "I dwell in possibility." After the tour, Fritz sold one Anchor belt buckle and seven cases of his newly released Old Foghorn, including four for Ken Grossman's homebrew shop. "With just a light spritzy finish and a deep mellow color," noted Fred Eckhardt in his *Amateur Brewer* newsletter, "we found this beer a real delight."

On June 11, 1978, Anchor got another unsolicited lift, this time thanks to Iowan and veteran wine-writer Robert Lawrence Balzer of the *Los Angeles Times*. It was another blind tasting, which had been judged by six international experts, including Fritz Maytag. They evaluated thirty-four beers from all over the world on body, foam, color, aroma, taste, bitterness, and general quality. As in the *New West* tasting, Anchor Steam was the clear winner of this so-called beer bout. Fritz was still rationing his beer, so he was flattered but conflicted about receiving top honors on such a big stage. Balzer was not the only wine writer that year to write about Anchor Steam, which had recently become available in New Jersey. In August 1978, Frank J. Prial began his *New York Times* review, "Some say it is the best beer in the United States. . . . Anchor Steam Beer, slightly darker than lager, is now made with only natural ingredients at a time when some American commercial beers have as many as 59 additives to improve the head, shelf life, and coloring."

Prial also wrote of "tiny 'boutique breweries' starting up around the country to provide an alternative to mass-produced mediocrity." Five years earlier, Philip Harding had used the term "boutique winery" to describe Paul Draper's Ridge Vineyards. To Paul and Fritz, saying "boutique winery" or "boutique brewery" was a little like saying "Frisco." Some journalists called Anchor a "boutique brewery" and some used Fritz's preferred nomenclature at the time, "American specialty brewer," but Fritz

can remember the moment when I said "microbrewers." I was at the new brewery, standing next to Linda in the office, when a reporter who was interviewing me used the term *boutique brewer*. It really bothered me because it seemed to put breweries like ours into a kind of a silly category that was of no consequence, whereas in fact we were breaking remarkable ground I would argue. So I said, "Let's call it microbrewers, OK?" There was our Apple II on the counter right behind Linda. My connection to microcomputers was through Steve Jobs and through the fact that I had bought one of the very first Apple IIs—you know, little guys versus big guys—even before I was introduced to Steve by Bob Noyce, the inventor of the microchip—we all served together on the Grinnell Board of Trustees. So why not just call us a microbrewery?

It caught on, though some preferred defining it numerically rather than philosophically—sales of X number of barrels per year, periodically increasing X as those microbreweries grew. In the early days, Fritz liked to joke that the definition of a microbrewery was any brewery that makes less beer than Anchor! And "to run a microbrewery," as Fritz would tell the National Homebrew and Microbrewery Conference in 1983, "it seems to me requires a degree of enthusiasm for excellence . . . and a theme of quality and integrity." Little did he know at the time that his idol, Jean De Clerck, had used the term microbrewery in 1969 to describe the pilot brewery his students used at the University of Louvain, telling an American reporter, "Visitors are astonished that a normal beer is brewed in a microbrewery, by students." Brits also used the term *microbrewery* for *pilot brewery*, at least as early as 1974, but neither use was ever meant to describe a small brewery making beer for sale.

Fritz's defines microbrewery as "a small brewery that is dedicated to traditional brewing, attitudes, and methods—utterly traditional, absolutely traditional, extreme traditional—combined with the most modern food technology, which has of course evolved dramatically in our time. What's unique about it is the combination." He feels the same way about craft. Bottom line, Anchor was the first boutique brewery before they were called boutique, the first microbrewery before they were called micro, and the first craft brewery before they were called craft.

HOMEBREWERS AND FAMILY BREWERS

The really big excitement in the brewing world in the summer of '78 came thanks to the advocacy of California homebrew clubs. State Assemblyman Tom Bates's AB 2797 was on its way to becoming state law. It allowed single adults to brew up to 100 gallons of beer at home, and households of two or more up to 200 gallons—all without the $828 manufacturer's license that McAuliffe and Maytag had fought to reform for small professional brewers. Governor Jerry Brown signed the Bates bill into law July 19, to take effect January 1, 1979.

On June 19, 1978, in Washington, DC, Lee Coe had testified before the US Senate on behalf of another California-born movement, the Cranston Bill, S. 3191. Just as Tom Bates had backed the homebrewers at home in California, Senator Alan Cranston was fighting the good fight on a national scale. And Lee Coe was there to testify for the passage of the Cranston Bill on behalf of the Home Wine Merchants Association and five California homebrew clubs: Maltose Falcons, Santa Clara Valley Brewers, San Andreas Malts, Redwood Lagers, and Yeast Bay Brewers. Coe's simple, effective message of parity between homebrewers and home winemakers was similar to what Fritz and

Jack had been proposing for the pros: "We want just one thing," Coe testified. "We want equality of treatment for home brewers and home winemakers." On October 14, 1978, President Jimmy Carter signed the Cranston Bill into law. Ironically, it was just two days after Falls City Brewing Co.—the last remaining brewery in Louisville, Kentucky—brewed its last batch of beer. G. Heileman Brewing Co. had bought two of their labels and recipes, but turned down one, the beer that made Carter's younger brother famous: Billy Beer.

In July '78, Fritz was on the road again, searching for ideas and equipment for his new brewery, like a treasure hunt for pieces of a colossal jigsaw puzzle. On July 18 he traveled to Pennsylvania to visit the Erie Brewing Co., which had closed March 10, after C. Schmidt & Sons Inc., a huge Philadelphia brewery, bought the family-owned brewery's brand names and recipes—including Koehler ("the good life beer"). Fritz met Erie's brewmaster, Charles Bauer, as well as its president J. M. (Marty) Magenau, who attributed the decline and fall of his brewery to the sway of TV advertising, which introduced national brands into local markets. Fritz always felt terribly uncomfortable at such "brewery estate sales," but he bought Erie's old American Peerless ("ABSOLUTELY SUPREME") Six Roll Malt Mill that day. By the time it was shipped and installed in his new brewery, this single jigsaw puzzle piece would set him back $14,500 (about $62,000 today).

THIS IS MY BELOVED SON

After a number of family meetings at their Mill Valley home, Lucy and Fritz had agreed to let Fritz's stepson Matthew climb another mountain. Matthew, age seventeen, had just graduated high school, but had plenty of experience mountaineering. This summer's goal would be to summit Canada's highest peak: Mount Logan in Yukon's Kluane National Park. It was particularly challenging, not so much because of its incredible height,

19,551 feet, but because of its awe-inspiring massiveness—by base circumference it is the world's largest nonvolcanic mountain—as well as its remoteness and isolation, necessitating drop-off and pickup by private plane. In early June, Matthew, at seventeen, and the five other members of their expedition, all in their twenties, were dropped off at Seward Glacier, to be picked up six weeks later. They would take the Warbler Ridge route, named the year before by the only other expedition to use this direct but treacherous route to the mountaintop. Fritz and Lucy had faith in the team leader. "I interviewed him, and he did impress me," Fritz recalls, but no parent would rest easy until they were all home safe and sound.

When Fritz returned to Anchor from Philadelphia on July 21, the brewery was bustling, its bottle shop chugging away, a Steam in the brewhouse, Porter and Steam in the fermentors, and the whole building as redolent as the Conservatory of Flowers in Golden Gate Park. He sat at his desk, removed the fountain pen from his shirt pocket, and began to write a letter, in his cryptic mix of print and cursive. It was to Marty Magenau. Fritz tried always to write thank-you notes to those who had welcomed him into their breweries and homes with warmth, generosity, and hospitality, and he encouraged his employees to do the same. But this note was different, almost a condolence.

Most of the shuttered breweries Fritz had seen looked like everyone had just dropped their tools and walked out the moment the last whistle blew. Erie Brewing was different.

I cannot resist telling you what a fine impression your brewery made on me. I have visited many, many breweries around the world, big and small. Many of them had, alas, closed as yours has. But never have I seen a brewery that reflected more care and pride. When I saw that all your brewing vessels were spotlessly clean, I was thrilled to see such an attitude of respect for the idle equipment, and proud to have known you as an active

member of our industry. It is truly a tragic thing when giant companies with no love of the brewing art or respect for its traditions can thrive, while companies such as yours are forced to close. I will never forget the intensity of the feeling that I experienced in your quiet brewhouse. I hope that you will not retire completely from your contacts and friends in the industry, and that I will have the pleasure of seeing you soon.

Fritz put down his pen, lost in another thought, wondering why he hadn't heard from Matthew yet. The climbers should have been picked up by then. Unbeknownst to Fritz or Lucy, two weeks before—on the evening of July 7—the six-man team had been setting up camp on Warbler Ridge at about 14,000 feet. Matthew and two of his fellow hikers were standing on what looked to be a safe cornice, when part of it gave way, taking their tents, their radio, and most of their gear down with them. One of them landed on a ledge about 500 feet below, from which his companions were able to rescue him. But Matthew and a longtime hiking companion were not so fortunate. They fell about 4,000 feet to the glacier below.

By July 17, the four remaining climbers had made their way to base camp, where they were finally spotted and rescued July 29. When Fritz got the call, he immediately flew to nearby Whitehorse, joined by two eagle-eyed friends, Sam Armstrong and Lars Speyer, to assist him in an aerial search. Sadly, the lost climbers were never found.

"You can't imagine what a thing it was. It was just absolutely horrible. Every now and then I can sort of imagine putting myself back in that situation, when he was killed. It's an infinite. It's not possible to go there. I can't imagine." Bereft and devastated, Fritz took some time off to grieve with and comfort his family.

***

When Fritz finally returned to work, he was reminded of the wonderful second family he had at

Anchor: Gordon, Mark, Linda. Paul Michaels, head brewer, had begun working for Anchor in 1973. His duties included ordering brewing materials and supplies, supervising brewhouse employees, and quality control/lab work. San Francisco-born USF-grad Chris (Solo) Solomon, who joined in 1974, served as racking supervisor and assisted Mark in running the bottle shop. He was also qualified as a brewer. Brewers Al Kornhauser and Tim Morse, both graduates of Beloit College, started at Anchor in 1977. J. Michael (Mike) Lee, a University of Northern Colorado grad, and UConn grad Sue Anders both started out in 1977 as bottlers, like most Anchor employees, and ended up working throughout the brewery over the course of their long careers. Fritz proudly called Sue Anchor's first "brewster," a Middle English word for female brewer in the same way that baxter is to baker. Aaron Donald and Greg Kimball, brewers, also joined in 1977, the same year Phil Canevari left after six and a half fun-filled years. As a former school-teacher, Phil was especially appreciative of "what amazing teachers Fritz and Gordon were, and we couldn't have done what we did without teamwork—and humor." Fritz's new hires in 1978—he interviewed and made the final decision on every employee—included bottler Michael Heiner and, in charge of maintenance, Wayne Filloon, whose "Wayneisms" made him Anchor's Yogi Berra.

In autumn 1978, Fritz asked all eleven of his current employees to gather in the taproom for an Anchor family portrait (see page 167). Inspired by the nineteenth-century photos hanging on the brewery's taproom walls, it is an eloquent tribute to the people who made Anchor such a special place.

LOOKING FORWARD

By fall 1978, Fritz had invested more than $600,000 of his own money in the finest machinery and equipment available for his brewery. But that was for 541 8th Street. Now, even as general contractor

Plant Bros. Corp. was finishing demolition and beginning conversion of 1705 Mariposa Street, Fritz was still trying to get a loan. And a lot of people depended on him, including both his Maytag and Anchor families.

In December, he put the finishing touches on the loan proposal that he hoped, if accepted, would get his new brewery up and running in early 1979. He wanted the loan package to include a real estate loan, equipment loan, secured loan, and working capital line of credit, and he had a good case for it. Interest in Anchor was high, and sales in 1978 would soar to 12,524 barrels—2,500 barrels beyond 8th Street's "capacity." Anchor was now selling beer in Alaska, Arizona, California, Colorado, Idaho, Minnesota, Nevada, New Jersey, New Mexico, Oregon, Texas, Washington, and Wyoming, with plans to expand to the major metropolitan areas in the Central and Eastern states as soon as production could be increased.

To achieve this, Fritz proposed to install a new brewhouse, lab, offices, fermentors, cellar tanks, finishing room, racking room, and a state-of-the-art bottling line "so that approximately 25,000 barrels of beer can be made readily with no additional labor. Additional increases up to a total of 50,000 barrels can be made readily with modest additions to equipment and staff. The building can accommodate even larger increases handily, although there are no current plans to exceed 50,000 barrels." That made sense, at least in part, because in 1976 the USBA's Henry King had successfully convinced the nation's biggest brewers to support an amendment to the Internal Revenue Code, reducing the tax on the first 60,000 barrels of beer sold by breweries producing less than two million barrels annually from $9 to $7 per barrel. Congress, with eyes wide open thanks to King, understood how consolidation had led to the precipitous decline of the small brewers, especially family-owned businesses, and that this tax break was a way to help them compete. For Anchor, it represented yet another advantage of being a very small brewer.

Consolidation set the stage for America's bicentennial year, in which there were just 49 brewing companies (94 breweries). America's top five brewing companies (AB, Schlitz, Miller, Pabst, and Coors) accounted for 68% of US beer sales (excluding imports) and the top ten accounted for 85%. Total sales were 150,426,000 barrels (88% bottles and cans; 12% kegs), of which Anchor accounted for 7,861 barrels (68% bottles; 32% kegs), 0.005% of the market. The largest brewer was AB at 29,047,000 barrels (19.31% of the market), including their new Fairfield, California plant, which opened in 1975. AB's sales in 1976 were 3,695 times that of Anchor.

From the start, Fritz intended his new brewery to be the physical exemplar of his philosophy of business and brewing. "The style in which the building will be remodeled and the type of equipment to be installed will both complement our public image of tradition and quality. We expect the brewery to be a showplace—a model of cleanliness and efficiency in a setting of tradition and charm." That came with a price tag. The projected cost of Anchor's expansion project was over $4.6 million (over $19.7 million today) for the building and equipment. Fritz planned to provide 25% of the building and built-in equipment cost, as well as 33% of the other equipment costs. To complete his expansion project, then, he proposed a building/built-in equipment loan of $2,550,000 and an equipment loan of $800,000, totaling $3,350,000. He would then lease the building and all its equipment back to the brewery.

By December 1, 1978, Fritz had already advanced Anchor about $1.5 million, leaving him at the end of the year with just $15,400 personal net cash. And both the prime rate and inflation were climbing. When he bought the brewery in 1965, they were 4.5% and below 2% respectively. By the end of 1978, even as he was still seeking a loan to make his new brewery possible, they were 11.75% and above 9%, headed toward 1980 highs of 21.5% and 15%. Fritz recalls, "One story that I like to tell with pleasure and some awe really, was at the worst of it in the new brewery project when I still didn't have any written note—it was all demand notes. And John Clow had just desperately tried to find someone to give us a note that had some substance to it, some time. We failed, and I said to Lucy at one point, 'you realize we may lose everything,' and she said, bless her heart, 'I know. I can live in a tent.'"

The last six months of 1978 were filled with *Sturm und Drang*, with but a few brief moments of calm. One of them was on December 15, when Paul Camusi stopped by the brewery for another visit. The first brew of Sierra Nevada Pale Ale was still almost two years away, and Paul was eager to try the 1978 Christmas Ale, bottled December 12, which Anchor had made with "plenty of Cascades" and "English malt" from Peach. "Our theme for the Christmas Ale from the very beginning was not just that the label would change but that the *brew* would change. We did things that only a brewer would be interested in, but that a brewer would be *very* interested in. And we never mentioned it. We kept it a secret. But it was an ongoing experimental process that we enjoyed. And we learned that that was the whole point: To take a chance." Fritz happily welcomed Paul back and gave him his full attention and a second tour. Such days were as gratifying to Fritz as they were to his guests, always reminding him, as he saw the brewery through their wide eyes, of the

THE ANCHOR BREWING STORY

Front L to R: Linda Rowe, Chris Solomon, Gordon MacDermott, Aaron Donald
Back: Tim Morse, Mike Lee, Mark Carpenter, Fritz, Al Kornhauser, Sue Anders, Michael Heiner, Paul Michaels

profound joy and wonder that brewing brought him. After the tour, Fritz sold Paul two cases of Christmas Ale and one of Old Foghorn, as proudly as a corn farmer at the Newton Farmers Market.

The snow-covered tree that Fritz asked Jim Stitt to create for Our Special Ale in 1978 is their favorite, and unlike any other before or since. Its arresting beauty comes from Fritz's concept for the label and Jim's mastery of negative space, what the Japanese call 間 (*ma*), whose kanji character is derived from the combination of 門 (*gate*) and the 日 (*sun*) that pokes through it. Like a jazz improvisation by Miles Davis, where the space between the notes is as meaningful as the notes themselves, this tree's transcendent, eternal beauty flows from what isn't there.

PART FOUR

FRITZ MAYTAG'S REVOLUTIONARY NEW BREWERY

THE PALACE OF STEAM BEER
(1979)

The rediscovery of American beer began in the West, in California, . . . the unwitting prophet of its beer revival, Fritz Maytag. . . . The brewery was no plaything: it demanded great faith and dedication. . . . Today, gleaming in copper, with brass trim, his is the most beautiful small brew-house in the world, . . . but the quality and distinctiveness of Anchor's products represent the company's truest claim to fame. . . . Anchor Steam Beer . . . is a world classic. . . . This is a "Premier Cru" brewery.

—Michael Jackson, *The New World Guide to Beer* (1988)

January 1979 was a busy month for Anchor, with brewing scheduled for twenty-nine of its thirty-one days, a futile attempt to keep up with demand. Fritz was busy too. In addition to his role as owner, president, and brewmaster of Anchor, he was chairman of the board of Maytag Dairy Farms and Grinnell College, director and first vice president of the USBA, and incoming president of the Brewers' Association of America, having been elected to a two-year term the previous fall. The BAA was a trade group of small brewers "dedicated to the best interests of the brewing industry." Its key-to-success mantra was simply "good management and good beer," and if Fritz was going to practice what the BAA preached, he would need to focus on two urgent and important priorities: the trademark battle brewing with Richard Dye and the opening of his new brewery, financed or not.

In January, Don Saccani called Fritz to let him know that Dye was selling a stout to liquor stores called "California Steam Beer Stout." It was in the same bottle as Anchor Steam Beer, with a label, as Fritz would soon describe in an affidavit,

using colors and old-fashioned typography similar to the colors and typography used on my labels. My distributors reported that the California Steam Beer Stout was being displayed on shelves next to my Steam Beer, Porter, and Ale. They also reported that storeowners were solicited to buy California Steam Beer Stout to fill the orders for my Anchor Steam Beer, which was in short supply. The final blow to me occurred when liquor-store owners reported that the quality of California Steam Beer Stout was poor and asked my distributors to take back the California Steam Beer Stout, under the misunderstanding that it was a product brewed and sold by my company.

Fritz's attorney sent repeated requests to Dye to "cease use of my tradename and trademark," but Dye's attorney responded that he "would not discontinue use of my trademarks and tradenames 'Steam Beer' and 'California Steam Beer,'" even though both were already in commerce as Anchor's brands. Fritz was not surprised by reports of the poor quality of Dye's product, continuing

it took me many years of learning and a very substantial sum of money invested in equipment and operations to attain the present high quality of my Anchor Steam Beer. I am dismayed, however, because consumers in my opinion will be misled into thinking that Dye's "California Steam Beer Stout" is the "Steam Beer" which they have read about in the *New York Times*, the *Los Angeles Times*, or the *Chicago Sun-Times*; or is a new product—Stout—which my brewery has come out with to supplement our present products of Steam Beer, Porter, and Ale. Any customer who drinks "California Steam Beer Stout" and forms an adverse opinion of its quality will inevitably be turned off and turned away from my products, which are the true "Steam Beer," Anchor Porter, and Anchor Christmas Ale. In my experience a beer drinker who gets one or at the most two bad bottles of beer from one brewer turns his trade to another brewer.

But even if Dye's beer had been drinkable, his opportunistic usurpation of Fritz's brand would still have been crystal clear. Fritz: "A common thread of my brewery is that during its entire

history it brewed and sold steam beer," and "how other breweries brewed 'Steam Beer' at the turn of the century and before Prohibition is really a matter more of speculation rather than of information. The only things that I can say for sure about the method of brewing 'Steam Beer' are that such methods are the ones that I use in brewing my Steam Beer." And since the 1930s, *no other brewery* has brewed or sold beer under the name "Steam Beer" in San Francisco or anywhere else in the United States.

In 1965, Fritz had rescued an obscure beer, brand name, and brewery from extinction, over the next fourteen years building all three up to a level such that "I believe that it is fair to say that to a beer drinker in 1979 (as well as to beer distributors, liquor-store owners, bartenders, and others in the industry), 'Steam Beer' is the beer brewed and sold by my brewing company and nothing else. I have spent fourteen years of my life and all of my money developing the reputation of my Steam Beer for quality and reliability and I am heartsick that the reputation of my brewery and my Steam Beer should be jeopardized by the thoughtless and unfair use of my tradenames and trademarks."

Fritz wished Dye and his brewery "every success in their venture of brewing and selling stout—or beer—or whatever they wish to brew and sell. I ask only, however, that they adopt any tradename and trademark other than the ones 'Steam Beer' and 'California Steam Beer'—that I have spent so much effort, time, and money in developing." This was Fritz's first trademark dispute, and his case and determination proved much stronger than Dye imagined. It would take nearly a year, though, with the Sword of Damocles hanging over Fritz all the while, before the case made its way through the courts and a judge ruled in favor of Fritz, his company, its brands, and its trademarks.

A TANGIBLE, PHYSICAL SOMETHING

By spring 1979, the new brewery was coming together, even though Fritz's ability to pay for it wasn't. In May, a friend sent Fritz an F. Scott Fitzgerald quote for moral support: "The test of a first-rate intelligence is the ability to hold two opposed ideas in the mind at the same time, and still retain the ability to function. One should, for example, be able to see that things are hopeless and yet be determined to make them otherwise."

The art deco features of the old coffee roastery building were to be preserved wherever possible, including its entrance, rooftop tower, glass-block panels, and even the staircase railings, which had been stripped of their old paint to reveal the original brass. Architect/artist Richard Elmore, who had illustrated the 1976 Christmas Ale label, helped Fritz design the unique layout of the third-floor offices, taproom, and lab, which made an L-shaped wrap around the copper brewhouse. This was critical to Fritz's concept, in part because at the old brewery everyone was bumping into each other all the time, which, by default, promoted good communication and teamwork. He feared that the new building, at nearly ten times the size, would feel like a desert, with tumbleweed blowing down its long hallways. So, to preserve esprit de corps, he made the brewhouse physically as well as metaphorically central to everything going on around it. Everyone could not only see each other but would be continuously reminded of their true employer: the beer. Even years later, as Fritz and I met in the warmth of his office, he would sometimes look through its huge windows toward the brewhouse and ask, "Well, Dave, before we decide, shall we check with corporate?"

The brewery was meant to be just like the beer, "aesthetically pleasing and wholly superior in every respect." The Erie Brewing malt mill was ensconced behind a wall for safety, but also so it did not distract from the copper kettles, grant, and sink,

gleaming against a backdrop of industrial concrete and the custom "Anchor Steam Blue" tile wet-floor. Fritz repositioned the door through which all visitors enter the third-floor office/taproom/brewhouse area, so that it directed them toward a stunning, panoramic wow! moment as they enter the space. "I used to say, 'when they walk in, I want them to fall down. On the floor.' Because it looks exactly like they had dreamed a brewery would look. There was nothing like it in the world of brewing. And all the people in their little glass booths, looking at each other across the kettle where we make the stuff—I was so proud." The entire building was redesigned with tours in mind, following the beer's odyssey from brewhouse to beer glass. The taproom, with its custom mahogany and marble bar and brass bar rail, featured—from the old Crystal Palace Market—a brass trough under the taps and bar stools. Plus, there were plenty of vintage beer trays, signs, barrels, and photographs, many of which had been at Anchor for decades, in this time machine back to an 1896 San Francisco saloon—minus the spittoons.

Leaving the taproom, guests were greeted by the sights, sounds, and smells of the brewhouse up close, experiencing the traditional art of brewing vicariously through watching Anchor's white-coveralled brewers at work. In coming up with his plan, Fritz had made dozens of sketches of the brewhouse installation, which included the mash tun, lauter tun, grant, brew kettle, and sink. The

This shallow, open-pan fermentor, prior to the addition of its skirt, looks like the ones on page 15.

coppersmithing of craftsman Fred Zaft made it look as if they were brand new. Beneath the Ziemann brewhouse were the new spent-grain tank as well as a replacement for the old hop jack, the hop separator. Spent grain went to dairy farmers for feed and spent hops to gardeners for mulch, just as they had at 8th Street.

Just down the hall to the right, past the brewery's small state-of–the art lab, guests could see the stainless steel hot wort tank, as well as the heat exchanger (short time) that cooled the wort. But their eyes were drawn to another wow! view: Four 20 by 30-ft shallow, open-pan fermentors for the primary fermentation of Anchor Steam and Anchor Porter. Like much at Anchor, these pans were unique and had to be custom-made. Bulling Metal Works built the stainless steel fermentors and

THE ANCHOR BREWING STORY

their skirts in the East Bay and assembled them onsite. Behind the back wall of the fermentor room was the Klimatic, aka the King unit, which filtered and maintained the air in the room at 55°F, something brewers from Gottlieb Brekle's day could only have dreamed about. Further down the hall was the hop room, where guests could walk right in, immersed in the aroma of fresh, whole hops. There, nylon mesh hop bags were filled for dry-hopping in the cellar.

At the end of the hall today, there are two open ale fermentors for the primary fermentation of Anchor's ales, much deeper than the steam beer fermentors in order to retain heat for ale fermentation that the shallow fermentors allow to escape. When the new brewery opened in 1979, Fritz didn't have the money for even one ale fermentor, so that had to wait. Next, before they headed down to the cellar, guests got to see the lunchroom and the carefree camaraderie that typifies Anchor's work environment. The beer tap in the lunchroom dispensed cold, bubbly water, but employees were free to have a beer or two on their break or after work—a longtime tradition in the brewing industry. And employees got to take home "shorts"—unsaleable cases of beer with short-filled bottles, crooked labels, scratched crowns, and so forth.

In the cellar, guests could see how beer from a fermentor upstairs was dropped by gravity through a stainless steel pipe into a hose and then into a cellar tank for secondary fermentation. Fritz had Dairy Craft ("Craftsmen in Stainless Steel Fabrication") from Minnesota custom-make eight 1,800-gallon round, vertical cellar tanks and Crepaco in Wisconsin make six new 3,600-gallon horizontal, cylindrical cellar tanks. The temperature in the cellar was controlled, as was the temperature of each individual tank. For the adjacent finishing room, Fritz bought a new centrifuge, plate-and-frame filter, and flash pasteurizer, which were utilized the same way regardless of whether the beer's destination was a bottle or a keg.

The new bottle shop on the second floor, engineered by Dave Orton of Sierra Design & Manufacturing, played a key role in the quality and shelf life of the beer. Bottling had to be aseptic, because Anchor's beers had no chemical additives or preservatives and were flash pasteurized before bottling rather tunnel pasteurized after the beer was already in the bottle. The bottling line was another wow! moment for guests who, when they first saw it, often broke into song—the theme from *Laverne & Shirley*. In order of appearance, the bottle shop's cast included an IAC uncaser, which removes the clean new bottles from an open case;

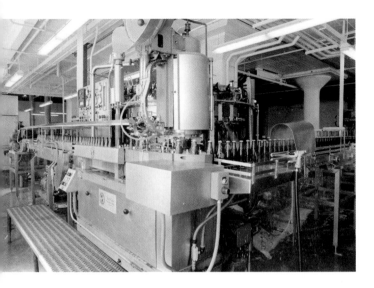

Standard-Knapp pocket-type bottle rinser, which rinses and sterilizes the bottles and looks like a shooting gallery at a county fair; Holstein & Kappert 30-valve bottle filler, which rotates like a merry-go-round, filling and crowning bottles; the World Rotary labeler from 8th Street, linked in tandem with three World Tandem labelers, which apply the neck and face labels; John Burton case conveyors and Tonko bottle conveyors; Packstar drop packer (also from Standard-Knapp), which drops the filled, crowned, labeled bottles into the empty cases using metal fingers that guide each bottle into each of the four 6-packs' cells; and Sealstar hot-melt case sealer, a big improvement over Phil Canevari's glue gun. At speeds of 240-280 bottles per minute, the line was four times as fast as 8th Street, but, like 8th Street, the cases were hand-palletized and either loaded into the brewery's own cold storage or onto a distributor's refrigerated truck. "The way beer is stored and shipped in commerce," wrote Fritz to Roger Protz, editor of the Campaign for Real Ale's *Good Beer Guide*, "may be far more important than almost anything. Quality belongs to the consumer. If I tell you our dinner was cooked by a great chef, you may not know the 'whole story,' especially if you discover that it was actually cooked 6 months ago and stored in a malfunctioning refrigerator!" Just seven or eight people made the bottle shop run: glass thrower, filler operator, labeler operator, 2 inspectors, case-packer operator, palletizer, forklift driver, and rover.

Fritz kept some of the 8th Street equipment for parts and sold some of it. Ken Grossman and Paul Camusi bought the old Sieben's bottle filler. It was the first of many hand-me-downs that went to up-and-coming brewers. The Crepaco pump, for example, went to Don Barkley at Mendocino Brewing in 1985. "Happy plumbing," Fritz typically wished brewers setting up shop. The rest was either stored offsite, displayed in the brewhouse hallway, or moved upstairs to what came to be known affectionately as the Fritzonian. The line, like everything in the new brewery, was designed to be functional, cleanable, and beautiful. For example, in most breweries, after the bottles are removed from their cases they head into the rinser while the empty cases travel around overhead, waiting to be reunited with filled, crowned, labeled bottles. But Fritz didn't like the way that looked, so he had Orton route the empty cases downstairs out of sight.

The racking room provided the penultimate wow! moment before the tour returned to the taproom for the pièce de résistance, a glass of Anchor Steam. In the early years at Mariposa, the brewery's draught beer was still sold only in half-barrel Golden Gate kegs, and the new racking room looked much

as it had in Joe Allen's time. A Golden Gate keg is an open system keg that has two valves, one for adding CO_2 and one for dispensing beer, as well as a bunghole for access. Before refilling a keg, it had to be debunged on a drill press and drained; cleaned outside on a keg washer that brushed it as it rotated; washed and rinsed inside on a machine that, with a large lever, moved the keg from station to station; inspected via the bunghole using a lightbulb dangling from a cord; filled and bunged on the racker; and palletized. A full Golden Gate keg weighs over 160 lb. The German Enzinger-Union-Werke racker Anchor used in the early days at Mariposa was the one that Fritz had bought from the Peter Bub Brewery in 1969, refurbished along with an ancient barrel washer. One of the highlights of the tour came when whatever large person doing the racking that day banged the wooden bung into a full keg with a large mallet, beer shooting everywhere. Often, the unlucky (or lucky, depending on their

point of view) guest standing closest to the action got more free beer than he or she expected. Then it was back up to the taproom for a cold Steam.

But even in June 1979, these brewery tours were only taking place in Fritz's imagination. "Moving the brewery to the new location has taken just about twice as long and cost about twice as much as I estimated," he admitted. And his loan had still not come through. Fritz got a bit of good news, at least, when Robert Balzer and the *Los Angeles Times* reprised their "Judgment of LA"— same criteria, new panel of tasters. Anchor Steam, on a roll from its *New West* 1977 and *Los Angeles Times* 1978 wins, was again victorious, in a field of thirty-five beers from all over the world.

Meanwhile, Fritz was still waiting for his loan. And it was a long, long, scary wait. He had passed the point of no return, signified by the sign on the 8th Street brewery's front door: "All Visitors: Our Small Staff Is Extraordinarily Busy Preparing to Move. Please Postpone Your Visit for a Month or So If You Can. Thank You. The Management." By July 28, the last Brew Day at 8th Street, Fritz could finally exhale. Wells Fargo had approved his loan proposal—one Gold Rush company helping another. They even gave him a scale model of a Wells Fargo stagecoach, hand-carved by Chilean immigrant Oscar M. Cortes. "You know, the brewery, well, *I* was basically bankrupt, head over heels in debt." So Fritz quietly put that stagecoach on his office bookshelf, where it remained until he finished paying off Wells Fargo twenty years later.

At long last, it was time for a celebration, but one in which Fritz and some of his guests would be put to work. Once the brewhouse installation was complete, there was lots and lots of tarnished copper to be cleaned. So Linda helped organize a polishing party, sending out invitations to consultants, contractors, engineers, electricians, plumbers, accountants, bankers, and friends. Most of the guests drank beer and watched as a few hardy souls—including Fritz—vigorously burnished the copper kettles, grant, and sink to stunning resplendence. One very special new hire was there too, which gave Fritz great solace. It was his daughter Alexandra, working the first of her several summers at Anchor.

There were just three things left to do in the brewhouse before the brewery was officially up and running. The first was to hang Dave Lyon's painting of St. Nicholas, patron saint of brewers, on the new brewhouse wall. The second was even closer to Fritz's heart and faith: the "Blessing of the Brewhouse" before the first brew, given by Malcolm Manson with a small group assembled. A friend of Fritz's, he was newly an Episcopal priest and also headmaster of Marin Country Day School, where Fritz had been on the board. Then finally, at 7:35 a.m. on August 13, 1979, Anchor ushered in a new era in its—and craft brewing's—history, with Test Brew #1 of Anchor Steam Beer at 1705 Mariposa Street. Fritz still remembers the early morning light bouncing off the gleaming copper kettles. "It was a jewel, just a jewel."

A year before, John Segal had come to San Francisco for a visit. Fritz, exuding the optimism that John so admired in him, had taken John over to Mariposa Street to share his vision for the handsome building. Upon returning home, John thanked him for the time they'd spent together, adding prophetically: "Your new brewery will become the Palace of Steam Beer."

PARADIGM
(1979–1985)

Your new brewery is quite beautiful in every respect. It will stand as an inspiration for all small brewers.

—Ken Grossman, letter to Fritz (1979)

Fritz's dream of a shining brewery on the Hill had finally become a reality. Longtime friend of the brewery Fred Eckhardt hailed it as "the queen of small breweries . . . a story-book brewery—the way it's spozed to be!" But in the summer of '79, when the old brewery was closed and they were moving into the new brewery and getting ready to start brewing, Anchor beer, which had been in short supply for months, disappeared from retailers' shelves. And it would take weeks of trial brews, fermentations, finishing, racking, and bottling before Fritz could say that his new brewery was truly up and running. But for Anchor and the entire brewing industry, an unanticipated challenge loomed ahead.

THE NITROSAMINE SCARE

In the summer of 1978, an ongoing study at the German Cancer Institute in Heidelberg indicated for the first time that low levels of dimethylnitrosamine (DMN) were present in certain European beers. Fritz recalls,

New technology, of a type that had existed before but had suddenly been improved, could now detect nitrosamines, which are known to increase the likelihood of cancer, and they were present in beers at a level higher than they had

ever thought before, because now you could measure parts per billion. [By comparison, during the 1966 cobalt scare the discussion was about parts per million.] As I understood it, some Americans were in Germany and heard from the German brewers about this. To my great delight, as you might expect if you know anything about American business and laws and responsibilities, the Americans went straight to the telephone and called their breweries and the USBA and said, "We need to be public about the fact that there are nitrosamines in beers at levels higher than we had thought before."

A few brewers scoffed at the idea, thinking nitrosamines were additives of some kind. Joseph Pickett Jr., of Pickett's Brewery in Dubuque, Iowa, remarked, "I just can't think of anyone who would use those things. I know we sure don't." But Henry King and the USBA (working with the Brewers Association of Canada) knew better, grasping the gravity of the situation well before the source of nitrosamines in beer was understood. They immediately issued a statement to the press and established an ad hoc committee to determine causes and remedies and report the results of their investigation to the ATF, the US Food and Drug Administration (FDA), and the Canadian Ministry of Health for further study. Fritz continues,

ANCHOR

Now, there are nitrosamines in all kinds of things; it's the result of cooking or burning and the air that's in the presence of the flames coming in contact with a substance. There are high nitrosamines in bacon, for example. It turned out that there were nitrosamines in whiskey and in beer because of the flames that were used to dry the barley malt. After the malting process you dry the grain and they were using air warmed up by flames, and so the NOx, molecular combinations of nitrogen and oxygen at various different numbers, causes these nitrosamines.

The problem was pervasive. In September, the FDA released the results of their study of thirty beers, only two of which—Coors and Guinness Stout—showed no sign of nitrosamines. Anchor's beers were not tested. "We had the only all-malt beer in America, and our numbers would have been much higher, and it would have been front-page news. But we were not brewing. The brewery was closed. And we were absolutely relieved that our beer was not available; it was not easy to find *any*, so it wouldn't have been testable. But we were about to start brewing again."

As this malting problem became a brewing crisis, Fritz called John Segal, who recommended the third helpful Otto of Fritz's career: maltster Otto Seidenberg. Otto had been president and then owner of Kreiner Malting Corp. in Buffalo, and helped Fritz with malting advice and sourcing. Fritz personally called every maltster and nearly every brewer in the United States, which helped him understand the economic reasons behind the malting industry's sluggish response, noting that it cost "one-tenth of the money for direct fired and 30% less fuel." Fritz asked brewery president Peter Stroh, "Can you, or the USBA, or others apply some pressure or persuasion to the whole malting industry? Only a handful of nonbrewer maltsters have even ordered low-nox burners, and the maltsters have yet to feel the heat. Ultimately the solution is in their hands, upon which I believe most are sitting." It turned out there were four malting solutions to the problem: use sulfur during kilning, use a low NOx emission burner, a combination of those two solutions, or the best choice: indirect firing of the malt.

Roger Briess reassured Fritz that nitrosamines in the caramel and black malt he'd been buying from Briess Malting in Chilton, Wisconsin, since 1977 were "non-detectable." By the second week of October, Fritz had persuaded Anchor's pale malt supplier, Bauer-Schweitzer, to transition to sulfured malt, which reduced the nitrosamines in their malt by up to 94%. Fritz told them it was essential to produce a beer with no detectable nitrosamines. He tried talking them and other maltsters into installing low-nox burners, which was "not a popular idea." Otto Seidenberg told Fritz there were just two sources of barley malt without nitrosamines. Ladish Malting of Spiritwood, North Dakota used air that was electrically heated indirectly; the malt never entered the presence of a flame. But of course, their malt was all booked up. Coors also had nitrosamine-free malt. Otto arranged with Pete Coors, who was in charge of brewing, for them to ship malt to Anchor at the brewery. Coors shipped the malt in railcars

Front L to R: Richard Gossett, Bette Riley, Bruce Joseph, Chris Solomon, Sue Anders, Mike Lee, Tim Morse
Back L to R: Dennis Kellett, Ed Dalton, Mark Carpenter, Tim Herring, Al Kornhauser, Gordon MacDermott, Linda Rowe, Fritz

and charged a premium because they had to put it through their malt cleaner again before loading. Fritz also had to pay Western Pacific Railroad every time Anchor used their spur track.

"We had sized our malt holding system to accept railcars, so that was fortunate, and here came the malt." The first brew with Coors malt took place on November 27, 1979. With a few minor adjustments to the recipe and the grind, it was a success—and a testament to Anchor's resilience. Fritz "called Ken Grossman at Sierra Nevada and Jack McAuliffe at New Albion and told them that Anchor had nitrosamine-free malt and they were welcome to come and buy it at Anchor's cost. Both did, and they were the only other microbrewers at

that point I think." So, for a time, Coors, Anchor, Sierra Nevada, and New Albion were the only nitrosamine-free breweries in America. Coors had done Anchor a great favor, and Anchor had paid it forward.

In the fall of 1979, Fritz made it clear to Bauer-Schweitzer that, despite their long history together, Anchor's future purchases of malt from them would depend on the nitrosamine levels, the government regulations that might develop, and the nitrosamine levels of other malt sources. He was disappointed that Bauer-Schweitzer seemed to lose interest in Anchor after that. By 1981, the historic malthouse had closed. Its building became a registered San Francisco landmark that year, along

with the Old Spaghetti Factory, which celebrated "a quarter century of fun, food, fad, and fetish" on October 19. For one day only, Fred Kuh served "Steam Beer at 1956 prices." Two bits a glass. Fritz continued using Coors malt for two years, until he struck a deal on pale malt with LA's Great Western Malting, which also passed the nitrosamine test with flying colors. Problem solved.

Less than three years after its silver anniversary, Fred Kuh—one of Anchor's greatest champions—sold the Old Spaghetti Factory and retired. Fritz had been to dozens of brewery auctions by that time. Now, on the day after St. Patrick's Day, 1984, he paid a bittersweet visit to 478 Green Street for the Old Spaghetti Factory auction. Fred had paid just $10 for the antique stained-glass Anchor Steam sign that hung in the OSF all those years. As with his Mariposa Street building, Fritz would have paid any fair price for it. And he happily did, installing it in the Palace of Steam Beer, where it has hung ever since.

MALT MECCA

Not surprisingly, what with the slow and hardly seamless transition from 8th Street to Mariposa, Anchor's sales were flat in 1979, up a modest fifty-one barrels from Anchor's last full year at the old brewery. But in 1980, the Palace of Steam Beer began to catch up to John Segal's prognostications and Fritz's expectations. The brewery was beautiful, and the beer was better and more consistent than ever before. And Anchor was becoming a sort of malt beverage mecca, just as Fritz had hoped, attracting beer pilgrims from all over the world. A lengthy conversation with Fritz at Mariposa prompted perceptive freelancer Anthony Brandt to write in the July/August issue of *Quest/80* magazine of "a certain calmness" in Fritz, "the kind that comes when you're truly comfortable with what you're doing with your life. He has settled convictions, *believes* in smallness, in quality, in tradition, and exhibits no interest whatever in sacrificing his beliefs to a more conventional kind of success." But it was the article's headline that caught everyone's attention: "Craftsmanship: Best Beer in America." It was high praise, and everyone at Anchor got a kick out of the fact that the best beer in America was made with Coors malt!

But if you were to ask Fritz in private, he might tell you that his favorite words about Anchor in 1980 came from aspiring brewers. Early on in his career, knowing firsthand how hard it was, Fritz discouraged entrepreneurs from going into the beer business. Even in 1979, he was still offering more words of caution than encouragement, ending one letter: "Many people have asked for my opinion in this regard, and I am in the curious position of always recommending against such a venture, while actively proceeding myself." But when he met them face to face and saw the enthusiastic spark in their eyes, Fritz was only too happy to share his wisdom and moral support. Sometimes he'd get a thank-you note, like this one from an Ed Janus, who opened Capital Brewery in Madison, Wisconsin, six years after their meeting: "Thank you for your advice and counsel. Perhaps a great part of the benefit which I derived from our meeting was the sense that 'it could be done'; that you had succeeded in a 'righteous' course and, I think, have expressed the possibilities of the time. Whether I can also succeed is, of course, another question. I intend to persist!"

MENTEE AND MENTOR

Behind the scenes—as incoming president of the USBA's little brother, the BAA, during the nitrosamine scare—Fritz had demonstrated the magnanimity of his moxie. Dozens of calls, telegrams, and letters moved the ball forward not just for his newly christened brewery, but for his fellow brewers. Part of what drove Fritz to be so obliging was all the help he'd received over the years. And part of it was having role models like Edward Seidensticker and Henry King. *Chicago Sun-Times* columnist Irv Kupcinet had praised King's USBA for the "great gusto" of its quick, decisive, forthright, responsible response to the "villain nitrosamines." Fritz had already been the recipient of King's kindness and generosity and the beneficiary of his leadership, advocacy, and bold can-doism on behalf of consumers—as well as brewers big and small.

Lieutenant Henry B. King, United States Naval Reserve, served during WW II as gunnery officer on a US Navy tank landing ship (LST) in the South Pacific, for which he received the Silver Star for gallantry and "outstanding control of inexperienced gunners" and the Purple Heart for wounds suffered in combat. One of his proudest war memories was when his LST carried a fellow navy lieutenant, John F. Kennedy, and his PT 109 crew back to base. King had happily given up his bunk to the valiant young sailor. When King became president of the USBA in 1962, a century after its founding, the public's perception of the beer business was still rooted in the gangster days of Prohibition. Over the next twenty-one years, King shattered that image, transforming the USBA into a strong, vibrant, effective, and quintessentially American organization. In the

1990s he would reprise his USBA success, becoming executive director of the BAA, representing hundreds of breweries that had not existed during his USBA tenure—and a few that had. Fritz respected King's integrity and tenacity, telling *The New Brewer* in 2004, "the brewing industry should get together and award Henry a 'Brewer's Gold Star' to go with his Silver Star. There is no question he was in combat for the brewers. We won most of the battles, always coming out with more honor and respectability than we had gone in with, due overwhelmingly to Henry King."

On October 26, 1981, upon Fritz's retirement from his two-year term as president of the BAA, its grateful membership presented him with a beautifully bound volume of tributes. Henry King was among the fifty-six who saluted him, writing, "The brewing industry needs more Fritz Maytags to remind it, not only of its proud traditions, but of the bright future it offers to those willing to bring dedication and hard work to the profession." Others included Jack McAuliffe, who wrote,

You have shown by that best of teachers, example, how a brewery is properly operated and managed. Beginning brewers would do well to take note of the progress of your traditional firm. Benjamin Franklin once observed that to be remembered, a man must do either of two things: write something worth reading, or do something worth writing about. I think it is safe to say you will be remembered as an exceptional brewer.

And Paul Camusi and Ken Grossman wrote that, "We appreciate your setting such a fine example for we 'new wave' brewers. Through your efforts you have cleared the way for others and shown them what is possible."

Encomia notwithstanding, Fritz would continue to play an active role in the brewing industry writ large and small, from the USBA, BAA, and MBAA to new organizations emerging as a consequence of the resurgence of beer in America. And he couldn't wait to participate in the BAA's

Marketing Meeting that same day, at which he shared his newfound enthusiasm for tech. He called his presentation "How to Select a Small Computer," though it was as much about the why as the how. As he would later tell Theresa McCulla in an interview for the National Museum of American History's American Brewing History Initiative, "I had one of the very first Apple II's; long before I knew Steve [Jobs] I had an Apple II, and we had used it at the brewery and I was very aware of the whole . . . micro-computer world. IBM . . . were the big guys, and Apple was making little computers for little guys like us."

MICROCOMPUTING MEETS MICROBREWING

There are a lot of similarities between the microcomputer and microbrewery revolutions. The Homebrew Computer Club (HCC), a hotbed of intellectual and technical curiosity, had its first informal meeting on March 5, 1975, in Menlo Park, not far from the Oasis, to which they would often adjourn for enthusiastic discourse over a pitcher of Anchor Steam. In fact, one of the original names discussed for this group of talented, skilled, and imaginative people was the Steam Beer Computer Group. The club's theme, according to Wozniak, was "give help to others," and even the schematics of Woz's Apple I were passed around freely. The open-source atmosphere was not unlike that of a homebrew club or a visit to Anchor, where Fritz freely shared his brewing knowledge and epiphanies. Like Anchor, the HCC had the autonomy of creators, and members of the club saw the big revolution coming, even though the rest of the world wasn't aware of it yet. In 1977, the same year Steam Beer Brewing reincorporated as Anchor, Apple Computer, Inc. became a California corporation. Notably, even with the release of Apple II, Apple's sales for the 1977 fiscal year, at $773,000, were *below* Anchor's—for the first and last time. "But we were just real people," Fritz told Theresa, "and [thanks to Apple] we had our own computers."

One of the first real people Fritz met online was jazz musician Herbie Hancock, who bought an Apple II Plus in 1979. After setting it up, Herbie decided to explore the chat function, which he recounts in his appropriately titled memoir *Possibilities*:

I typed "Hi," on the screen, and whoever it was typed "Hi" back. I typed, "We just got an Apple II! This is my first time chatting." And whoever it was typed back, "Congratulations! My name is Fritz." This was cool! I had no idea who or where this guy Fritz was, but here we were, just chatting with each other over our computers. What an amazing invention! We kept typing, this slow back-and-forth of green letters on a black screen, and Fritz asked me what I did for a living. I typed that I was a piano player. "Do you have any records?" he asked. I typed, "Yes, about twenty of them. What do you do?" He wrote, "I make beer. Kind of like you with your records—I make a lot of beer." And then he typed, "Actually, I'm the owner of the Anchor Brewing Company." Wow! This blew my mind, that the owner of Anchor Steam beer and I could randomly meet over the computer. The idea that he was up in San Francisco, typing away, and I was sitting in my studio in L.A., and we were getting to know each other—it was like science fiction.

In 1980, Steve Jobs joined the Grinnell College board of trustees, thanks to the encouragement of longtime trustee Bob Noyce and chairman Fritz Maytag. For the next eight years, Jobs contributed to the school's progress and financial security. In many ways, Noyce meant to Jobs what King meant to Fritz. Fritz and Steve quickly became lifelong friends, Fritz proudly running his brewery from a desk sporting three-hundred-year-old brewing books and an Apple II. And Steve gave Fritz one of the first copies of VisiCalc, the visible calculator spreadsheet program that became known as the first "killer app," which Fritz proudly ran on his Apple II.

ALL ABOUT BEER

Almost as soon as Fritz and his staff moved into Mariposa Street, the sheer volume of visitors, calls, and letters of inquiry convinced him that his brewery needed to be more than a paradigm; it should also be a place for the exchange of ideas, knowledge, and experience. If the Homebrew Computer Club could meet at the Stanford Linear Accelerator Center, why couldn't brewers of all stripes, alongside businesspeople, salespeople, marketing people, and entrepreneurs, meet at Anchor? Fritz had cautioned one hopeful young entrepreneur, "All too often, a new brewery will fail because of

lack of experience of the people running the company. One of the most important requirements for brewing a quality beer is a thorough knowledge of chemistry and microbiology. Often this is overlooked or underestimated by people starting breweries." Why not share what Anchor had to offer—not in a classroom, but in the taproom, just a few feet from the brewhouse?

In November 1979, Fritz met with biochemist Dr. Joseph L. Owades, who was already known for his seminal role in the development of light beer, as well as what Joe called his "technical and strategic consulting to the fermentation industries." Fritz's idea was for a "course on brewing technology and theory—*in a brewery!* You talk about mashing; you go out and look *in the mash tun.* There was nothing like it in the world." A month later, Joe wrote, "I've given your idea of having a beer seminar at your brewery some thought." The two-day seminar would "cover the history of brewing, the practice of brewing—including water, malt, hops, brewhouse, fermentation, aging, etc., types of beers, with their advantages. We would go through your plant and see the brewing operations. Later, we would taste beers and show how tasting should be done and what to look for." But Joe was concerned that finding an audience would be a problem. It was not. All Fritz had to do was to reach out to the folks who had written, called, or visited him in the past year.

The first annual Center for Brewing Studies "All About Beer" seminar took place at Anchor on October 16 and 17, 1980. Joe's "All About Beer" handout was just twenty-four pages long and included a straightforward mission statement by way of introduction: "It is our purpose here to explain beer and brewing, and to impart an understanding and appreciation of the many types and tastes of beer." Over the ensuing years, the mission remained the same, although by the time I took the course in 1993, the handout had grown to forty-five pages. The look of the attendees, Fritz observed, was changing too: more suits, less flannel (i.e., more entrepreneurs, fewer homebrewers), which

STEVE JOBS:
OUT OF THE MAIN FRAME

On the back cover of Walter Isaacson's biography of Steve Jobs is a captivating Norman Seeff photo of Steve at home with his "baby," the Macintosh. Because the photo is cropped, what you don't see is the bottle of Anchor Steam next to him. In 2017, I asked Norman to tell me about his memories of the shoot:

In January 1984, I was asked by Rolling Stone to shoot a visual story on the launch of the new Macintosh computer. . . . I got a number of shots of Steve [at work] and then said that I wanted to shoot him in his home in Woodside. I didn't know at the time that he had this large home [designed by Richard Elmore], which he hadn't furnished, but we ended up in this large living room with no furniture, sitting on the floor discussing creativity.

I remember together going very deeply into dreaming and visioning, drinking Anchor Steam Beer. We weren't over-indulging but having fun and there was this moment when he suddenly jumped up, left the room, returned with the Mac, and plopped down on the floor with it on his lap. It was a totally spontaneous moment, nothing preconceived to make Steve look like a guru—and in the typical world of advertising, holding the product. He then put the Mac on the floor and threw his head back laughing. We got a series of sequences of really wonderful imagery—all with an authenticity that came in the moment. In the business world, this might seem to be conceptually perfect, but the truth is that it was spontaneous and real, and not stiff or forced, just beautiful and natural. Two guys hanging out drinking beer and bonding and talking about creativity and vision. What I saw when he brought the Mac in was a beautiful sense of accomplishment, a very tender experience.

mirrored not only the rapid growth of microbrewing but also the increased attention Fritz was getting from the likes of *Inc.* magazine and the *Harvard Business Review*.

Joe became a great friend of the brewery. In 1981, he shared his hop-aroma trick with Gordon:

A good way to evaluate hop aroma is to prepare a "hop tea," by weighing 10 gm of hops into a Waring blender, adding 200 ml of distilled water, and running the blender for 30 seconds at high speed. The liquid should be poured into a 400 ml (or larger) beaker and covered with foil. Rinse the blender between hop samples. When all hop samples have been prepared, smell each of them. Old hops smell cheesy. Cascade hops should smell "sweeter," or less sharp, than Clusters or Galena.

After moving West in the early '80s, Joe enjoyed dropping by the brewery and could often be seen hanging out where he was most at ease—the Anchor lab.

In fall 1981, Fritz got a handwritten letter from twenty-six-year-old Tom Burns of Boulder Brewing, thanking him for the personal and public welcomes that Fritz had extended to him at the BAA convention. He confided, "So I am back here in Longmont [Colorado] trying to make this thing work. The future is uncertain; nobody is very enthusiastic about the brewery except me. And I am an (the only?) employee." But Tom proudly shared with Fritz that "my tenure as GM and Brewmaster has resulted in the longest stretch of uninfected beer in the brewery's history. The beer is clean. Sales are stable, and that is with virtually no marketing campaign." The following February, Tom wrote, "I have been recruited by Charlie Papazian to help organize the 1982 Great American Beer Festival [GABF]."

Charlie had founded the American Homebrewers Association, Inc. (AHA) and its journal *zymurgy* in 1978, and the Association of Brewers in 1979 (it would merge with the Brewers Association

of America to become the Brewers Association in 2005). The word zymurgy resonates with brewers because it's all about fermentation, from the Greek *zymē* (a leaven) + *-ourgia* (a working). Charlie's experience at CAMRA's Great British Beer Festival inspired him to create, in Tom's words, "an annual event of national stature where America's unique and quality beers are showcased. The Beer Festival is not necessarily limited to America's small brewers; and smallness is no guarantee of participation. Although as things stand, most of America's unique and quality beers are produced by small brewers."

Tom trained to be an attorney and used his expertise to help legalize brewpubs. When he passed the bar exam in 1981, he had told Fritz "I get a lot of 'Why are you working in a brewery instead of practicing law?'" Tom was still in his thirties when a cancer diagnosis reversed that question to "Why are you practicing law instead of brewing?" After all, brewing was his real love. In 1992, he opened the Detroit & Mackinac Brewery, the first new brewery to open in the Motor City since Prohibition. Just as Fritz had done thirteen years before, Tom asked a pastor to bless his brewhouse. Sadly, Tom passed away in 1994, the day after friends and family celebrated his thirty-ninth birthday at the brewery he'd built.

Flowing right out of the AHA's fourth annual conference, the first GABF continued through Saturday, June 5, 1982. Anchor was one of twenty-four breweries represented, pouring two (Anchor Steam and Anchor Porter) of the forty-seven beers listed, for the 800 festivalgoers. Anchor, Boulder, River City, and Sierra Nevada were the only microbreweries that year. As the belly dancers—yes, belly dancers—completed their gyrations, Charlie Papazian—who in 1984 would write the homebrewers' bible, *The Complete Joy of Home Brewing*—brought the groundbreaking event to a close with an effervescent benediction, as quoted in the AHA's 1982 *Beer•Bloid*: "Let's wish ourselves the right spirit, the proper attitude, and the luck to

guide us into making great homebrew until we meet again next year." His congregation's amen-like response: "FOAM."

Although Anchor was well represented at the first GABF, Fritz—now forty-four years old—did not go. The unfathomable loss of Matthew, compounded by Fritz's sister Ellen's cancer diagnosis at just forty-five, his protracted struggle to get the new brewery up and running, the trademark dispute, the nitrosamine scare, and the very real possibility of financial ruin, were catching up with him, taking a toll on both Fritz and his marriage. He and Lucy separated. In March 1984, after nearly seventeen years of marriage, they were divorced. Fritz credits Lucy with being "supportive, understanding, and I would even say exemplary in the sense that I was a very irresponsible, classic example of the entrepreneur, whose life is so chaotic."

It was in early 1981 that Fritz knew he needed a sabbatical, "but I was on four boards, chairman of all four, and I couldn't." Besides his ongoing leadership of Maytag Dairy Farms and SF's Community Music Center, he had the BAA until fall '81 and Grinnell until summer '82. Then he would finally be free to take a sabbatical, as far away from Iowa cornfields and San Francisco fog as possible.

THE LIGHT OF GREECE

A friend, attorney/artist George Hellyer, had recently returned from a decade in Corfu, a Greek island in the Ionian Sea, where he had a Victorian-era stone villa. Fritz rented it in early '81. Entranced, he bought it shortly thereafter:

When I go to Corfu, I'm reborn every time. That's what saved my life. I was transformed. It was so different, so simple, so primitive. I found the

whole thing just transporting, but paradoxically. If you're in your car in the hinterland of Greece and your wheel falls off or you have a blowout with no spare, if you know Greece, along with your thought, which is *oh shit*, will come the thought, *ah, we're going to have an adventure, somebody's gonna come and help us*. There's something about Greece. There's a generosity there, a respect, a courtesy for the individual. It's beyond rational. Corfu had a profound effect on me.

Corfu is the reason that the olive tree on the 1981 Christmas Ale label has nothing to do with California. Although Fritz had planted Mission olive trees at his vineyard a few years before, he wouldn't make his first olive oil—for private use—until winter 1984/85. Instead, it's his nod to what artist/limericist Edward Lear called Corfu's "endless speaking olives. (I say speaking because every olive [tree] has more individual character than any other tree I have ever seen.)"

The 1983 Christmas Ale label is also rooted in Corfu, and it's the first time Fritz used the Latin name of a tree on a label, *Abies cephalonica* in this case: Greek fir. He sailed to Cephalonia from Corfu several times, first on a small fiberglass boat and then on *Aqualeo*, both of which he bought in Corfu. The label represents a memory of sailing the western islands and a visit to "that enormous, glorious forest on top of Mount Ainos."

THE THREE ROCKS

Fritz made several trips a year to Corfu in the early '80s, with trust and confidence in his "three rocks," Gordon, Mark, and Linda, as well as the employees under their supervision. After weeks or even months away, he happily returned to a brewery that was "humming along" as if he'd just stepped out for the afternoon. In fact, his time away from Anchor brought into a lovely light one of his greatest accomplishments as its leader:

Linda, Fritz, Gordon, and Mark in Europe

choosing good people and encouraging them to become the best of themselves. "They were the only reason I ever succeeded, because although I could think stuff up, I didn't have the thoroughness and the detail-oriented follow-through that Gordon, who was my original rock of course, and later Mark and Linda had."

In production, Gordon and Mark led by example. Bruce Joseph, who joined the Anchor team in 1980, remembers,

I never worked for anyone where bosses worked harder and would do anything. I remember one day when someone said, "Hey, come on, malt truck's here." We used to get the Briess malt in 100-pound bags, but it wasn't palletized, just loaded into the truck. You open the back of it and palletize them and the forklift would take them away. So Tim Herring [a new-hire who would one day become head brewer] and I started to do it and Mark and Gordon are pushing us out of the way to get at the malt bags 'cause they want to do it. And man, I'd never worked where the bosses—usually it's like "Well, I'm a boss now; I don't do that shit." And I think Fritz instilled that whole thing of "if you see something that needs to be done, do it." And I like that, the feeling of teamwork, that we're all in this together.

Fritz recalls that,

at some point, I think during my sabbatical, when I got home from Corfu, Mark and Gordon came to me and said, "in your absence, we have decided to switch roles, and we hope you're not upset by it, but we think it's the right thing." And it certainly was the right thing because Gordon, I would say, his genius is with things, this just unbelievable ability to focus and finish with a project to be done perfectly. He also has incredible integrity and honesty and we just had total trust. Mark's obvious ability is as a kind of—you know, there's that famous thing I learned at the

Maytag Company about what a foreman has—a dual loyalty. If you're a foreman, you have to relate to the employees. They have to trust you, but you also have to relate to the owner or to management, and it's a very challenging role, and a good foreman is good at both. And Mark has had the ability to manage people, to inspire people. I think that was just remarkable. It was a magical role. Plus, it didn't hurt, in terms of his relationship with Gordon, I think, that Mark is a master mechanic also—not in the way Gordon is, but they clearly had that in common, mutual respect for stuff, and if we were going to put in a new labeler [as they would do in 1991], it would be a joint effort and they would respect each other's point of view and they would trust each other and help each other and make it happen. God, we did amazing things, and all of us just completely ignorant—not stupid but ignorant—and innocent, and hippies, you know! I was very proud of it.

Fritz continues,

I don't think there's any question what Linda's role was. She was it. She was the center of it all, at the center of the company. Her fingers were on everything. She was like the den mother. She was the organizing factor for everyone, including me, in terms of appointments and phone calls and letters and bills. I think a normal company might have had three people doing what she did. She was my right hand too—they were all my right hand.

Fritz liked to draw a little picture of what he called "the spokes." It was a wheel with a hub in the middle representing Fritz, and three spokes representing Gordon, Mark, and Linda. "Each of them has their own area of responsibility and reports to me, but when I'm not here, then they are a committee. In any given crisis, the leadership goes to the person whose territory that is. If a decision has to be made, he or she should listen to everybody

because they're ultimately a team. And they understood that and worked together as a team—with almost no competitive stuff. It was amazing."

NEW WINE, NEW BEER

In the fall of 1982, Fritz returned from his sabbatical in time for the grape harvest at York Creek. Although he was still selling grapes to vintners like Paul Draper at Ridge, the Cabernet Sauvignon fruit was especially important that year. He was selling it to Peter Friedman, husband of Carolyn Estes. Peter had recently founded Belvedere Wine Co., where he would serve as what the French call *negociant*, buying grapes from four top-notch California vineyards to create four distinctive wines for his "Grapemaker Series." Peter's plan was novel in that the face label, rather than featuring the winemaker, featured the "grapemaker." Fritz's 1982 York Creek Cabernet Sauvignon debuted as a part of this exclusive series in 1986.

Earlier in 1982, Fritz had brewed the first Foghorns at Mariposa, using the steam beer fermentors. Even though he still didn't have federal label approval, he was able to do a special bottling of Old Foghorn for California only, featuring "Jubilee Ale" neckhangers on the 6.4-oz green bottles. Dated April 7, 1983, this release celebrated the fiftieth anniversary of "the day beer came back." The idea for jubilee brews came out of a conversation between Fritz and Stuart Wilson, who was brewmaster at the Fred Koch Brewery in Dunkirk, NY and made a Jubilee Porter for the occasion. Other small brewers followed suit, making the toasts to April 7 all the more jovial and local.

The 1982 Christmas Ale was brewed for the first time on October 5 and bottled by the end of the month. It was the seventh annual variation on Fritz's 1975 Christmas Ale theme: a single-malt (pale) and single-hop (Cascade) Ale. 1982's recipe used over 95 lb of Cascade hops (from both the Segal and Haas farms) in the kettle, plus 40 lb for dry-hopping. The ale yeast that year was from Molson in Canada. At that time, Fritz was still fermenting his ales in shallow, open-pan fermentors like the ones at 8th Street because he was still waiting on an ale fermentor, which would be open but deeper in order to facilitate somewhat warmer fermentations more suitable for the ale yeast.

To everyone's delight, the '82 Christmas Ale was the best yet, so Fritz decided that as soon as the new ale fermentor arrived, he could repurpose that recipe for the return of Liberty Ale. Of course, Liberty Ale had really been there all along, with each iteration of Christmas Ale a step toward the perfection of its recipe. Jim Stitt updated the original Liberty artwork to full color, changing Steam Beer Brewing to Anchor Brewing and superimposing an anchor on the eagle's shield. Other than the ale yeast, which would come for the time being from Schmidt's in Philadelphia (home of the Liberty Bell), this year-round Liberty Ale recipe was identical to the '82 Christmas Ale. Unfortunately, the new ale fermentor did not arrive in time for the first brew on May 24, 1983, so Fritz opted to go ahead and ferment the first few brews of this Liberty Ale in a steam beer fermentor. The first bottling, at 5.75% ABV, took place on July 21, 1983. Joe Owades, who tried it the following January, had very little to say about it: "I just tasted Liberty Ale. It's the best ale I've ever tasted."

WHOLISTIC BREWING

On June 3, 1983, Fritz was in Denver, giving a talk at the AHA's fifth annual National Homebrew and Microbrewery Conference, as a sort of prelude to the GABF. "When I went to Colorado to speak, it was kind of like the lead talk and I took it seriously." Fritz's unique ability to connect with any audience is based on one of his favorite maxims: "Never underestimate your audience's intelligence or overestimate their knowledge." And his diverse audience that day—from beer drinkers to beer

makers, buyers to sellers, was the ultimate test. He called his talk (later transcribed and reprinted by the AHA), "Wholistic Brewing." Its big-picture message was, "you have to do everything, and I mean everything, right. Do it better than anyone else has done it. And then do it again, even better. Ninety-five percent of what you've done will literally never be seen or appreciated by anyone other than maybe your employees or your wife." To run a microbrewery "requires a degree of enthusiasm for excellence . . . and a theme of quality and integrity, that many people don't appreciate. . . . You should be the tip of the iceberg of what the public sees of quality. And you should know that you have a reservoir of quality below that is so deep you can just hold up your head anywhere and your employees will hold up their heads."

BROWN ALE FROM ANCHOR

After his stirring talk, Fritz headed to Corfu. He returned to the Bay Area in October for the grape harvest but his mind was on Christmas Ale. Fritz had always maintained that his beers, though all from the same brewery, should each have their own distinct personality—from liquid to label. So, with the release of Liberty Ale that summer, 1983's Christmas Ale would have to be a departure from its 1975-1982 run as a pale ale brewed and dry-hopped with Cascade.

Fritz, Mark, and Mike Lee

Brown ale, like barley wine, had fallen out of favor, so it was ideal fodder for Fritz and the 1983 Christmas Ale. Americans were already somewhat familiar with English import Newcastle, which Michael Jackson likened to more of a Viennese amber than the traditionally darker and sweeter brown ale. "If we were talking about making something new or different," Mark recalls, "Fritz didn't hesitate to say, 'Well, let's take a trip.' And so you really had an opportunity to learn. Breweries, equipment shows in Europe. He was so generous." The spring of 1983 was the first such trip for the brewery quartet of Fritz, Gordon, Mark, and Linda. It included the International Brewex and Packex Exhibition in Birmingham, England, and half a dozen British breweries, including Vaux in northeastern England, whose chairman, Paul Nicholson, was great friends with Fritz. Vaux had a strong brown ale, Double Maxim, which gave Fritz an idea for the 1983 Christmas Ale—a brown ale that would distinguish itself from Vaux's and all others by being all-malt.

The grain bill for the '83 Christmas Ale created luscious notes of chocolate and toffee from a combination of pale malt, 20°L and 120°L (Lovibond) caramel malt, and Munich malt. The color was dark brown, with a hint of red from the Munich malt. The hop choices were also a radical departure from the 1982 Christmas Ale. The bittering hop was Galena from John Segal's Yakima Valley farm. The hop used for aroma in the kettle and for dry–hopping in the cellar was East Kent Goldings, from the Borden, East Kent farm of A. Hinge & Sons. This hop contributed subtly tantalizing aromas of lemon, spice, flowers, earth, and honey. By the time of the first '83 Christmas Ale brew on October 11, the new, open ale fermentor was up and running. The yeast was the same as the 1983 Liberty Ale, and the wort was cooled to 63°F before pitching. The ABV was 6.25%, just slightly higher than 1982's 6.1%. This complex, flavor-packed but not heavy, all-malt brown ale and the ensuing 1984–1986 variations on its theme are fondly remembered by Anchor's staff as among the best beers Anchor ever made.

ANCHOR WHEAT BEER

In the summer of 1984, Fritz decided he needed a new brew with which to toast Anchor's fifth anniversary at Mariposa. His friend and colleague Bill Leinenkugel drank wheat beers in Germany—there weren't any in the United States—and talked about them at a BAA board meeting. "And that got me interested," recalls Fritz. The two most popular wheat beers in Germany were Weissbier (white beer), found mostly in northern Germany, and Weizenbier (wheat beer), from southern Germany. The former usually contains a smaller percentage of wheat malt in the mash and is fermented with traditional top-fermenting yeast and a lactic-acid producing bacteria, which gives it its customary sour flavor. Weizenbier has a higher percentage of wheat malt and is fermented with traditional top-fermenting yeast, plus a second, "wild" yeast, which contributes a distinctive flavor of its own. Fritz, ever the contrarian, chose to ferment his wheat beer without either of these additional fermentation organisms, but rather to use Anchor's ale yeast alone. He preferred the clean, pure flavors developed by this yeast in conjunction with a very high percentage of wheat malt. Fritz had Mark source the ingredients and work with Briess Malting on a pilot brew—the first time Anchor had made a test brew outside the brewery. In the end, it convinced everyone that the best test—for this brew and all others in Fritz's tenure—was to just fire up the boiler and brew a full batch on-site.

The first brew of Anchor Wheat Beer—the first wheat beer in America since Prohibition—began at 7:30 a.m. on July 17, 1984. The mash was 61% wheat malt and 39% pale malt—about as much wheat as possible. Barley malt has a husk, and wheat malt doesn't, so some of the former is needed to maintain a porous filter bed for the wort as it runs out of the lauter tun on its way to the brew kettle. To help with the runoff, they successfully tried adding some spent hops to the lauter tun. And because of all the protein in all that wheat, this beer developed an unusually abundant head, like whipped egg whites. Fritz chose Bavarian Hallertau hops for this brew for its mild bittering qualities and subtle aromas, so as not to let the hops overshadow the dry, clean flavors of the wheat. This first brew of Anchor Wheat Beer was not dry-hopped, though some later brews would be. And, like Liberty Ale, it was bunged rather than kräusened, which meant the entire brew was dropped from the ale fermentor to the cellar after only two days of primary fermentation, giving it a delicate, champagne-like bubble. Nor did Fritz, who had drunk all the cloudy beer he cared to in his early days at Anchor, want to make a German-style Hefeweizen, where the yeast is deliberately kept in suspension in the finished beer. This quintessentially American wheat beer would be filtered like Liberty Ale. Anchor Wheat Beer was bottled on August 10, just in time for Anchor's "First Brew Day" anniversary party August 13. And everyone got a commemorative bottle to take home. "My idea was that we would give the wheat beer in special-mold bottles to all our trusted friends and supporters and helpers who had made our new brewery a success."

So how was a tiny brewery able to afford a custom bottle mold for just 127 cases of beer? "The bottle company," Fritz recalls, "offered me a special one-of-a-kind mold, in a limited edition. The bottle molds were wearing out and would soon need to be replaced, so they came to me and said it would be possible to make a special engraving on these old molds, run them once and briefly, and then throw them away."

The little key on the bottles is called a *Zwickelschlüssel*, German for sampling-valve key. "It's an old device," explains Fritz. "Only the brewmaster would have one, and maybe a few trusted associates. It was needed to open the sample valves on cellar tanks, which had a triangular or other odd-shaped inner stem that could only be opened by the key. It's not uncommon for a water spigot in parks or similar places to use a comparable device today." At Anchor, the sampling valve on a cellar tank is still called a "Zwickel"—although, to everyone's sampling delight, they do not lock. Beer critic Michael Jackson praised Anchor's "clean, dry Wheat beer, very delicate, but with light honey and apple notes." But to Fritz, this beer, at under 4.6%

FOR THE BREW-CURIOUS: THE LOVIBOND SCALE

In 1883, Irish-born physicist/mathematician William Thomson, Lord Kelvin, said that "when you can measure what you are speaking about, and express it in numbers, you know something about it; but when you cannot measure it, when you cannot express it in numbers, your knowledge is of a meagre and unsatisfactory kind: it may be the beginning of knowledge, but you have scarcely, in your thoughts, advanced to the stage of *science*." Forward-thinking brewers such as Balling and Lovibond did much to advance the science of brewing, which in turn advanced science itself.

In the late nineteenth century, British brewer Joseph Williams Lovibond created a system of color classification for grading and enumerating color, which used a tintometer, an instrument he invented, "for ascertaining the colour of malt and of beer." Brewers and maltsters could choose from a reference set of glass discs (later slides) and insert them into the tintometer to compare and evaluate the hue and lightness to darkness of their products. Until recently, malt was measured in degrees Lovibond on a scale from 2-3°L for pale malt to more than 500°L for black malt, which demonstrates numerically how a little dark malt goes a long way in brewing color-wise. Today, the tintometer and the Lovibond scale have been widely replaced in the industry by the more accurate spectrophotometer and Standard Reference Method (SRM) numbering system.

ABV, was his "lawnmower beer," which for years to come would occupy a spot in his vineyard fridge—right next to the Coors Light.

Fritz would continue to experiment with the grain bill (up to more than 70% wheat malt), hops (including a staff favorite, Saaz from the Czech Republic), ABV (as low as the mid-3s), and label for his Anchor Wheat Beer (a local label in 1984/85, followed by a national label in 1985/86, both beautifully designed by Jim Stitt). "Everyone at the brewery is most excited about the Wheat Beer," wrote Fritz in summer 1986. "It seems like it is the beer of choice around here when work is done and people gather in the taproom. We certainly hope our consumers like it as much as we do." And they did, including the "mixed drink" made with it and dubbed "Jolly Solly Dunkelweizen" in honor of its namesake and creator, bottling superintendent Chris "Solly" Solomon. It was a refreshing blend of Anchor Wheat and Anchor Porter. Simply fill your glass about one-half to two-thirds full of Anchor Wheat, then carefully pour Anchor Porter

down the side of the glass to push the white head up to the top of this deliciously light, dark beer. It was a great way to celebrate not only the fifth anniversary of Mariposa Street, but the near tripling of Anchor's sales in that short time, from 12,575 barrels in 1979 to 37,349 in 1984.

Fritz has had a love of music since childhood. And he sees the parallels between a great musician and a great business, especially their dedication to continuous improvement, what in Japanese is called *kaizen*. Violinist Jascha Heifetz described it this way: "Always in my playing I strive to surpass myself, and it is this constant struggle that makes music fascinating to me." Fritz had seen it at the Maytag Company and made a successful effort to instill it in his staff at Anchor. He also saw the parallels between great chamber music and great small business, especially the synergy of teamwork. By 1981, the brewery already had its own in-house rock band, the Hysters (named after the brewery's forklift). Now it would have its own professional chamber group. Called the Anchor Chamber Players and made up mostly of musicians from the SF Opera and SF Ballet, their 14-year run of free concerts began just a block from the brewery away at Potrero Hill Middle School. In 1983, following the untimely passing of Fritz's sister Ellen, he reminisced about her piano practice in their "very musical home," which blossomed into Ellen's lifelong dedication to music and music-making. With the support of his family, Fritz commissioned a local instrument maker, Francis Kuttner, to build a matching string quartet of instruments in her memory. Crafted from the same wood, the instruments would be loaned out to student and professional players during the year, in what Fritz liked to call "their secret life." But once a year, they would be reunited in a Bay Area performance as a quartet.

EVERYTHING FOR A REASON

(1985-1991)

Success has only spurred Maytag into looking more deeply into the lore and legends of beer.

—**Dan Berger,** *Los Angeles Times* (1990)

With the addition of wheat beer in 1984, the Anchor family of beers was set at six: Steam, Porter, Liberty, Christmas, Foghorn, and Wheat. Fritz's idea was that if you lined up a glass of each on the taproom bar, you could easily pick out which was which—one reason, for example, that there was no Anchor Stout. And though they all came from the same brewery, each also had its own distinctive story, personality, flavor, aroma, and label.

With the 1985 Christmas Ale came a new backstory and a new Anchor tradition: having all the pale malt in Christmas Ale come from a single California source, the Woodman family farm in Tulelake. And Fritz wanted to take everyone to the harvest. He had read in *Brewing and Beer Traditions in Norway* about the ancient connection between Christmas ales and the harvest. Author Odd Nordland discussed Norwegian traditions such as the pouring of homebrewed Christmas ale "into the grain field. The underlying idea must be a kind of thanksgiving for the harvest from the fields." And Fritz hoped an annual trip would reinforce for himself and his staff what had been ingrained in him growing up in Iowa: "There is a risk with the harvest. And the supply of our raw materials doesn't just come from the telephone; it comes from the season, from *this* season."

Fritz, who knows his Shakespeare, knows "strong reasons make strong actions." So the 1986 Christmas Ale would be the last of Anchor's

Yuletide run of four brown ales. The reason was not that his fiancée, Beverly Horn, disliked brown ales, but rather that the two of them had a better idea. A graduate of UC Davis, Beverly had first met Fritz while she was working for Potrero Hill businessman Frank Buttine, whose aphorisms she and Fritz both admired. "One of the things he told her was 'If things don't make sense, you don't have all the facts.' Brilliant!" Beverly's "dad ran the PG&E

---

office in Coalinga. So she has and had a very sympathetic attitude toward business and to entrepreneurs. She's been extremely understanding and supportive, been great, and she knows it—I tell her everything." Both knew their marriage would be a good one because, in the words of one of Fritz's favorite writers, Rainer Maria Rilke, "a good marriage is one in which each partner appoints the other to be the guardian of his solitude, and thus they show each other the greatest possible trust." Fritz and Beverly were scheduled to march down the aisle—to the music of the Anchor Chamber Players—on January 10, 1987. But what to serve the guests at the reception? It would have to be Bridale.

The word *bridal* comes from the Old English *brýd-ealo*, which means wedding-ale or wedding feast, and Fritz and Beverly thought it would be fun if each of them came up with a special ingredient for this Bridale. And together they would choose a special hop for brewing/dry-hopping, all of which would forever remain their secret. The grain bill, a blend of pale, caramel, and Munich malts, was similar to the 1986 Christmas Ale. Bridale, brewed on December 31, 1986, was Anchor's first spiced brown ale. It was a hit at the reception, and bottles of it, with their elegant letterpress labels, made tasty thank-you gifts for Fritz and Beverly's guests.

In the fall, Bridale served as inspiration for Anchor's 1987 Christmas Ale and all the Christmas Ales to follow it—each a little different from the other, but all *spiced* brown ales, a wish list in a glass. Appropriately for the newlyweds, the '87 Christmas Ale label featured two trees: a Douglas fir and a coast redwood. This was also the first year for Christmas Ale neck labels, which proclaimed "WASSAIL! Every year since 1975 the brewers at Anchor have produced a special ale which we sell from early December to early January. These ales are different each year, and we hope our friends and customers enjoy the variety as we do. This year we offer a 'wassail,' following an ancient tradition of spiced ales at Christmas time." Wassail, from the Old English salutation *wes hál*—good health!— was the spiced ale created for Christmas Eve, New Years, and Twelfth Night celebrations, drunk from a wassail bowl, as wassailers made merry with song and drink.

CALIFORNIA'S SMALL BREWERS UNITE

By 1989, the prediction Fritz had shared with Mark Carpenter in 1973, that "down the road you're going to see *hundreds* of small breweries around the US," was coming true. And so was the need for what Fritz had begun discussing with Ken Grossman ten years before—in Ken's words, "pursuing the idea of a small brewers' organization for the West Coast. It seems like the time is right to revitalize traditional brewing practices. The feasibility of localized breweries may again soon become a reality. If we can keep our standards above the rest of the industry, we can continue to popularize quality brewed American beer." The reasoning was right in 1979, but the time was not—until 1989.

Indeed, of the 247 breweries in the US in 1989, forty-two were in California, producing a total of about 135,000 barrels a year, less than 0.5% of all the beer sold in California. Of those forty-two, eight (Anchor, Sierra Nevada, Los Angeles, Pete's, Mendocino, Stanislaus, Anderson Valley, Devil Mountain) sold bottled beer off-premise (to take home, as opposed to on-premise, to drink at a bar or restaurant), using between six (Devil Mountain) and seventy (Anchor) independent wholesalers to do it. And in 1990, it was expected that these breweries alone would account for 99,000 barrels in total sales (bottle and draught). With a 55% share of those sales, Fritz saw a rising tide lifting all boats and the opportunity (1) for Anchor to continue leading the way on quality and price, (2) to caution the micros against cannibalization, and (3) to warn them against denigrating their wholesalers or big beer. In short, the common good of California small brewers was best served by working together. It was time to organize.

To do this, Fritz started the California Small Brewers Association (CSBA) and found Bob Judd, who was president of Cal-Tech Management Associates in Sacramento, to help manage, counsel, and lobby for it. The nonprofit CSBA filed articles of incorporation on September 18, 1989, cognizant, in Judd's words, that "small breweries are breathing a spark of life into a troubled and stagnant beer market. We represent moderation and quality, and our presence creates consumer interest in all beers, not just our own. There are big issues that are a common threat to the brewers and wholesalers (tax increases, neo-Prohibition). Let's focus on fighting these together rather than fighting each other."

Fritz became president, and Steve Harrison from Sierra Nevada served as secretary. Vice President Michael Laybourn from Mendocino Brewing and Treasurer John Martin from Triple Rock Brewing helped give voice to the blossoming California brewpub movement. Mendocino had started it in 1983, thanks to a little groundwork by Fritz and Jack McAuliffe, carried forward by state assemblyman Tom Bates, who paved the legislative way for brewpubs in 1982.

One of the CSBA's early successes was the "First California Small Brewers Festival" in October '89. A benefit for the Santa Clara County Chapter of the National Multiple Sclerosis Society, it provided an opportunity to promote the CSBA, "formed to promote the development and appreciation of fine, all-natural, hand-crafted beers," as well as the more than thirty breweries and brewpubs pouring at the event. The CSBA's first legislative triumph was the resounding defeat of Proposition 134 in 1990, which would have raised the state tax on beer by 1,400%. It lost, thanks in part to the CSBA's "MICRO-BREW MACRO-TAX VOTE NO" buttons, reminiscent of anti-Prohibition campaigns, and ads in Tom Dalldorf's entrepreneurial California brewspaper, *Celebrator*

Beer News: "REMEMBER, DRINKING GOOD BEER IS NOT A SIN!—Yet."

By the early '80s, when Fritz was making frequent trips to Corfu, Mark Carpenter had blossomed into an effective pinch hitter. Mark exuded the depth of knowledge and joy of brewing of someone who had worked alongside Fritz for years. Plus, with Fritz reluctant to blow his own horn, Mark could extol Fritz's accomplishments without seeming immodest. And he could drop a hint with near-Fritzian élan, as he did at the 1987 National Conference for Quality Beer and Brewing. There, in a talk later reprinted by Brewers Publications, he told his audience, "It is true that there is currently a love affair with good beer, but it is an old love affair with beer. . . . The love of beer is an ancient tradition."

THE NINKASI PROJECT: RE-CREATING AN ANCIENT BEER

The 1988 Christmas Ale was the first to feature a botanical illustration on its neck label, initiating a new Anchor tradition. On the face label was something more intriguing, a tiny pictogram nearly six thousand years old. It was another hint about Anchor's Ninkasi Project, already underway, which would culminate in the re-creation of an ancient beer. This undertaking would become one of the proudest and profoundest achievements of Fritz's lifetime—and the perfect way to celebrate Anchor's tenth anniversary at Mariposa. Fritz, who can connect equally with a warehouse full of beer distributors or a museum full of archaeologists, described it in one of the tag-team talks we did, where I told the story of Anchor and he told the story of Ninkasi, the ancient Sumerian goddess of beer:

Why did the earliest people settle down to farm and grow grain? Did they grow the grain to bake bread or to brew beer? I got so intrigued by this

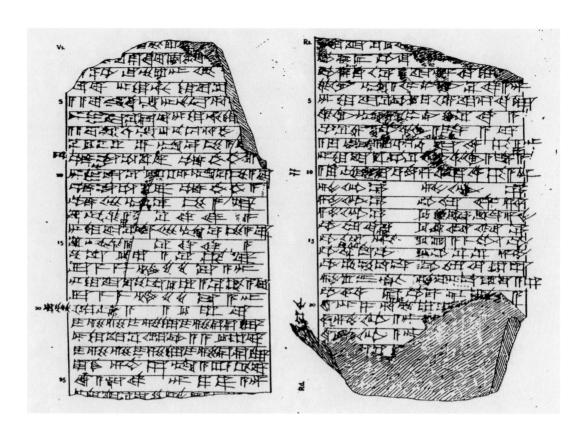

beer/bread question that I sought out the key scholar, Dr. Solomon Katz. Anchor had been invited by the Institute for Brewing Studies to brew a special beer for a convention of small brewers in San Francisco, and I formed the idea of studying how these earliest beers were made, and making one for this convention. The goddess of brewing in ancient Sumeria—from around 1800 BC, and possibly much earlier—

We were the first brewers in modern times who ever read the *Hymn to Ninkasi*. We realized that this is a remarkably accurate, linear story about the process of making beer, from malt to fermentation to *the filtering vat* (probably a mash/lauter tun), *which makes a pleasant sound*. This just intrigued us, and the more we studied it, the more we decided that the translation was not made by a brewer and could be improved. I flew to Chicago see Dr. Miguel Civil, the *Hymn's* translator.

This is bappir. And it turns out that the earliest beer was made primarily from bread. In other words, if they grew grain to make beer, they went through a process of making a kind of bread from it first, because bread will keep almost indefinitely. You can turn bread into sugar and start fermenting it almost within a few hours, so if you discover that cousin Charlie is coming for the weekend, you could, if you have the right kind of bread, the bappir, make beer. When I was a boy, we had zwieback for young children, which means "twice-baked," and "biscuit" is from the Italian *biscotti*, which means "twice-baked." So we decided that bappir would have been twice-baked. And these Sumerians were

was called Ninkasi, a young woman who, according to the ancient Sumerian text, "fills the mouth," in other words, someone who quenches your thirst.

Our Ninkasi neck label features an ancient pictogram, the earliest known depiction of human beings drinking an alcoholic beverage. It dates from around 4000 BC. Those are two guys drinking beer out of a big jug through straws in ancient Sumeria. Straws would most certainly have helped in straining out the grain from the gruel that you were drinking from a jug. We pounced on this as a research project and became the world's experts on ancient brewing, because no brewers had ever really studied it, and the scholars knew nothing about brewing. One of the documents we found was the *Hymn to Ninkasi*, a kind of celebrating hymn, a song of praise or thanksgiving, to the Sumerian goddess of brewing and beer. Its evocative verses include:

*Ninkasi, you are the one who soaks
the malt in a jar,
The waves rise, the waves fall.*

*You are the one who spreads the cooked
mash on large reed mats,
Coolness overcomes . . .*

PART FOUR: FRITZ MAYTAG'S REVOLUTIONARY NEW BREWERY   201

raisins?" "Yes." Well, that made a whole lot of sense to me, because in the poem, at the point where Ninkasi adds gestin, it's exactly where a brewer would want to add yeast. So it made tremendous sense to me to have the raisins be the yeast starter for the brew.

Here's the owner and he's thinking about how much all of this is going to cost! Brew Day—we called them Bake Day and Brew Day—was August 17, 1989. We had only one chance, like a watercolor painting, and we did not want to screw up!

With me in my office were Miguel Civil to my right and to his right, Solomon Katz, the scholar at the University of Pennsylvania who had written a beer/bread article. Professor Civil showed

serious, sophisticated, professional brewers. So we decided to put dark malt into our bappir dough. We made perhaps a hundred significant decisions, none of which we were sure of, but we were sure that we were the first really knowledgeable brewers who had read these documents and who had tried to think it through and make a decision. And so we found, in a kind of living experience, what many modern archaeologists take for granted: that if you are studying something in ancient history, *you go do it*.

In the *Hymn to Ninkasi* there is a reference to something sweet. I asked Professor Civil, "Some of these words I want to know more about; for example, lar; what does it mean?" He said, "Well, it just means sweet." And I said, "Well, what would they have had that was sweet?" "Honey and dates." So we put some honey in the bappir and dates in the brew. I also asked him about another word, gestin (wine). "*The Hymn* says that Ninkasi is putting wine in the beer. That doesn't seem right to me. What does it really mean, gestin? Isn't there a dictionary where we could go and look up some synonyms and things for these words?" And he looked at me and said, "*I* am the dictionary." Then he said, "It just means grapes; anything to do with grapes." "Could it be

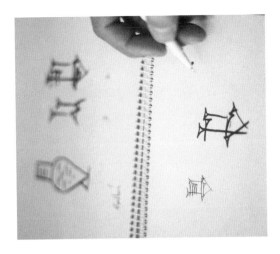

us about ancient Sumerian cuneiform writing. On the right is the character for beer, as it evolved. With the figure on the lower left, he showed us the etymology of the word for beer. It comes from a picture of a jug (amphora) on its side, just the sort of vessel out of which one might enjoy a beer.

We adjourned to the Anchor brewhouse, just a few feet away. As we tipped in the bappir, Sol Katz and I, we felt a thrill—4,000 years of brewing tradition relived. While we were putting the dates in, some of our brewers were kidding around, and this became known at Anchor as the "Sumerian Date Dance."

They didn't have hops in ancient Sumeria. There is no record of hops anywhere until around

AD 800. And in 1989, when we did this project, it was actually illegal to make beer in America without hops. So, I'm the brewmaster, and I told everybody, "Now turn your backs while I add the hops." And, of course, I put the hops in my pocket. At least there were no witnesses.

We let the mash run off the way a normal brew's mash does. And we decided not to boil the wort. Boiling would have been extremely costly back then, and unnecessary if the beer was going to be fermented and consumed right away. We let it cool overnight, the way all beers used to be made. You just waited for them to cool down. It was late afternoon, the San Francisco Giants were playing the Expos that night, and we had tickets to the ballgame. And so I assembled my troops, and said, "Now we have to ask ourselves, what would the ancient Sumerians do? Would they stand around all night watching this stuff cool, or would they go to the ballpark?" Once the wort had cooled, we fermented it with brewer's yeast and prepared for the banquet.

We got some gigantic, 9-liter bottles, called Salmanazars, and some long tubes to serve as straws. With the help of Richard Elmore, we created a wrap-around label for these bottles. The

R to L: Michael Jackson, Jim Fristoe, Bob Brewer, Mark Carpenter, Jerry Van Atta

narrative of the *Hymn to Ninkasi* served as inspiration for each of its six images. At the National Microbrewers Conference banquet, all the small brewers from all across America were there. I got up and said, "Now we are going to have a beer that is a serious attempt to re-create the beers of ancient Sumeria, from four thousand years ago."

And at that point, the doors to the kitchen opened and the waiters came out, each carrying one of these big jugs, and everyone laughed and cheered, because it was weird and wonderful. And the waiters put a jug down in the center of each table. "What we've done," I said, "is a serious attempt at scholarship, and we've named it after the ancient Sumerian goddess of brewing, whose name was Ninkasi. And they drank their beer through tubes, so, each of you, choose a tube. And now may I suggest that we stand, everybody take a tube, and suck a little beer from the jug, and we will drink a toast to Ninkasi, who is the goddess of our trade." A chill goes through me as I retell this. It was a magic moment.

Here was a whole room full of brewers, cele-brating the brewers of four thousand years ago, and, yes, we probably weren't totally accurate on *any* of our decisions, but we were the first people who had used Sumerian brewing termi-nology in four thousand years, and we had tried our best to make all of these decisions based on practical knowledge. It was thrilling.

An oil painting, *Brewers' Icon*, has hung in Anchor's brewhouse since the early 1960s. It was created by an employee, Dave Lyon, and was his attempt to depict St. Nicholas, one of several saints reputed to be a patron saint of brewers. He is holding a little hop cluster in one hand. Like many saints, perhaps he wasn't so saintly, or didn't even really exist. Only after brewing Ninkasi and thinking about the god-dess of our trade—we don't have gods and goddesses floating around, but we do have patron saints, don't we?—I think this is a way to relate to what it meant, in pagan times, when they had a god of this or a god of that, someone who looks over you in your trade. Suddenly I

realized, well, we have St. Nicholas in the brewhouse, and there is no way we would ever take him down. He is the patron saint of our trade, much as Ninkasi was once a goddess to the brewers of ancient Sumeria.

Everyone who participated in Anchor's Ninkasi Project came away with a renewed sense of what it means to be a brewer. But Fritz's research was by no means over. In 1992, Ninkasi was born again, with an even more historically accurate recipe that included emmer wheat and bappir baked in a wood-fired oven. As before, bottles of Ninkasi were quickly snatched up by the curious. But the real triumph of the whole project was that the story lives on, told and retold as a story not only about Ninkasi but about what makes Anchor, Anchor.

THE BEER HUNTER

A few days after Brew Day, Fritz got the call that it was harvest time in Tulelake. That would be the first lesson—the barley is ready when the barley is ready. And this time, in August 1989, writer Michael Jackson would have a seat on the bus. Anchor was to be featured in the *California Pilgrimage* episode of Michael's six-part television series *The Beer Hunter*. Originally prepared for British Channel 4, it would debut in the United States on The Discovery Channel, which described it as "a thirst-quenching adventure in search of the world's finest beers," hosted by the "world's leading authority on malt." After its premiere, Bard of Beer Michael Jackson would forever be known as the Beer Hunter.

Although the episode, through the magic of TV, appears to have been shot all in one day, it was actually shot in five, August 21 through 25, including pit/pint stops at Calistoga's Napa Valley Brewing and Mendocino's Hopland Brewery. On the bus, members of the Hysters, the Anchor rock band, provided the impromptu soundtrack for Michael's relaxed conversation with Fritz, who told him, "People want the beer to come from a good place. They hope that it comes from a good place. They want to trust the people that make the beer. It gives us an identity with our Christmas Ale that relates to an actual farm. And I think when our brewers put the malt into the mash tun, they remember that that's the stuff. There it is. It gives our company something that's hard to duplicate."

Michael got it. So did Bob Brewer, who had been hired by Fritz in 1985 to be one of Anchor's "ambassadors" (a job title Fritz preferred to salesperson): "Most people who work in a factory or a manufacturing plant, they just mix ingredients and make something, but here we're actually getting our hands on and we're seeing the barley as it's actually harvested. And it gives somewhat of a feeling of the origination of the product. I can smell it. I can taste it." In later years, Fritz would add

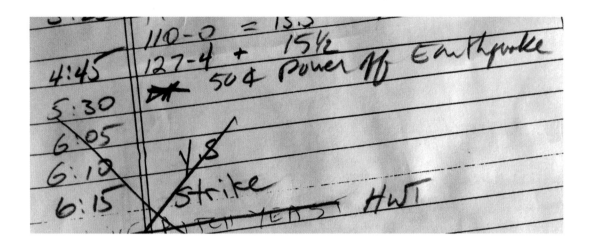

California hops to the Christmas Ale and another annual trip to Anchor's harvest itinerary—to the Signorotti Hop Ranch near Sacramento.

EARTHQUAKE BEER

From harvesting a field to hoisting a glass, brewing requires planning. But every brewer, particularly in the Bay Area, knows that even the best laid plans can go awry. At 5 p.m. on October 17, 1989, the Giants were at Candlestick, warming up for Game 3 of their Bay Bridge World Series against the A's. Brewer Richard Gossett was in the brewhouse, with two brews on base—Steam Beer in the mash tun and another in the brew kettle. At 5:04:15 p.m. he felt it, as the magnitude 6.9 Loma Prieta earthquake rocked the greater SF Bay Area like nothing since 1906. About fifteen seconds later he scribbled "504 Power off Earthquake" on his brew-chart and headed to the taproom. Outside, freeways collapsed, sirens roared, and huge fires, which could be seen from Anchor's rooftop, broke out in the Marina District.

Miraculously, unlike 1906, Anchor was shaken but spared. Not a single bottle fell from its perch. But no power meant no pumps, so the third brew of the day was trapped in the brew kettle, and the fourth, fully converted and ready for transfer to the lauter tun, was stuck in the mash tun. Fritz suggested that as soon as the power came back on, "why not just pick up where you left off?" With the bridges closed anyway, Richard and Mark volunteered to wait it out. The power came back on at 9:45 p.m. Finally, at 4:11 a.m. Richard noted that the last brew was "ALL IN" and headed home.

The resulting beer, of course, didn't look or taste very much like Anchor Steam. Sugars had caramelized; hops had languished in the beer for hours. But on November 16, Fritz couldn't resist bottling Anchor's "Earthquake Beer"—but with its oval labels upside down. "We limited distribution to the immediate Bay Area, where we had *felt* the earthquake, and where we were *aware* of the earthquake, and where the theme of the day was 'keep going.' That was the spirit of it. We divided the beer into small lots, so that every distributor got

On August 15, 1990, Anchor hosted a *Beer Hunter* sneak-preview party. The show was a sensation, well beyond even Michael and Fritz's vivid imaginations. Michael had captured on video the sort of thing that Anchor had been doing for years. Yet it was so novel—that a company should shut down to go harvest barley—that it resonated with a public just beginning to take an interest in micro- and brewpub-brewed beers, as well as the food that could be made and/or served with them. At the preview, there was Maytag Blue Cheese and a light lunch. And there was plenty of fine beer, including Anchor Wheat, Ninkasi, and a vertical tasting of Christmas Ales. There was also a new brew, Potrero Commons Ale. It was a sumptuous brown ale with a bucolic Jim Stitt label, named after a public green space or "commons" on Potrero Hill that was threatened by development. Villagers in medieval England often brewed such ales together to raise money for village projects and promote a festive spirit of neighborly cooperation. In that spirit, this ale was brewed on the Hill by neighbors for neighbors. But the developers won, replacing much of the open space with high-end housing. So, in 1995, Fritz donated proceeds from the sale of Potrero Commons Ale—$16,496—to nearby Starr King Park, a similar open space.

With everything that was going on in 1990, the twenty-fifth anniversary of Fritz's purchase of Steam Beer Brewing came and went, without fanfare, hot-air balloons, or sour beer. But not by accident. Like Hokusai's *Thirty-six Views of Mt. Fuji*, Fritz viewed Anchor from many angles. As he mulled over the recipe for his sixteenth Christmas Ale, his imagination kicked into overdrive, toward a view beyond Anchor Brewing.

some—just a little bit mixed in with their regular beer. And we told nobody about it, until it was going out onto the shelves. And then we told Herb Caen. And he just loved it, and everybody loved it." Local Melba Moeck got a 6-pack: "Who knew that an upside-down label on a bottle of beer would become a topic of conversation?" Fritz knew. As in 1906, Anchor and San Francisco remain resilient, indomitable—we keep going.

Anchor finished 1989 with sales of 58,572 barrels, more than four and a half times its sales just a decade before. And Anchor Steam was more widely distributed than ever before. It had made it to Canada in 1985 and the UK in 1987, and would soon be found in Sweden, the Netherlands, Italy, France, China, and Japan. And by the early '90s, Anchor would be available in all fifty states, becoming what Fritz calls "America's first little national brewery."

ANCHOR DISTILLING
(1991–2000)

When I first met Fritz, the very first thing he ever talked about was the quality of a product. He didn't talk about mass production. He always discussed how could he produce something that hadn't been seen for a long, long time, reintroduce a whiskey, a flavor, a style that may have been lost to the American nation—been lost to the world in fact.

—**Jim Murray, James Beard Foundation video tribute to Fritz** (2008)

In 1976, the year Joe Allen died, Lawrence Steese had moved to Costa Rica with his and Frances's children. He bought a small farm in the countryside east of the capital city of San José, married his fourth wife, and began growing everything from coffee, pineapple, and bananas to the indigenous star fruit. In 1991, when news reached Fritz and Gordon of Lawrence's April 19 death in a car accident, it instantly conjured up memories of a man without whom Anchor might have disappeared long ago. "He put his heart and soul into the job. A remarkable, wonderful man," Fritz told me. Gordon, with a wistful grin, nodded, then shook his head. "Glad I met him. What a character."

SPRUCE BEER

On August 2, 1991, exactly twenty-six years after he met Lawrence Steese, Fritz created another draft of brewing history, Anchor Spruce Beer. It is exemplary of many of the beers popular in pre-industrial Europe and America, brewed at home with locally available natural flavors and spices, a tradition that includes everything from root beer to wassail. Spruce beer played an important low-alcohol role in the American Revolution. In 1775, General Washington's soldiers' rations included "One Quart of Spruce Beer Pr Day," which was safe to drink and helped prevent scurvy.

Anchor Spruce Beer, as Fritz described it in 1991, "is a gesture of exploration and celebration. It's an essay, an attempt to reach back into brewing history to honor the tenth anniversary of The Great American Beer Festival, and to celebrate our modern brewing Renaissance." As with the Ninkasi project two years before, Fritz put the word *essay* right on the label, to indicate that this product was made for its own sake and the concomitant joy of following curiosity wherever it led. Anchor's spruce beer would be created by adding a few ounces of natural spruce extract to Anchor Wheat Beer in the cellar. But the burning brewing question was: how much spruce? Would Fritz and Mark risk too much or too little spruce flavor and aroma in this one-off historical brew? Well, the label said Anchor Spruce Beer, so they chose the former. And it was a lot of spruce. Like the hops in the original Liberty Ale, it mellowed a bit over time, but it was still an eye-opener at the GABF, which had no outbreaks of scurvy that year.

The unusual fishtail shape of the Spruce Beer label, like those of the 1990 Christmas and Potrero Commons ales before it, was Anchor's stopgap to

adhere to new federal labeling regulations, specifically the addition of the GOVERNMENT WARNING. Anchor's World Tandem labelers couldn't apply a back label, so until a new labeler could be purchased, these would have to do. Gordon, Mark, and their teams worked together to install a new, state-of-the-art Krones labeler over Labor Day weekend, 1991. The top speed of the new labeler was limited by the top speed of the old filler, but it still provided more consistent application and the back-label option. Soon, there would be more label requirements, all of which were anathema to Fritz, who wanted to preserve the original, clean look of Anchor's bottles. So the warning, recycling info, UPC, and even a three-digit code for the bottled-on date would all go on an innocuous grey-blue back label, designed by Fritz to look like it had been supplied by the Government Printing Office.

In addition to Anchor Spruce Beer, Anchor's other beers were well received at the 1991 GABF, with a gold for Old Foghorn and a bronze for the 1990 Christmas Ale. Prior to 1987, there had been no judging of the participating breweries' beers—just a consumer preference poll. But from 1987 (the first adjudication year) on, Anchor has won a total of nineteen medals—including four

golds—and each of Anchor's six original beers (Steam, Porter, Liberty, Foghorn, Christmas, Wheat) has medaled.

A quick look at the GABF's and Anchor's numbers sheds light on the astounding growth and transformation of American brewing. The first GABF was held in 1982 in a Boulder ballroom, with 800 attendees, 24 breweries, and 47 beers. The tenth GABF was held in 1991 at Denver's Merchandise Mart, with 7,000 attendees, 150 breweries, and 500 beers. In 1982, Anchor sold 28,752 barrels of beer, about 2,000 barrels per employee. In 1991, Anchor sold 70,419 barrels of beer, 20,000 barrels more than Fritz's "ultimate goal" for his brewery. And he was still at about 2,000 barrels per employee, showing how even steady growth at a small brewery does not necessarily translate to economies of scale.

Anchor's boat had once been the only one on the water. Now, in 1991, Fritz was leading a flotilla on a flood tide. "We [had been] all alone," Fritz had told *Brewer's Digest* in 1988. "We tried to hide from the industry. We didn't want everyone to catch on to us. Now everyone is either doing what we were doing or faking it. We can't assume we can stay the same and keep up." Fritz had always preached the gospel of small (but profitable). But Anchor continued to defy gravity—even when he raised prices—in its seemingly inevitable ascent toward 100,000 barrels of beer a year or more. How could Anchor grow like this and retain its foundational ethos? How could it continue to be a place where he and his employees didn't feel they *had* to go to work every day, but rather a place where they felt they *got* to go to work every day? Fritz concluded, "My real goal is to build a company people will admire. They'll say, 'Hey, that's the Anchor Brewing Co.'" And that meant building different.

TO GO PUBLIC OR NOT TO GO PUBLIC

In 1991, Fritz heard about a new book he thought might help. It was *Take Your Company Public! The Entrepreneur's Guide to Alternative Capital Sources*. In it, San Francisco securities lawyer/direct marketing consultant Drew Field showed that, with seven hundred thousand new incorporations a year and fewer than three hundred companies going public, there was a wealth of capital just waiting to be tapped, all without having to go through the financial labyrinth of a traditional underwritten initial public offering (IPO). Instead, Field favored the direct public offering (DPO), where the company itself sells shares to investors through a direct marketing appeal. But could Fritz's loyal *customers* be turned into loyal—but not too impatient—*investors*?

"I read the book—devoured it—got in touch with him and hired him." There were some puzzles that Fritz hoped Field might help him solve. Even though the brewery was situated in one of the last M-1 light-industrial zones in the city, the voracious development of Potrero Commons had been a cautionary tale about the coming gentrification of Potrero Hill. When Fritz found out that the soy sauce factory across Mariposa Street from Anchor was going to move out, he thought about buying the property and building. "Every owl needs its forest," as Fritz likes to say. "And there we were, terrified about growth—even thinking about building a new brewhouse above the brewery's loading dock." An Anchor Brewery annex across the street could keep the developers at bay and provide a viable option for expansion, but it would take capital.

Drew, Fritz, Gordon, Mark, and Linda went full Fritzian, exploring every angle and consequence. A DPO was an idea that couldn't be rushed. Would it be a great idea that was also a good idea? In the end, says Fritz, "I just got cold feet. To his

NET CONT. 50.7 FL. OZ. (1 QT. 1 PT. 2.7 OZ.)

credit, Drew waited a respectful amount of time before finding another company and taking Mendocino Brewing public in 1994." Without investors, Fritz would once again be pushing all his chips to the middle of the table. In 1992, he convinced his friend Dave Hall to lease him the Wing Nien property and building with an option to buy. That freed Fritz to dream—not big, which held little interest for him, but different, which appealed to his insatiable curiosity.

Paul Draper, who has known Fritz as long and well as just about anybody, has "seldom known people that are more curious about how things work, what the world is about, everything that they come in contact with." And Fritz recognizes that he had "a fabulous advantage: I learned the ropes myself. I can walk out into the brewhouse and say, 'Guess what we're going to do? We're going to make a new beer.'" Fritz loved to start new things, get them going, and then step back, although stepping back wasn't always easy for him. And he had

unshakable faith in the employees he'd handpicked for his company and their ability to transform his dreams into reality. But by the early '90s, everybody in the beer business, including big beer, had "new things," from Amber to Zima, all vying for attention and shelf space.

Fritz still had a few new things up his sleeve. When he received a 1.5-liter magnum of sparkling wine from fellow vintner Jack Davies for Christmas, rather than return the favor with a 6-pack of Christmas Ale, he had a better idea: Why not fill magnums with Christmas Ale and surprise him? On December 12, Anchor bottled 103 magnums (including two for the lab) off a keg in the cellar. It was a fine example of trying something out with people power before committing to it with machine power. Fritz asked me how many I thought I could sell on the tour that afternoon. I said, "How many would you like me to sell?" "Fifty" he replied. And fifty it was. By fall 1994, Anchor's magnum sales had grown to the point that Fritz could justify buying a second bottling line, which included a filler from SMB Technik GmbH and a Krones Universella labeler. It could bottle anything from 7-oz bottles to magnums. Anchor sold 10,302 Christmas magnums in 1994. Brewer Bruce Joseph "always liked that attitude that, 'We're Anchor. We can do anything we want. We're one team and proud of what we make. There's nothing we can't do.'" Though the company had grown, its core values had not changed.

A NEW REVOLUTION

What really intrigued Fritz was the idea of reprising his triumphs of the 1960s, '70s, and '80s, with the same enthusiasm, creativity, and rigor, but in a completely new category. It would set his brewery apart from all others, big or small, and give his newer employees the opportunity to be revolutionaries too, just like Fritz, Gordon, Mark, Linda, and others from the "old brewery." Fritz chose to take Winston Churchill's words, that "it seems

even more difficult to carry forward a revolution than to start one," as a challenge. It was time for him and his employees, old and new, to do two things at once: carry the original revolution forward *and* start a new one.

But what did Fritz have in mind for his next revolution? What new company did he want to be chairman of the board of? On the bus to Tulelake, less than a week after brewing Ninkasi, Fritz had told Michael Jackson, "Beer is like painting in watercolors. You do it and that's it. And making wine is like painting in oils. You make the wine, and then you analyze it, and you blend it, and you fine it, and age it, and you put it in one oak barrel and then another oak barrel, and you go on and on and then finally you bottle it and even then you say, 'Well, please don't drink it for five years.'" What Fritz didn't tell Michael that day was that, since the 1970s, he had been thinking about becoming a sculptor! Rather than building up like painting, he wanted to create sculpture, in Michelangelo's words, "fashioned by the effort of cutting away." Fritz wanted to distill—to release the angel in the marble. He wanted to make rye whiskey. And he longed to replace what his friend Steve Jobs called "the heaviness of being successful" with the lightness of being a novitiate again.

From his early days as a brewer, Fritz had been drawn to neglected history like a moth to flame. He had essayed at becoming the alchemist of steam,

porter, ale, barley wine, and more, turning forgotten, unrecognized, unappreciated "lead" into gold. From that time on, he'd dreamed of taking beer to the next step. To Fritz, whiskey represented the natural apotheosis of beer. Both begin with a mash, but with whiskey, it's the mash itself that undergoes fermentation. The mash goes into a pot still, where it is heated, creating a vapor containing water and alcohol. Because alcohol is lighter than water, the water falls back into the still. The alcohol, however, rises up and out of the still into a coiled condenser where, as it cools, it becomes liquid and *trickles down* or *falls in drops*—the original meanings of the word *distill*. Surprisingly, what comes out of the still looks nothing like whiskey—it gets its color from the barrel—but as the distillate flows from the condenser, the distiller gets to choose what will be saved, what will be redistilled, and what will be discarded. It's called the distiller's cuts—a sculptor's decision. The initial runoff is called *heads*, the final runoff *tails*, and the middle—the angel in the marble—*hearts*, and making that decision is one of the great joys of distilling.

But why *rye* whiskey? In his time on the board of Grinnell College, Fritz got to know Warren Buffett, who admonished his fellow contrarian

THE ANCHOR BREWING STORY

investors to "be fearful when others are greedy, and greedy when others are fearful." In other words, when you find something that has fallen out of favor but still has intrinsic value, invest! And, Fritz knew, "rye was *so* out of favor!" Over the years, Fritz enjoyed the occasional Manhattan (originally made with rye, not bourbon) and the occasional martini (originally made with gin, not vodka). But when it came to rye, he was never a true believer, never satisfied that the ryes he was drinking were as authentic or as tasty as they once were or could be. So he began researching the subject (more of a challenge then, five years before Google). Fritz soon learned that rye whiskey was the original American whiskey, predating bourbon. Rye was the grain of choice along the East Coast, and when the early eastern settlers began to switch distilling from rum to whiskey, they made whiskey primarily from rye. George Washington distilled rye whiskey—one more reason he was a hero to Fritz. Fritz wanted to actually re-create these original rye whiskies, but to make that happen he needed to know more.

Fritz wanted to become as expert a historical distiller as he was a historical brewer. He began in his Anchor office, reading and studying and talking to various consultants. Anyone taking inventory of his antiquarian books on distilling might have guessed what he was up to. He traveled to Washington, DC, where he spent hours at the Library of Congress and the Distilled Spirits Council of the United States (DISCUS), a trade association similar to the USBA. He also traveled to Europe. Fritz had a motto for whenever he or his staff headed "across the pond" for work: "Just tell 'em you're going back East—no one needs to know how far." He went to England, home of distilled dry gin; Holland, home of genever gin; and Scotland, home not only to Scotch whisky, but also to whisky experts Harry Riffkin and Jim Swan, who would later travel to San Francisco to help with Fritz's rye whiskey project. "Ahh, Jim Swan. He was the one who helped the most." Known deservedly in the industry as the Einstein of Whisky, Swan would be instrumental in helping Fritz's rye whiskey attain the remarkable flavor and aroma that belied its young age. Harry was "the distilling guy, who taught me how to do a double distillation, the wash, and all the rest of it."

Anchor's distillery was deliberately built in a distant corner of the warehouse, far away from prying eyes. The space had been a pallet repair station, though it was more appreciated for its basketball hoop. Fritz served as *spiritus rector*, having Gordon and Mark and their teams set up the wet-floor, tiling, platform, mash tuns, still, and barrel room. Linda and her team took care of the accounting and compliance, which, because there was no precedent of a brewery having its own in-house distillery, was as new to the government as barley wine had been in 1975. But it was particularly important to Fritz to involve employees who had never worked at the old brewery, including brewer Bruce Joseph, who had been at Anchor since 1980, as head distiller; Phil Rogers, who was hired in 1992, to assist Fritz with public relations; and me, who had started in 1991, to assist Fritz with research, story, label design, and packaging. Phil's Napa Valley Brewing Company—where he was chef turned brewmaster, years before Wolfgang Puck (whose favorite beer was Anchor Steam) opened his Los Angeles Brewing Company brewpub—had been featured in *The Beer Hunter*. PR was a cinch for Phil Rogers. But for the distillery, it was a conundrum, because it would have no public relations at all until there was a product to sell. Phil's job was to keep it a secret.

Fritz loved to provide fringe benefits for his employees, and one of the most coveted was being in on a company secret. "It's not just that secrets keep your product safe—there is a sense of camaraderie when you have secrets." And Fritz's employees had always kept their part of the bargain—as the ongoing mystery surrounding the ingredients in the Christmas Ales attests. They weren't the nuclear codes, but it seemed everybody wanted the inside scoop on what was new at Anchor—especially the copycats. So, as an additional precaution, the "gadget" (code for Anchor's

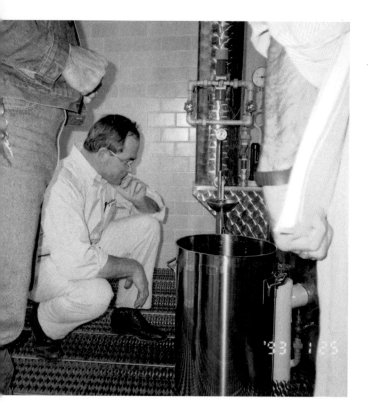

reapply those methods, honed by decades of study and experience, to a brand-new essay.

POT-DISTILLED SINGLE MALT RYE WHISKEY

The excavation of rye farmer/distiller George Washington's Mount Vernon distillery would not begin until 1999, but it was well known that his rye whiskey was made one batch at a time in a copper pot still. Pot stills remained the still of choice for American distillers until the late nineteenth century, when column stills, which allowed for continuous distillation and the efficient creation of a purer, higher-proof distillate, began to replace them, hastening the disappearance of pot-distilled American whiskey. "When we started our project, we were making the only pot-distilled whiskey in America, but then I realized I had to say the only *legal* pot-distilled whiskey, because of course the art of making whiskey in little batches still exists—it's just way up in the hills where the revenuers can't find it."

Fritz began with one small copper pot still, for which he later had local coppersmith Willard "Willy" Stryker make a custom whiskey top to match Fritz's sketches. Its still charge was just 250 liters (about 66 gallons). "Making whiskey in a pot still is really a more complicated affair than it might seem, because each time we distill we actually put some things back into what we are going to distill next time. It takes quite a few runs of this before it begins to even out, but eventually we're actually distilling pretty much the same type of material each time. We typically do two runs. The proof is lower on the first. On the final run we get the new spirit that we put in the barrel. The Bud bottle was kind of a joke," but it was the perfect container to help Fritz learn about the distiller's cuts:

You've heard about heads and tails and the middle cut and all that sort of thing. We had too, but

pot still) was safely ensconced out of sight behind two huge roll-up doors. Nevertheless, while Anchor's rye whiskey project was still under wraps, one of Anchor's maltsters couldn't resist tipping off another brewer that Anchor was buying rye malt. Assuming that Anchor must be about to release a rye beer, *they* released a rye beer, much to the Anchor crew's clandestine amusement.

On Tax Day, April 15, 1992, Fritz signed Anchor Brewing Company's application to register its distilled spirits plant. On January 6, 1993, Anchor Brewing, doing business as (d/b/a) Anchor Distilling Company (ADC), became licensed distiller #DSP-CA-199, the only known brewery to have its own in-house distillery. On January 25, as Fritz fired up his copper pot still for the first time, he couldn't help thinking of his chemistry set, his childhood, and his mom, explaining to him how alcohol was a "gift from God." He also thought of his first day brewing and all of the years he'd spent perfecting Steam Beer. Now he would need to

we needed to know, what happens during a run? We made several test runs where we separated each quart of distillate and kept it separate and numbered it, so that we could go back later and see what happened quart by quart during the run. So then we could go back later and say, with this run we saw that at quart #8, between 8 and 9, we began to see a change in such and such a direction. It just enabled us to get a linear view of what a typical distillation run would be.

Fritz's modern-day brewing knowledge and experience had impacted the historical decisions he made in re-creating a 4,000-year-old Sumerian beer, bringing a new perspective and vocabulary to the Hymn to Ninkasi. Now he would apply that same logic to re-creating 150- to 200-year-old American whiskeys. Legally, you could make rye whiskey with as little as 51% rye and still call it rye whiskey. The rest could be corn or some other source of fermentable sugar. But Fritz was going to make the only all-rye whiskey in America and the only whiskey made with all-rye malt. He didn't have to, but Fritz, who had pioneered the return of all-malt beers to American brewing, didn't see why, other than cost perhaps, anyone *wouldn't* make all-malt rye whiskey. "Today, for example, in Scotland, the single malt whiskies are all barley malt. Once upon a time, you couldn't really make a brew without using all malt, because the grain wasn't great, and the malting wasn't great, and the enzymes just weren't there. So I think the early distillers would also have used all malt, and that's why we're using all-rye malt."

Correspondence between George Washington and his nephew, William Augustine Washington, when George was at Mount Vernon, confirms Fritz's theory, at least for what appears to have been the most prized of G. W.'s rye whiskeys: "If you have any Whiskey of fine quality made intirely of Rye," wrote William to George in 1799, "you would oblige me by sending me a Barrel, it is the only Spirit I make use of, when I can get it good." George replied, "I thot the Whiskey had been sent; but Captn Bowcock postponed taking it on board it seems, until he made his second trip. Now, he has two barrels according to your desire; and if you should want *more*, or any of your neighbours want *any*, it would be convenient, & always in my power, to supply you."

Fritz's whiskey experiments kept him at the distillery for hours on end, where he worked hands-on and side-by-side with his employees, much as he had at 8th Street. Meanwhile, his brewery was chugging along on its way to a significant milestone. It had taken Fritz until 1986 to transform Anchor into a 500-brew-a-year brewery. Now, on December 2, 1993, the brewery achieved something that none of its brewmasters—from Brekle to Maytag—had dared dream: "We made brew

#1,000"—the first time that Anchor had ever brewed a thousandth batch of beer in one calendar year. For Fritz, it was like landing on the moon.

On December 4, every Anchor employee received a surprise "joy and gratitude bonus," a check for exactly $1,000—*after* taxes. With it came a handwritten note from Fritz, as well as a letter in which he wrote,

Together we have achieved something which is the wonder of the American brewing industry. You were there, you are a very real part of it, we did it together, we can all be very proud. So let's celebrate! We have become famous for making wonderful beers and pioneering a world brewing renaissance. We can all take pride in this. But I am especially proud of all of you for the way you work together. I often wonder if you all know how many people admire this company for our spirit of friendly cooperation and self-reliant working atmosphere. Constantly I hear very sincere compliments on the integrity and politeness and enthusiasm of Anchor employees. I love to hear it, and I think making 1,000 brews by early December is just an outer sign of our company's inner success. And that success is your achievement. I truly believe that this is terribly important, because I believe that our company's personality is our most valuable asset. I am very proud to be working with each of you.

RYE WHISKEY, ESSAY 1

A little over a year later, on December 9, 1994, Fritz bounded up the brewery stairs two at a time as usual. But he didn't tarry in his office. Fritz celebrated his fifty-seventh birthday in the distillery, transferring Essay 1 of his rye whiskey to barrels— but not just any barrels.

We had learned that as far back as the *eighteenth* century, when rye whiskey was first being

made, the barrels were made the way some fine wine barrels are made today, with a little oak-chip fire in the middle to soften the wood and help the cooper bend down the staves while putting it together. So there's some toasting that goes on, which would just occur naturally in a handmade barrel process. But the idea of *charred* barrels didn't occur until the *nineteenth* century.

Sometime around the 1820s, '30s, '40s, whiskey apparently began to be aged—and also aged in charred barrels—for the first time. The charring seems to have an effect in terms of mellowing, but it also makes for a darker whiskey, with more of an oaky character. Legally, rye whiskey must be aged in new, *charred* oak bar-

rels. So I had the idea of making the most traditional whiskey in America, and maybe in some ways the most traditional in the world, using nineteenth-century-style *oak-chip-fire-charred* oak barrels. And I went to a cooperage in Missouri, and I told them what I wanted, and they agreed to do it. Bruce, Mark, and I were there when they made them.

The rye whiskey that went in barrel on December 9, 1994, distilled in a small copper pot still from a mash of 100% rye malt, would be aged in those unique barrels—the only ones in the world at the time. On December 27, 1995, while Essay 1 was still aging, Essay 2 went into the same kind of barrels as Essay 1. The key difference was that Essay 2 would be aged longer—for the three years legally required to call it "straight rye whiskey" in California.

Fritz has a favorite saying: "How do you make a lot of water move? You just tip it a little bit." After repeated tastings to be sure it was ready, he put that saying into action on January 18, 1996. It was bottling day for 290 unfiltered gallons of Essay 4-RW-ARM-1-A of Old Potrero Single Malt Rye Whiskey, aged for one year and forty days and bottled at barrel strength of 124 proof (62% ABV). Fritz designed his label with the help of his Design Committee: artist Jim Stitt, graphic designer Jack Martin, and me, the project shepherd from design to bottling. It featured a small embossed copper still

with the letter A—which stood for Anchor Distilling, of course, but metaphorically for alpha as well, since the distillery represented the beginning of something new for Anchor. The essay number on the shoulder label 4-RW-ARM-1-A, indicated that the bottle's contents went in barrel in 1994, was **R**ye **W**hiskey made from **A**ll **R**ye **M**alt, and was Essay **1A**, Anchor Distilling's first. In California though, without being aged for three years in charred oak barrels, it could not be called whiskey. So there were two labels for the initial release—one said RYE WHISKEY and the other, for California only, said RYE. Single Malt? "Because we were from a single distillery and it was all malt." Old Potrero? Potrero for Potrero Hill and old because, as with Old Foghorn, the word *old* was not government regulated, and Fritz liked the "slightly naughty" idea of legally calling something that had only been in barrel for a year *old*.

With all his labeling ducks in a row, Fritz had 1,448 bottles of Old Potrero to sell, which he would do "one drink at a time." He knew that if he sent a pallet here and another there, his infinitesimal

inventory would disappear in an afternoon—to who knew where. So he sold Old Potrero to bars and restaurants only, from San Francisco to Washington, DC, *one bottle*—that's fifteen 50-ml pours—*at a time*. That way there would be no "hoarder's dram," and he'd maximize the number of people who'd get to sample this rare product.

There was a little education needed too. The first releases of Old Potrero were bottled at barrel strength. "I did that because I thought in the eighteenth and nineteenth centuries there was no point in shipping water around. If you can ship strong whiskey around, well, let the next guy water it down, right?" Scotch whisky aficionados knew that barrel-strength whiskey was best enjoyed with a little water, a ritual that had the dual effect of opening up its flavors and aromas for leisurely appreciation and avoiding consumption of this potent potable like a gold miner in a wild-west saloon. Those who heeded this advice were rewarded with a unique gustatory experience, described by Jim Murray, one of the few to whom Phil Rogers had revealed Anchor's secret distillery, as "honey, honeysuckle, and spice. Massively intense on the palate; fruit and delicious oils, rich and complex. A lengthy, oily finish with more honey, chocolate, and telltale rye hardness. Brilliant."

On April 18, 1996, four months after the first bottling of Anchor's *nineteenth*-century-style rye

whiskey, Essay 3 went in barrel. Coming out of the still, it was the same spirit as before. But instead of fire-*charred* barrels, Essay 3 would be aged in fire-*toasted* barrels, just as George Washington would have done in the *eighteenth* century, creating an "even more traditional rye whiskey." And since his Mount Vernon distillery had been G. W.'s way of quickly turning a field full of rye into a wagon full of whiskey, Fritz knew that this rye whiskey, like Washington's, had to be a young whiskey, sold not when it was old, but when it was *ready*. After one year, eight months in barrel, Essay 3 of Old Potrero Single Malt Whiskey was bottled on January 8, 1998. And it was delicious. There were more labeling challenges, of course, as could be expected with such a completely novel product. So Anchor called it Single Malt Spirit in California and Single Malt Whiskey everywhere else.

On January 14, 1999, after more than three years in barrel, Essay 2 was finally bottled. By that time, Essay 1A was already sold out. However, since both Essay 2 and 3 were for sale concurrently (on- and off-premise), rye whiskey enthusiasts now had the opportunity to compare them side-by-side. There was Essay 3: Old Potrero Single Malt Whiskey, Anchor's *Eighteenth*-Century-Style "*Revolutionary* Whiskey," aged in fire-toasted barrels "the way rye whiskey was made when George Washington was making rye whiskey." Michael Jackson described it

as "a peppery, oily dram with mint and chocolate notes." And there was Essay 2: Old Potrero Single Malt Straight Rye Whiskey, Anchor's *Nineteenth-Century-Style "Evolutionary* Whiskey," aged in fire-charred barrels. By contrast, Michael called it "spicy, buttery, and sweet." And there would be more essays to come, forever changing the way the world drinks and thinks about rye whiskey. Michael summed it up as "the most noteworthy development in American whiskey in living memory."

ANOTHER BREWING MILESTONE

In 1994, while Anchor Distilling was still in its infancy, Anchor Brewing reached another milestone. That year marked the first of four consecutive 100,000+ barrel years. Anchor was riding a wave that seemed would never crest. On December 11, 1994, Fritz sent a celebratory letter to his forty-eight employees. "For many years I have dreamed of a really nice 'Company Jacket,' informal but sharp, a jacket that would be special and fun, and something the public would not be able to get, only our employees and a few very special people who have lent us a helping hand over the years," from Fred Kuh to Don Saccani, John Segal to Otto

Seidenberg, Bill Hyde to Jim Stitt. The concept was a lot like the special-mold wheat beer bottles in 1984, which Fritz had reprised in 1989: "Only the brewery's inner circle" would get them. The idea for a jacket was based on one that Fritz's friend, Chef Barry Wine (an early supporter of Anchor Steam), had done for his Quilted Giraffe restaurant in Manhattan years before. Fritz and I designed Anchor's "killer jackets," as they came to be known, with the able assistance of Beverly Maytag. They were custom tailored, proudly worn, never sold, and even handed down from generation to generation. After the death of Fred Kuh in 1997, Fritz, Beverly, and I were especially touched to learn that Fred had bequeathed his jacket to his nephew.

INNOVATION IN A CHANGING INDUSTRY

In 1995, though Christmas Ale magnum sales were on the upswing, Fritz wanted to find year-round uses for Anchor's SMB bottling line. In 1995, Fritz, Jim, Jack, and I created a new look for Old Foghorn, inspired by Fritz's collection of old California fruit-crate labels. The unique 6-packs of 7-oz amber bottles looked like kid brothers to Anchor's 12-oz packaging. And Fritz loved the radically traditional twist for this throwback label, which was the first beer label printed using the cutting-edge technology of stochastic screening.

PHILLIPS STUDIOS

1995 marked the thirtieth anniversary of Fritz Maytag and Anchor. It also marked the thirtieth anniversary of Chet Helms and The Family Dog, which began producing dance concerts in the Bay Area in 1965. Fritz and I met with Chet and graphic artist Jim Phillips to design a commemorative label. Unfortunately but understandably, the California Department of Alcoholic Beverage Control rejected the label—not because they didn't care for rock and roll but because The Family Dog was an Anchor account and as such, couldn't receive something of value from the brewery like this custom label.

By 1996, the 22-oz "bomber" bottle had caught on, serving as entry-level, off-premise packaging for up-and-coming small brewers. So Anchor created a custom-mold 22-oz bottle—big brother to its 12-oz bottle—for Steam, Porter, Liberty, and Wheat, all bottled on the SMB line. Readers of history might ask if the release of this new packaging was in celebration of Anchor's centennial—or perhaps the 125th anniversary of Gottlieb Brekle's Golden City Brewery. But Fritz let those milestones come and go with barely a nod. Even without a birthday party, the brewery would sell 107,840 barrels of beer in 1996, more than Fritz's first fifteen years combined. Anchor had once again reached capacity. But Fritz did not wish to

relive the '70s by turning away new business, which centennial publicity would most certainly have generated. Plus, a brewery celebration would take the spotlight off a distillery debut: the 1996 release of Old Potrero, an innovation of which no other brewery could boast.

The wave that had lifted the craft beer industry—including its share of irrationally exuberant, opportunistic entrepreneurs—to unsustainable 58% growth in 1995, crested, crashing to 26% in '96 and 2.2% in '97. Fortunately for Anchor, it was a shakeout that Fritz, Nostradamus-like, had anticipated, and he was prepared for a relatively gentle landing based on the strength of Anchor's preeminence in the marketplace; its healthy, longtime relationships with its wholesalers; and especially his new distillery.

GINNING UP A NEW PRODUCT: JUNÍPERO GIN

Fritz had another idea for his copper pot still: gin. Like olive oil, "you could make it in the morning and enjoy it that night." And gin had a history, going back at least to the mid-1600s in Holland. Its true antecedents are even earlier, those first experiments in the ancient and mysterious art of distilling in the presence of herbs and spices. I was curious why Fritz hadn't started with gin and then gone to whiskey. "Simple," Fritz replied. "I wanted them to take us seriously. A gin distiller that makes whiskey on the side? Forget it. But a whiskey distiller that makes gin on the side, no problem."

When Churchill wrote about the scaffolding of rhetoric, he might well have been writing about the scaffolding of gin: "The subtle art of combining the various elements that separately mean nothing and collectively mean so much in an harmonious proportion is known to a very few." That scaffolding was in plain sight twice a week in the brewery lab. Fritz, Mark, Mike Lee, and Bruce convened every Tuesday and Thursday morning at 10 a.m. to blind-taste gin. First, they tasted gins from all over the world, with the goal of developing the same acute sense of taste and smell for gin—with vocabulary to match—that they already had for beer.

By law and tradition, gin must be made with juniper, the dried berries of *Juniperus communis*. "But the wonderful challenge for the distiller," as Fritz would later write for his gin label, "is in selecting and blending from a wide variety of additional botanicals, in order to impart a uniquely satisfying, balanced character" to one's gin. So, as Bruce recalls, "When we were working on the gin recipe, Fritz had a plan. We came up with a very basic gin recipe using four standard botanicals: juniper berry, orris root, angelica root, and coriander. And then to that recipe we would add one botanical and do distillations. And then the ones that we liked we would start using more."

Fritz recalls: "At one point I looked up and said, 'Well, it's not gin exactly, but we're in the ballpark.' And then we went back to work. We tasted and we tasted. And I'd look up at the group, and I usually went first, because it's a key question: if you're the boss, do you go first or last? So I think it's usually polite to go first and say, 'So this is my impression, and I can't wait to hear what everybody else thinks.' And that sets the tone."

Bruce continues: "For months, we continued meeting in the lab to taste what had been distilled. And we'd be sitting there, and we had the glasses of clear liquid." One morning, Fritz looked up and saw the brewery tour peering at them as if they were fish in an aquarium. "And I think Fritz—you know how he kinda likes to run with something—said, 'Oh, tell them that the most important thing in a brewery is the water and we have to test the water, and we don't want to let anything get by us for making Anchor Steam. The water has to be top notch.' And I think the tour guides started telling people that's what was going on in the lab. So Fritz dubbed us 'The Water Committee.'"

Anchor's gin would be made in a pot still from 100% grain neutral spirits, a base spirit that provides a sort of blank canvas for the flavors and aromas of the botanicals. Grain neutral spirits, which must be at or above 190 proof (95% ABV) in the US, cannot be made in a pot still, so they were distilled offsite in continuous column stills. This high-proof base spirit would then be *redistilled* at Anchor with juniper berries and all-natural botanicals. No extracts, essences, sugars, or flavors were added, nor would soaking, steeping, infusion, percolation, or maceration be involved. Bruce, as head distiller, would simply take the berries and botanicals in their natural state and mix them in a blender. Then he would add them directly to the grain neutral spirits in the pot still (which had its own special gin top). By redistilling just this once and then not filtering, Anchor was able to maintain the fresh botanical quality that would make its gin unique.

On Fritz's fifty-ninth birthday, December 9, 1996, the Water Committee gave Linda the recipe, which called for juniper berries plus fourteen botanicals, so she could submit it to the ATF for approval as what was called the formula. Each ingredient was listed with a range of possible amounts. By using a lower range of zero for several of the ingredients, Anchor gave itself the option not to use that ingredient at all and did its legal best to keep the exact recipe a secret. The final recipe would call for juniper berries plus a dozen botanicals. Having learned the lesson of the rye beer, Fritz established a separate company, which became what Bruce calls "the secret botanical-ordering arm of Anchor Brewing." It would serve Anchor well for everything from gin to Christmas Ale. The formula was approved December 18, by which time the Water Committee was already fine-tuning the relative proportions of the botanicals, tasting after tasting. It was a long but never tedious process. One morning, Fritz looked up at the Water Committee and said, "It's beautiful. We could keep going like this for years, fiddling around. But this is beautiful stuff. Let's stop and put this in the bottle!" And they did.

Fritz said almost the same thing to the Design Committee, finishing with something like, "Let's stop and put this on the bottle!" The clean, elegant look of the label, with Jim's graceful script *Junípero Gin*, would be as singular as the product itself. Deciding on the final proof was easy and fun. Like his whiskey, Fritz's gin was unfiltered, so a higher proof would help avoid haziness in the product when chilled. With tongue in cheek, he chose a proof of 98.6 to match a normal body temperature of 98.6: "You won't even know you're drinking it!"

On December 30, 1997, Anchor bottled its unfiltered, pot-distilled Junípero Gin, Essay 7-DDG-GNS-1 (for 1997—the year the recipe was finalized, **D**istilled **D**ry **G**in, **G**rain **N**eutral **S**pirits, Essay **1**). To price it, Fritz recalls,

Mark and I went to the Liquor Barn. All of the gins were $13, $14 a bottle. And then we went

to the vodkas, which were right next to the gins. And, wow, there were the special label vodkas and what are they selling for? $30. And there were lightbulbs over each of our heads, but it was the *same lightbulb*. And then Mark took it one lightbulb further: "A bartender who knows how to charge for a $30-a-bottle-vodka martini will know how to charge for a $30-a-bottle-gin martini."

Eric Asimov of the *New York Times* called Junípero Gin "smooth, clean, and very dry, with assertive, classic flavors of juniper and citrus: a martini with one eyebrow raised." Lawrence Marcus of *Variety* said, "This does the London Dry style better than anything from the UK. Power, spice, perfume, and balance. It might be the most perfect gin around." And *Departure*

Magazine's Oliver Schwaner-Albright called it, "arguably America's greatest gin." Ringing endorsements all, but Fritz and Mark wanted to hear from mixologist Dale DeGroff, the King of Cocktails, whose court was the Rainbow Room, high atop Manhattan's Rockefeller Center. After all, gin was all about martinis, and martinis were all about gin. But sometimes, even at its high proof, Junípero could still take on a little haze in an ice-cold martini. Dale expressed his concern that, as good as Junípero tasted with your eyes closed, the world was just not ready for an unfiltered gin, especially in anything other than a dirty martini. Fritz, with unflappable resolve, stuck to his gins. Remembering Ron Siebel's sage advice about unfiltered Guinness, he came up with not one but two bewitching synonyms for chill haze, including them on a special neckhanger for every bottle of Junípero:

One interesting aspect of this essay, 7-DDG-GNS-I, is that we have chosen not to filter it, in order that the maximum amount of fresh and intense flavors and aromas may be carried over from the botanicals. As a result, a very slight veil, or opalescence, may develop when this gin is chilled and diluted with water, a sign that it is an utterly traditional product.

ANCHOR SMALL BEER

In the 1990s, as Fritz hoped, the attention Anchor Distilling attracted for its whiskey and gin spilled over onto Anchor Brewing. But the brewery was not resting on the distillery's laurels. Instead, Anchor Brewing was continuously improving equipment and processes throughout its beehive-like building, from a new line for 13.2- and 5.16-gal kegs to a second ale fermentor. The best example perhaps, for which Peter Kollnberger deserves a lot of credit, was the installation of a special tank under the brewhouse and the possibilities it created.

Hidden away beneath the brewhouse, this combo tank (CTK for short), served as a holding tank, reducing the gridlock that sometimes occurred on multiple-brew days. Anchor was making four brews a day, starting at 5 a.m. and finishing up around 11 p.m. Wednesday was ale day—two ale brews followed by the weekly polishing of the kettles. Like adding a burner to the kitchen stove, the CTK enabled Anchor to make five brews in the time it had taken to make four, without affecting the beer. But Fritz saw another use: the possibility of reviving an ancient tradition and another historic beer whose "stock was at 1."

The tradition of brewing two or three distinct beers from one mash has existed in homebrewing for thousands of years, and for centuries the term *small beer* was used to describe the lightest and weakest of these beers. Though it didn't prevent scurvy like spruce beer, this low-alcohol beverage provided British troops, the working class, mothers, wet-nurses, and even infants with a safe, dependable source of hydration and nutrition. Popular with the Continental Army during the American Revolution, small beer was a staple at Valley Forge. Even Thoreau, not known for his drinking, wrote his sister in summer 1852, "I would exchange my immortality for a glass of small beer this hot weather." By association and with an assist from Shakespeare, the term came to mean a triviality, something of little importance. The 1716 edition of *The Whole Art of Husbandry* offers a typical recipe:

For the Brewing of Small-Beer, or common Ale, take something above the quantity of a Barrel of Water scalding hot, which put into your Mashing-tub alone; let it cool 'till you can see your Face in it, and put to it four Bushels of Malt, pouring of it in by degrees, and stirring of it well: Let it stand on the Malt two Hours . . . then draw it off, and let it boil. . . . Of this first Wort you may make a Barrel of Ale: After this is boiled, scald about a Barrel of Water more, and put it upon your Malt, letting it stand an Hour and an half: This draw off, and put the same quantity of hot Water on again, observing the same Rules, as before directed, of this you may make an Hogshead [apx 64 US gallons] of Small-Beer.

Since 1975, Anchor had been making Old Foghorn from the rich first runnings of consecutive all-malt mashes. Until 1997, the configuration of the brewhouse made it virtually impossible to do anything with the leftover but still viable grain, other than have it trucked away to a dairy farm for cattle feed. But with the CTK tank and two ale fermentors, Anchor could make Old Foghorn as usual *and* make small beer. On March 5, 1997, Anchor gave it a try. It worked. Anchor Small Beer was born. Thanks to an extra dose of hops in the kettle, it is surprisingly full-flavored, almost like an English bitter, and thirst-quenching. When Fritz asked what kind of bottle to use for small beer, Mark chimed in: "Big 22-oz bottle, small label." Bottled for the first time on July 8, 1998, it was a delicious re-creation of a historical beer, with the added benefit that, at only 3.3% ABV, a big bottle of Small was the perfect midday refresher for Anchor's employees and guests.

SAN FRANCISCO'S BREWERY

Anchor provided good jobs for San Franciscans, who spent money every day at Potrero Hill coffee shops, bars, restaurants, supermarkets, barbershops, and dry cleaners. But in the 1990s, Fritz grew increasingly concerned that its hometown, once a vibrant hub of manufacturing, was on a path toward becoming "another Carmel." That could doom manufacturers like Anchor. Fritz contemplated moving the brewery to South San Francisco or Napa, "but gradually realized we should stay in the City. We really benefit from it, but we should figure out a way to benefit even more from the positive side of San Francisco." That led to new

ideas about how to embrace and celebrate Anchor's deep-rooted connection to the city of its birth. One of them was an Anchor Brewing San Francisco calendar.

In December 1997, Fritz sauntered into my office with a familiar "great idea" look on his face. "I bought a picture and have an idea for an Anchor calendar."

"For 1998?"

"Yep. Let me show you. It's in my office."

The moment I saw it, I understood. It was one of Fritz's many great ideas that was also a good idea. It was an original nineteenth-century tinted lithograph printed by Edward Bosqui, who had arrived in San Francisco in 1850. Its title: *View of San Francisco, Formerly Yerba Buena, in 1846-7 Before the Discovery of Gold* (see page 5 [EPIGRAPH]). In early 1998, with the help of San Francisco designer Elaine Kwong, a new tradition began at Anchor: a San Francisco calendar that, from 1998 through 2010, told the story of San Francisco from

1842 through 1878. Anchor sent these free of charge to everyone in its orbit who could legally receive one. "It was magical. It was expensive. It was a brilliant success. We benefited. *Everybody's favorite city*. And so that was where the calendar idea came from. That we would identify. And one of the biggest mistakes that I ever made was to not follow through with the idea of printing one where all of the dates were wrong, so it would have no intrinsic value and we could give it to our retailers—and it would be *legal!*"

GENEVIEVE GIN

In the late 1990s, Fritz's idea of offering two rye whiskeys from two different eras made him think to do a second gin. It would be a re-creation of the earliest gins, which are variously known as genever, jenever, Geneva gin, Hollands gin, or Schiedam-style gin. Like rye whiskey, there were a few modern-day examples of the product. But Fritz wanted to make his genever the way it was made in the seventeenth century: distilled, like whiskey, in a pot still from an all-grain mash. Anchor's pot still would get its own special genever top, handmade by Willy Stryker from sketches Fritz made in Holland while researching this ancient spirit. And Fritz decided on a historically appropriate combination of wheat, barley, and rye malts. Like Junípero, Anchor's genever would be made with juniper berries and other botanicals. But as a novel twist for this genever, Fritz opted to use *the same botanicals* as Junípero in *the same ratios*, facilitating comparison. As such, the two gins represented what I called "the alpha and omega of the gin story." Genevieve Gin was first made in 1999 and stored in stainless steel until 2007, when it was bottled for the first time. Concerned that it might be confused with Junípero, Fritz simply wanted more time to think about the label. No one at Anchor minded the delay. They all understood that they were working not so much for one company as for one person.

FIN DE SIÈCLE

During Fritz's tenure at Anchor, the brewery collaborated extensively with local photographers Lars Speyer, Andree Abecassis, Kirk Amyx, and Terrence (Terry) McCarthy. In 1999, as the millennium drew to a close (for some, in 1999; for others, 2000), Fritz asked Terry to do a photo essay featuring each member of the Anchor team at work. The project culminated in two group photographs. Fritz wanted one of them to look like the original nineteenth-century photos in the taproom, suggesting that everyone study those pictures and make their own costumes for the shoot. Terry would take the photos in the Anchor Brewery Annex across the street, where Anchor's old brew kettle and Meyer-Dumore bottle cleaner were stored. First there would be the 1899-style photo, with stiff poses and serious faces to imply the long exposure times necessary back in the day. And there would be no bottles, because Anchor was draught only until 1933. Then there would be a break for lunch, beer, and a change of clothes. The 1999 shot would have everyone wearing what they normally wore at work—mostly the white Anchor coveralls that had been standard-issue since Fritz and Gordon started wearing them in the 1960s. And there would be wide smiles, lots of bottles, and even Liberty Ale.

When the day finally arrived, the phones were turned off, the front door locked, and a sign posted: "Closed Today for Company Meeting." After much merriment and a last-minute scramble to make more Magic Markered, cardboard-cutout mustaches, Terry quieted everyone down, got everyone into position—with open eyes—and started clicking away from his perch atop a brewery ladder. It was one of those unforgettable Anchor days. Terry, as mighty with the pen as with the Pentax, described it best:

At its visible surface, this brewery is a harmonic wonder of copper and bronze, steel, concrete, and glass; the beauty of its forms generated by the logic of their functions. Deeper, inside the process, brewing is all sun and rain, sowing and harvest. An ancient art. A storied practice. A tradition manifest here every day in fresh beer.

At the very heart of the enterprise are its people— their skill, diligence, pride of craft, and sense of history are everywhere apparent. Photographing here, I witnessed that purpose daily in the faces and bearing of the fifty-seven people who work at Anchor Brewing. These photographs mean to honor them. Men and women whose skill is self-evident, but whose pride in and loyalty to the Anchor tradition is the deeper, richer seam.

—Terrence McCarthy, December 1999

1. Steve Johnson	12. Alex White	24. Richard Gossett	35. Bayley Moynihan	47. Phil Rodriguez
2. Dave Burkhart	13. Lloyd Knight	25. Clem Off	36. Mike Moelter	48. Julia Damir
3. Chris Morgan	14. Sue Herring	26. Tom Holmes	37. Ellen Bergeron	49. Gilberto Coote
4. Eddie Heston	15. Robin Heston	27. Lynne Mangione	38. Bob Anders	50. Rodrigo Santos
5. Bill Kiebala	16. Tom Riley	28. Kevin West	39. Rick Hendricks	51. Gordon MacDermott
6. Eric Svendberg	17. Julio Peix	29. Ollie Lagomarsino	40. Andrea DeVries	52. Mark Carpenter
7. Phil Longenecker	18. Dave Bates	30. Darek Ochtera	41. Teresa Gordillo	53. Linda Rowe
8. Niels Legallet	19. Tim Herring	31. Ismael Lopez	42. Mike Lee	54. Bette Riley
9. Mario Gardin	20. Jim Glowner	32. Matt Cooper	43. Marie Goulet	55. Mitch Perry
10. Dan Mitchell	21. Dan Riley	33. Jerry Probert	44. Tom Littig	56. Kendra Scott
11. Marek Pastuszynski	22. Bruce Joseph	34. Bob Brewer	45. Fritz Maytag	57. Jason Ellis
	23. Phil Rogers		46. Chris Solomon	

UNENDING CURIOSITY
(2000–2010)

He has got an unending curiosity. He carefully, intelligently examines what makes quality and then goes out and produces it.

—**Paul Draper,** *San Francisco Chronicle* (2004)

In 1779, Ben Franklin wrote to French friend André Morrelet about everyday miracles: "Behold the rain which descends from heaven upon our vineyards, and which incorporates itself with the grapes to be changed into wine; a constant proof that God loves us, and loves to see us happy." Two hundred sixteen years later, during a talk Fritz gave to a group of beer marketers, he deliberately and playfully misquoted America's founding polymath: "Beer is living proof that God loves us and wants to see us happy." Reprinted in *Beverage World* in February 1996, Fritz's version took on a Franklinian life of its own. It amused Fritz no end, especially because his journey from winemaker to brewer to distiller was coming full circle. *In vino veritas*.

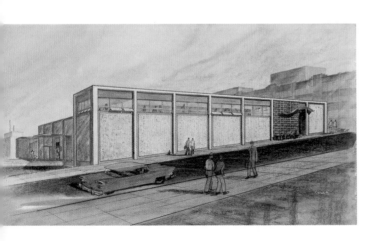

495 De Haro in 1960

Fritz had been home-winemaking at York Creek Vineyards for years, and in 1987 he even made a port. But in the early 1990s it was hard for him to resist turning this hobby into a business. So he asked up-and-coming young winemaker Cathy Corison to help him make wine from his York Creek grapes, but not at York Creek—he had vowed never to turn his family retreat into a winery. Fritz and Cathy both saw themselves as farmers who loved wine and winemaking. And, as Cathy told podcaster Doug Schafer in 2018, "layered in on top of that was the fact that it was a whole series of living systems that conspired to the alchemy in your glass."

The first fruits of their labors were the "York Creek Cellars" 1992 Port and 1992 Meritage Red Wine. Meritage is a new-world name for an old-world blend of Bordeaux varieties. It combines the words *merit* and *heritage*, and rhymes with *heritage*—not *arbitrage*. Beer, of course, is just beer—easy to drink and easy to pronounce. But wine? The irony of hearing faux-pas–phobic wine drinkers saying "meritahzh" with a thick French accent was not lost on Fritz. There was also Pinot Blanc, reviewed by Eric Asimov in the *New York Times* in 2001: "It is usually said that Pinot Blancs are best when young, and most wines now available are 1998's or 1999's. But I did run across a few 1996's from York Creek Cellars that had softened and smoothed out with age, proving once again that when it comes to wine, conventional wisdom is best left for conventions." And unconventional wisdom? That was Fritz all over.

A GROWER'S WINERY IN SAN FRANCISCO

In 1997, Fritz exercised his option to buy the old Wing Nien Foods property, hoping to use part of its 21,600-sq-ft building to open his very own San Francisco winery, a first in modern times. Built in 1960, the unassuming structure at 495 De Haro was designed by San Francisco–born architect Rollo Simpson Wheeler. Once Fritz had the building, plus a few more harvests and bottlings with Cathy under his belt, he applied for a license, which the ATF granted September 26, 2000, just in time for crush.

As with the distillery, the winery was a d/b/a of Anchor Brewing Company, so it was Gordon's crew that magically transformed about a quarter of the building's main floor to create a wet-floor and barrel room. Fritz designed special, round open-fermentation tanks, which were temperature controlled and could be used with or without their lids. And he "stole" brewer Tom Holmes out of the brewhouse to be his assistant winemaker. Tom, who'd started at Anchor in 1992, completed his BA and MBA while working at the brewery, thanks in part to the financial assistance Anchor still offered for employee education.

Fritz was inspired by California winemaker E. H. Rixford to create his own "Grower's Winery":

In about 1965, friends told me about a recent discovery in a collector's cellar, 1936 and '38 Cabernets from a winery on the San Francisco Peninsula called La Questa. When I tasted them, suddenly I had a newfound confidence that California could compete with the best from Bordeaux. Here was a true pioneering California

vintner! His winery was long gone, but I learned that there were a few giant, old Cabernet vines in the backyards of houses built years later amidst his original vineyard. By this time, I was planting my own vineyard, and in 1973 I went sneaking around in Woodside cutting "bud wood" for a few test rows of what I believe to be the original La Questa clone. I don't know where Mr. Rixford found his cuttings, but I am confident that it would have been from a fine Bordeaux vineyard, for he was a man with a mission.

Cabernet Franc, 100% Petit Verdot, and so on. He would do the same for his port blend. How many could say they'd made and bottled port varieties like Touriga Nacional or Tempranillo as wines in their own right, and how might tasting such bottled wines help him perfect his blends? In deference to Paul Draper, Fritz did not make a Zinfandel or Petite Sirah, but that did not stop Fritz from giving those grapes a tryout in his port. York Creek Port was especially fun because the unaged brandy used to fortify it was made across the street at Fritz's own distillery—and it doesn't get more "estate" than that! Fritz would also take advantage of his distillery to make a radically traditional York Creek Grappa from the pressed pomace of his Cabernet Sauvignon and Merlot wines, as well as experimental apple brandies from York Creek's apple trees.

Apple was just one of the more than twenty-four tree species that flourished at York Creek, "an

That mission including Rixford's groundbreaking 1883 book *The Wine Press and the Cellar*, in which he expressed the hope that every grower in the state will "devote a portion of his ground to the cultivation of the choicest varieties of grapes, making sure that he knows what he is cultivating, will use the best methods of vinification, preserve each kind of wine by itself, or keep a careful record of his blends, and will age and rear the different products according to the best and most intelligent methods." Fritz devoted the "Horseshoe Block" of his vineyard to the La Questa cuttings, and his York Creek Horseshoe Cabernet—distinctive, spicy, rich—became his liquid homage to the early days of California winemaking.

Fritz essayed winemaking using many of the exploratory methods he'd developed for beer, whiskey, and gin—with the help of his new camera-equipped microscope. He had about 125 acres planted at his vineyard, growing about fifteen varieties in fifty different blocks. Like Rixford, Fritz was insatiably curious about each grape variety, different soils, exposures, and clones, so made many small, experimental batches. If he were going to make a Bordeaux blend, for example, he felt it important to make and bottle separate wines from each grape: a York Creek 100% Merlot, 100%

extraordinary richness of flora," as Fritz described it, "perhaps unequaled anywhere in California's Coast Range." These trees, along with the Japanese scrolls he'd seen in Japan, inspired Fritz's concept for the York Creek label. He drove Jim Stitt and his sketchbook all over York Creek's some 850 acres. Jim's delicate tree illustrations reflect the idyllic beauty of the vineyard as well as the care with which Fritz created his fine wines.

The Cabernet Sauvignon Estate, Port, and Pinot Blanc became the three flagships of the YCV fleet. Bottlings took place inside a mobile bottling company's semitrailer, parked outside the winery. "Be nice to them," Fritz joked with me, "or they will unhook and drive away." Fritz's San Francisco winemaking endeavor continued for ten years. It was another example of making something in the City for its own sake, while contributing to the vibrance of SF's economy and workforce. And it was the winery that ultimately cemented Fritz's decision to keep Anchor in San Francisco—plus being "chairman of the board" of three companies with the same parking spot!

FRITZ'S MANY HATS

Fritz celebrated the birth of his twin grandchildren in 2000 with a special Christmas label that year, featuring two "California nutmeg" trees (*Torreya californica*). By that time, he was widely heralded as the "grandfather of craft brewing." To some, it was "godfather" or "father," as in founding father, or just OG. Personally, he preferred *father*—after all, he was only sixty-two—but accepted all such honorifics with his inimitable Middle Western modesty. Either way, Fritz remained very much on the cutting edge of brewing, as well as the cutting edge of tech.

So he was flattered when Microsoft approached him about "paying!" the brewery to do a special bottling of Anchor Steam in magnum and 7-oz bottles for the launch of Windows 2000 in San Francisco. Fortunately, no one from Microsoft noticed the iMac G3 in Fritz's office or the irony that, at the height of the dot-com bubble, Anchor didn't have a website. With the brewery, distillery, and winery all in the air like spinning plates, such things took time. Launched in February 2001, anchorbrewing.com would play a key role in stimulating worldwide interest in Anchor, its beers, its history, and its hometown.

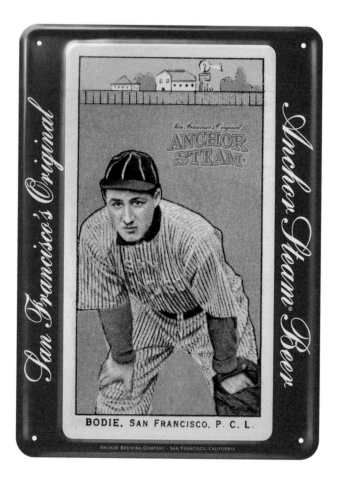

"Let's go for it," said Fritz. "But how will we be able to find rare, hundred-year-old baseball cards?"

"eBay," I replied.

"Have fun," said Fritz.

The restaurant's business turned around and heads turned in the Giants' front office. Anchor was helping them connect with San Francisco's baseball history, which goes back to the sandlot days. In 2001, Fritz took classic to plastic, introducing plastic bottles of Anchor Steam—which looked just like the glass ones—in the stands, where thousands of fans cheered Barry Bonds to his record-breaking seventy-third home run. Just as Fritz had hoped, Anchor was being seen more and more for what it had always been: meibutsu (the "fame-thing"), an integral part of what makes San Francisco such a special place to live, work, and play ball.

A CHANGING LANDSCAPE

Between 1990 and 2000, the number of US breweries had risen dramatically, if not recklessly, from 284 to 1,566. But annual growth of the craft beer industry had declined, from 29% to just 0.7%. During that same period, the Nasdaq Composite Stock Index soared like Icarus from 329 to 4,573. But by 2002, the dot-com bubble had burst and the economic impact of 9/11 was pervasive. The Nasdaq dropped to 1,172. For breweries, especially in tourism-dependent cities like San Francisco, the post 9/11 decline in the bar and restaurant business hit hard. As capital dried up, more breweries were closing than opening, the total number of US breweries dropping to 1,447 in 2005.

This second shakeout did not catch Fritz off guard. Paradoxically, the proliferation of US craft brewers in the 1990s had helped him manage the size of his brewery without huge price increases or significant out-of-stocks. By 2002, Anchor Brewing had returned to a sort of set point—in the

San Francisco's hometown baseball team, the Giants, celebrated their move from foggy Candlestick Park to sunny Pac Bell Park on Opening Day, April 11, 2000. Only a mile from the brewery, its scoreboard was visible from Anchor's roof. Anchor ambassador (as Fritz still called his salespeople) Dan Mitchell noticed that one of the ballpark's restaurants pouring Anchor Steam was struggling because their restaurant's decor didn't have anything to do with baseball. Dan suggested life-size San Francisco baseball cards. The only problem was that Giants baseball cards were subject to Major League Baseball restrictions and San Francisco Seals baseball cards from the great DiMaggio era were still in copyright. So I suggested cards from the City's legendary championship ball club, the 1909 San Francisco Seals.

ANCHOR SUMMER BEER

The craft beer revolution was turning beer consumers into beer enthusiasts, more knowledgeable than ever about a myriad of styles and flavors. And new platforms for self-posted ratings and reviews were democratizing the way beer drinkers consumed and disseminated information. When Anchor released its filtered wheat beer in 1984, it was the only beer of its kind. Few Americans had ever heard of wheat beer. And even fewer had ever heard of, let alone tried, Hefeweizen, an *unfiltered* wheat beer with the yeast left in suspension in the bottle. Eighteen years later, well-informed beer geeks bought Anchor's filtered wheat beer, only to be disappointed that it wasn't a Hefeweizen. Or they didn't buy it, because they didn't like Hefeweizens and assumed Anchor's wheat beer *was* one. Clearly, Anchor Wheat Beer, as tasty as always, needed a millennial makeover.

In 2002, after Fritz and I spent an afternoon surfing the internet, we decided it was time to give this twentieth-century brew a twenty-first-century name: Anchor Summer Beer. To test-market the name, we told a few friends that Anchor was thinking about releasing a summer beer. "Oh, I *love* summer beer," said everyone, as if that name told them all they needed to know about Anchor's lawnmower beer! "We've changed the brew," Fritz told his distributors, "as well as the name and the look, to better capture the 'feel' of this crisp, refreshing beer." The ABV went up, if only a little bit, to 4.2%. But since the label said "wheat and barley malt," the ATF reminded Anchor that "this product must be made with at least 25% malted wheat." No need. Anchor used over 50% malted wheat—one reason it was so crisp, clean, and refreshing. Soon, Anchor Summer Beer was the "summer seasonal" in demand year-round.

While Anchor Summer Beer was flying off the loading dock, Fritz was in New York City, nominated by the James Beard Foundation for its prestigious annual Outstanding Wine and Spirits

80,000- to 90,000-barrel range—the brewery equivalent of owning a small, profitable restaurant with a great reputation and a solid customer base. The distillery and winery arms of the business helped Anchor meet the challenges of the 2000s. And Fritz knew that maintaining a growth mindset would help inoculate the brewery against further decline. To do so it would be critical to activate and motivate all three tiers of the three-tier system—wholesalers, retailers, consumers. So Fritz asked his nephew John Dannerbeck, who would play a key role at Anchor for the next fourteen years, to help him with his "wholistic" approach to Anchor Brewing: integrity, authenticity, and quality combined with a "benign, benevolent, warm attitude toward brewing as a trade"—from the little brewpub down the street to the giant one across the Bay, and from the neophyte beer drinker to the jaded one—as well as being "absolutely gracious, polite, supportive, helpful, and straight" with all three tiers.

Professional Award. Fritz was not nervous. This was his ninth nomination in ten years at the so-called foodie Oscars, and when he lost again in 2002, it was just another "always a groomsman, never a groom" moment for him. A year later, though, back in his tux and back in Manhattan, Fritz was delighted to accept the 2003 Award, especially meaningful because it was the first Beard Award for a member of the brewing trade: a recognition that beer had finally taken its place at the table with wine, spirits, and good food.

Asked in March 1983 "how someone interested in Japanese philosophy found fulfillment in a brewery," Fritz told the *Chronicle*'s Blake Green of his "profound appreciation for a certain thread of philosophy that runs through Mahayana Buddhism . . . that is the type of thing that permeates the best of Japanese society. . . . Brewing is somehow related to that: You don't make the beer; you get everything ready and the beer makes itself." As the years went by, this became Fritz's philosophy for running his company: You get everyone ready, and the company makes itself. Early on in my time at Anchor, I noticed a 6-pack of Anchor Steam sitting in the center of the lunchroom table. I learned that day that if there was a 6-pack there, Fritz had put it there and something was wrong with it—could be a crooked label, short-filled bottle, or a scratched crown. Anything. There was no lecture, no meeting, no memo, no discussion. But by the end of the day the problem was solved.

In the 2000s, it seemed that Fritz gave his staff more responsibility and trust than ever before, which, of course, made everyone work that much harder to show how much they deserved it. No one at Anchor had ever suggested a tree for the Christmas Ale label until 2003, when I suggested the Sitka spruce for the two-hundredth

anniversary of the Lewis and Clark Expedition. Jim drew the tree, but thanks to the American Philosophical Society, the botanical illustration on the neck label came from Meriwether Lewis's journal, where he described this noble tree of the West for the first time. In 2009, it was brewer Kevin West who had a great idea that was too good to ignore: the monumental Monterey cypress at the eastern entrance to Golden Gate Park. Since its first lighting during the Depression, it has been known as the official San Francisco Christmas tree.

On January 6, 2005—Epiphany—Fritz received the sad news that his longtime friend John Segal had died from melanoma. Many times over the years, Fritz would get an idea for a historical beer, do extensive research, and slowly develop a recipe and label. In this case, that process happened in a flash. John, a lover of bock beer—a strong, malty beer first brewed in the Hanseatic League town of Einbeck in Lower Saxony and a favorite of Martin Luther—had thrown a bock party every year to celebrate the arrival of spring. And he'd begged Fritz to brew a bock for the occasion. On March 7, 2005, one day before what would have been John's seventy-seventh birthday, Anchor brewed a bock for the party, which would be a celebration of life and of spring. Most bocks feature a goat on the label, and most of them look fierce and intimidating. Fritz spent hours with the Design Committee trying to get Anchor Bock's goat just right—young and playful, but just slightly naughty. The colors on the label had to be just right too, "like a bouquet of flowers." Fritz's employees got such a kick out of Anchor Bock Beer that, after a little nudge from John Dannerbeck, he added it to the lineup later that year.

THINKING ABOUT RETIREMENT

The highs and lows of the first years of the new millennium got Fritz thinking, sometimes out loud:

We used to have a meeting every payday, and the original idea was it's a safety meeting; we'd provide lunch, and then we'd have safety. And the office staff had to come too because we're all in it together, and even though Bayley, for example, may feel perfectly safe sitting at her desk with a keyboard, she's part of a team where we're risking our lives, literally, down in the bottle shop. And I started to say at some point, "You realize, you guys, although we're doing well, there's no guarantee that a goofy little company like this can survive. We had our ups and downs, you know, there were years when we were—I was—very worried. And if you want a fulltime job with a guarantee, you should go to the post office." I used to say that. I thought I should sort of start reminding everybody. But then I started saying, "I'm not gonna be here forever. Something's gonna happen. I'm gonna die, or retire, or get sick." I don't remember why I started saying that or when exactly, but part of it was talking to myself. You know, you have to think out loud.

Since 1979, when the Mariposa Street brewery opened, Fritz had parked beneath the brewhouse and walked up the spiral stairs to his office. But since 2000, when he began spending a lot of time at the winery, Fritz would sometimes park and head directly across the street. And if you needed to ask him something, he never minded if you dropped by the winery for a quick chat. After a morning at the winery, he would walk back across the street and bound up the front stairs to his office, often to the excited surprise of people on their way in for a tour. "I used to think to myself, if I ever stop going up the stairs two at a time, I should retire. (I love this.) And then one day I noticed I was going up the stairs one step at a time. Yeah, I don't know. I'd worked for a *long* time."

Gordon, after thirty-six years, had retired in 2004, but not before spending time mentoring Niels Legallet, who had been with Anchor since 1993. Gordon was eager to spend more time windsurfing, skiing, drumming in a rock band, ballroom dancing with his wife, and welding. The latter he could now do as an independent contractor whenever and as long as he felt like it and then head back to the beach. From 2012 to 2013 Gordon was back at the brewery as a welder, four and a half decades after Lawrence Steese hired him to build a wall.

Gordon, Mark, and Linda knew what was on Fritz's mind, that he was looking to retire and looking to sell. Fritz had always said that secrets were a gift, and they were old hands at keeping a secret. For the brewery rank and file, the gift was *not* being in on a secret of this magnitude. With the help of a very discreet consultant, Fritz started trying to find a buyer, long before his interest in selling was known. But it wasn't easy. Fritz was looking for someone who wanted both a brewery and a distillery. And he wanted to make a clean break, knowing that if Anchor remained in the family, he would never end up truly retired. Fritz was in good health, but even though he'd already lived sixteen years longer than his father had, and twelve years longer than his grandfather, he was concerned that if something happened to him, the estate tax would create problems for his family.

A NEW SPIRIT

Fritz kept busy. In 2005, ABC celebrated its fortieth anniversary under his leadership as well as the thirtieth anniversaries of Liberty Ale, Christmas Ale, and Old Foghorn. Anchor Bock Beer took off, on its way to a strong ten-year run. And there was the 2005 Christmas Ale, with Jim's gorgeous coast live oak on the label. The YCV harvest netted fifteen different wines, twelve of which would be

bottled unblended. And in 2006, ADC released its third distinct rye whiskey.

Back in 1995, Fritz had put some of the new spirit for Old Potrero Straight Rye into new charred oak barrels to be aged like bourbon. Ready in a little over three years, it was bottled in 1999. Also in 1995, Fritz put some of the same new spirit into once-used charred oak bourbon barrels like scotch. Not knowing when it would be ready or what it would taste like, he couldn't resist checking it now and again. In addition to the angel's dram, there was always the taster's dram! But unlike the other Old Potreros, this whiskey didn't taste ready . . . didn't taste ready . . . didn't taste ready— until boom! Suddenly, after more than ten years in barrel, it was ready. And it was scrumptious. Rich, big, complex.

But Fritz, though he wanted to call it Old Potrero, wasn't sure how to distinguish it from his eighteenth- and nineteenth-century-style Old Potreros already on the market. He asked me for ideas. With the hundredth anniversary of the 1906 San Francisco earthquake and fire coming up on April 18, I had an answer: Call it Old Potrero

HOTALING'S WHISKEY

After the 1906 San Francisco earthquake and fire, several clergymen asserted that the catastrophe had been divine retribution, visited upon the City for its wicked ways. Yet A. P. Hotaling & Co.'s Jackson Street whiskey warehouse survived. On Thursday, April 19, 1906, two of Hotaling's managers, as later recounted to a San Francisco newspaper called *The Argonaut,* convinced the military that, if "permitted to remove the stocks of whisky in the warehouse, we could take them into the devastated area east of Battery Street, where no further risk of fire existed, and thus preserve our property and materially reduce the peril of a greater catastrophe if it became necessary to dynamite our [high-octane] premises." Eighty barrel-rollers were engaged. "Our lure was pay at the rate of a dollar an hour to every man that would lay hands on a barrel of Old Kirk whisky and roll it down, from our warehouse at Jackson Street and Jones Alley [now Hotaling Place], two blocks and a half to Battery Street." With the help of a fire hose, the navy tugboat *Leslie,* two wine pumps, and a shift in the wind, the warehouse was saved. On April 21, more rollers were engaged to roll the barrels back to Hotaling's forty-year-old building.

Anchor Distilling's first release of Old Potrero Hotaling's Whiskey, bottled in 2006 to commemorate the anniversary of the 1906 San Francisco earthquake and fire, next to an original, pre-quake A. P. Hotaling decanter.

And so, according to *The Argonaut,* "while millions of dollars worth of normally non-inflammable material was reduced to ashes" thousands of "barrels of highly inflammable whisky were preserved intact in the heart of the tremendous holocaust."

After the fire, UC Berkeley professor Jerome Barker Landfield bumped into poet and wit Charles Kellogg Field, a close friend of A. P. Hotaling's son Richard. Field "accompanied me to Berkeley," Landfield recalled, "and I put him up at the Faculty Club for the night. As we walked down to the station on our way back to San Francisco, Field asked me for a blank piece of paper on which to write. I handed him a used envelope. On the back he penned these lines:

If, as they say, God spanked the town
For being over frisky,
Why did He burn the churches down
And save Hotaling's whiskey?"

The path of the Hotaling barrel rollers

Hotaling's Whiskey, after one of the greatest stories to come out of the earthquake (see page 237); bottle it at 100 proof, and use this essay #: MCMVI–MMVI. Fritz, who knew the story and was always on the lookout for connections between Anchor and San Francisco, said yes without hesitation, inaugurating another Anchor tradition, that of releasing a barrel or two of Hotaling's every April.

For years, Bruce had been doing all the distilling himself. Fortunately, in 2005, another person moved over from the brewery to become a distiller. She was Kendra Scott, who had started at Anchor in 1997, and whose work was pivotal to the distillery's success. In 2007, the Design Committee finally finished its label for Genevieve Gin, which included a cartouche-like embossed image of the curious, custom still top Anchor used for this product. Anchor now had two gins: a modern, distilled dry gin called Junípero and a seventeenth-century-style gin called Genevieve. The gins themselves were as different as the Golden Gate Bridge and the Golden Gate Park Dutch Windmill. And the labels themselves were quite different. But both gins were in the same flint (clear) bottle, both said Anchor, and both said Gin. That was enough, unfortunately, to befuddle the bartender at Harris', one of Fritz and Beverly's favorite SF restaurants, who mistakenly served her a Genevieve martini one evening. The next day, Fritz, who'd created his share of peculiar products over the years, figured out how to make sure it never happened again. First, he had me order green bottles for Genevieve "stat." Then we came up with a Genevieve "no symbol" neckhanger, whose red circle/backslash overlaid a black martini glass. Its text read: "GIN? Yes, but NOT FOR MARTINIS!" That rectified the problem. In 2008, thanks to the California Historical Society, Fritz and I found a rare book that had recipes for cocktails made with genever (aka Hollands gin) that were *not* martinis. Written by legendary San Francisco mixologist William T. Boothby, *Cocktail Boothby's American Bar-tender* was originally published in 1891. Anchor Distilling reprinted it in 2008 and again, in an expanded edition, in 2009.

Fritz always tackled such problems with enthusiasm, as if they were the *New York Times* Sunday crossword. A new distillery problem presented itself when a rye drinker complained about his brand-new bottle of Old Potrero. Apparently, when he took it out of the trunk at the end of a hot summer day, he noticed that the bartop (cork), with tin capsule in tow, had pushed itself right out of the bottle. The obvious response would have been "Don't store whiskey in your trunk in the summertime." But Fritz was intrigued, as if he were back in Iowa with his chemistry set.

Fortunately, the bottles and bartops came from the same company. "Have they got a guy? Can we get them in here?" he asked me. Indeed, they had an "old-schooler" who, like Otto Wiesneth or Ken Hepler, might be able to help. He was Rod Smith, who had transported the very first pallet of glass bottles from Owens-Illinois to the 8th Street brewery. When he explained the volumetric thermal expansion coefficients of high-proof spirits, our eyes lit up. Turns out the bottle had been designed for low-proof brandy rather than barrel-strength whiskey and needed more ullage (headspace), an easy modification at the factory. It was the sort of day Fritz remembers as "a triumph."

NEW BREWS

Anchor released two completely new brews in 2008 and 2009, both of which spent important time in the cellar. The first was Our Barrel Ale ("O•B•A"), a name John proposed because Anchor, as far as anyone knew, was the only brewery on the planet that aged its own beer in its own used whiskey barrels. Notwithstanding the claims of some twenty-first-century brewers, barrel-aged ale is not a new thing. As I wrote for the label, "it is a centuries-old tradition, from a time when barrels were thought of simply as the containers in which

New Zealand hop with delightful fruity notes of gooseberry and grapefruit. An instant winner on draught in 2009 and in the bottle in 2010, Humming Ale put Nelson Sauvin on the map, much as Liberty had done for Cascade a quarter century before.

FINAL BREW

Fritz's last beer as owner, president, and brewmaster was the 2010 Christmas Ale—his thirty-sixth—for which, in consultation with Mark, he came up with the recipe. And he came up with the tree, the ginkgo tree, whose name comes from the Japanese words for silver apricot. The original label design used Fritz's handwritten kanji characters beneath the tree. Once the purview of the ATF, label approvals had been processed through the Alcohol and Tobacco Tax and Trade Bureau (TTB) since its creation in 2003. The TTB rejected Anchor's label because the supplement ginkgo biloba, even though it wasn't in the beer, was regulated by the FDA. The FDA referred Anchor back to the TTB. Fritz smiled a knowing smile at this regulatory alphabet soup. In the end, he opted for keeping the kanji characters on everything but the label, which was the only thing regulated by the federal government. The important thing was the tree itself, which Jim illustrated beautifully. There's a reason for everything at Anchor and the reason for the ginkgo tree was simple. As Fritz told me while we were working on the

beer was stored and transported from brewery to tavern." O•B•A was doubly fun, in that each bottling represented a carefully considered blend of several different ales, aged in several different kinds of ex-Old Potrero barrels. First bottled—in magnums—on December 23, 2008, it initiated an enduring Anchor tradition of barrel-aged brews.

On August 13, 2009, Anchor brewed Humming Ale in celebration of the thirtieth anniversary of its first Brew Day at 1705 Mariposa Street. From August 13, 1979 on, as Fritz liked to say, "we were finally humming along." He especially liked the name because it was, like Steam, a word in the dictionary, used for beers long ago, which no one was using, and about which very little was known. This ale's recipe was reminiscent of Fritz's "just change one thing" experiments, from Steam Beer Brewing Company to ADC and YCV. Humming had the same grain bill, number of hop additions to the kettle, dry-hopping, and even ABV as Liberty Ale. But to substitute for Cascade, Mark had found Nelson Sauvin, a wonderful, relatively unknown

label, "They're beautiful trees. We just planted some at our house. And since I'm gonna be there a lot more than here next year . . ."

Fritz is often asked what his favorite Anchor beer is. He demurs. But when describing what they all have in common, he sometimes quotes St. Francis de Sales, whose *Introduction to the Devout Life* he knows well. Seven words from this ageless text combine to illuminate Fritz Maytag's theme for himself and for his company. The last five words comprise his theme for his products: "Kindly, frank, sincere, straightforward, simple, and true." And it was fitting that Anchor's Christmas Ale would be his last brew at Anchor. Its seven-word message graced the first Christmas Ale label in 1975: "Merry Christmas and a Happy New Year."

We would never, I would never, get rid of the Christmas Ale. It's a brilliant idea. And it was a transforming product. And it was thrilling. And it was profitable. And it was fun. I'm proud that we say "newness of life" on the neck label. It's from *The Book of Common Prayer* of the Episcopal Church. And I'm very proud of tying the tree to "the winter solstice, when the earth, with its seasons, appears born anew."

A LIFETIME OF ACHIEVEMENT

On March 24, 2008, at a press breakfast at the historic James Beard House in Greenwich Village, the James Beard Foundation announced its nominations for the 2008 James Beard Awards. They also announced that Fritz Maytag would receive the 2008 James Beard Foundation Lifetime Achievement Award at the awards ceremony June 8. This prestigious award is given to "an individual whose body of work has had a significant impact on the way we cook, eat, and think about food in America." Previous winners included Robert Mondavi, Ernest Gallo, Alice Waters, and Jacques Pépin. And as of this writing, there has been no

other winner from the brewing trade, let alone someone who also did so much for whiskey, gin, wine, and cheese. The Foundation proclaimed,

In 1965, Fritz Maytag acquired the Anchor Brewing Company of San Francisco and became a pioneer of American microbrewing. Since then, he has not only preserved the tradition of Anchor Steam Beer, but he has also made Anchor a national brand without ever compromising his high standards. In the 1980s and 1990s, due in part to Maytag's example, more than 1,000 small breweries sprouted up all over the country. Today, American microbrewed beers rate among the finest beers in the world, and the return to traditional brewing methods has become a worldwide phenomenon, producing a veritable flood of creative and delicious brews.

The Foundation also feted Fritz for Old Potrero and Junípero, which "quickly became models for a burgeoning artisanal distilling movement in America and around the world." Of course, York Creek and Maytag Dairy Farms were also singled out for praise, but for Fritz, the hardest-won victory was the sweetest: that of seeing his company and its products recognized for their lasting contribution to the American renaissance of artisanal food.

FOND FAREWELL

Behind the scenes, Fritz was still trying to find a buyer, "and we had a deal, we thought we'd done it, in 2008. I was in Croatia when the stock market crash came and the new buyers said, 'Oh, don't worry about it. Believe me, we're fine.' Gradually, they said, 'Whoops, no deal.' And then when it finally was, 2010 I guess, it finally happened."

As the clock wound down to the end of what would be Fritz's forty-five-year-and-two-day Anchor odyssey, he reminisced about his very early days at the old brewery:

I gave all the tours, and poured the beers, and then I washed all the glasses, and then I went home. But one night I was walking out with the tour and I was in the brewhouse, when a nice older lady came up to me and said in a friendly, smiling way, "Did you grow up in the brewery?"— thinking, you know, maybe my dad had owned it and was the brewmaster, and I had just been there since I was a little boy, 'cause I seem to just know all there is about everything. I paused. And I said, "Yes. I did." Because I did, you know. The brewery was where I encountered the real world. And it was a gift that I didn't deserve, but I stumbled into it and it was a great, great gift. And for some reason I got so deeply committed to not failing that I ended up succeeding, really, in many ways. But it was a struggle. And I did. I grew up.

Fritz's employees wanted to throw him a party, but knew that he would never want a "retirement party." Retirement was not in his DNA.

Instead, on July 29, 2010, Anchor had its one and only "killer jacket party," an informal reunion of those on whom Fritz had bestowed the custom-made, elaborately embroidered, never-for-sale Anchor varsity jacket.

But how could his employees thank him in return? Everyone signed the mat for a framed original 1968 press sheet of Anchor Steam labels to give to Fritz. But there had to be something even more special, more personal. Linda asked me what that could possibly be. Much to Fritz's surprise, it would be a framed, original 261-year-old map of California, which Mark presented to Fritz at the party on behalf of the entire staff. Typical of its time, when few explorers—let alone mapmakers—knew much about the American West, it depicted California as an island. Some, of course, believe California is an island. Fritz—student of history and maker of history—smiled a smile as wide as the Golden Gate and pumped his fist with glee.

PART FIVE

GOLDEN PROSPECTS

ANCHOR BREWERS & DISTILLERS

(2010–2017)

Optimism before the future abides in the San Francisco psyche with an equally powerful tendency to conserve that which already is.

—**Kevin Starr,** *San Francisco* (2002)

In 1965, Fritz Maytag's "medieval" brewery sold just 880 barrels of beer. In 2010, Anchor finished the year with sales of 90,423 barrels, a 10,175% increase. If that sounds like a lot of beer, consider that in 2010 Anheuser-Busch InBev (ABI) sold 90,423 barrels every 140 minutes. During Fritz's entire forty-five-year run from 1965–2010, Anchor sold a grand total of 2,339,161 barrels. By comparison, in 2010 *alone*, ABI sold 2,339,161 barrels every 60 hours. Of course, Fritz never measured success

in barrels of beer, bottles of whiskey, glasses of wine, or wheels of cheese. His radically traditional bottom line was quality, not quantity. Fritz's influence ignited a revolution that was still playing out all over America and the world. One day in 2010, a visitor to the brewery who didn't recognize him asked, "What do you do here?" Fritz thought for a moment and then replied simply, "I'm the custodian."

ANCHOR'S NEW CUSTODIANS

Keith Greggor, born in Bournemouth, studied civil engineering and marketing. Tony Foglio, born in Brooklyn, studied sociology and marketing. Keith, who once worked as project manager for International Distillers and Vintners, was "the marketing guy." And Tony, who once sold Scott Paper and Hamm's Beer in Chicago, was "the sales guy." Together, first at Paddington Brands and then at Skyy Vodka, they became the dynamic duo of distilled spirits. As Tony recalls, "I've always had this thing about entrepreneurs and what

L to R: Keith Greggor, Tony Foglio, and Fritz

motivates them. We grow up in a world of business where it's all about business goals and business strategies, but entrepreneurs, their business goals are their personal goals." When they first spoke with Fritz in 2005, he asked if they might be interested in buying his brewery and distillery. In awe of Fritz and his years of experience with both, however, they declined. A few years later, having purchased Preiss Imports, a catalog of spirits and beers that included Coopers from Australia and Brewdog from England, Keith and Tony realized they'd passed up the opportunity of a lifetime. They remained intimidated by Fritz's incredible career and the worldwide respect that he and Anchor had earned. But they had what Keith calls a "bold and grand idea (being in San Francisco you're more likely to think like that)" and hoped it would appeal to the father of craft beer and distilling. It did.

Keith and Tony's idea was to have two separate companies under one umbrella: Anchor Brewers & Distillers. Anchor Brewing would continue making and selling beer, but now the plan included importing Brewdog (of which they were part owners) and Coopers to sell in the US. Anchor Distilling would continue making and selling whiskey and gin, but now it would also import and sell the distilled spirits in the Preiss catalog. The two companies would have separate sales and marketing teams but share production and accounting staff. Although neither the Coopers nor the Brewdog pieces would ultimately pan out, "the whole point," Keith recalls, "was being in San Francisco and building on what was here," which was what Fritz most wanted to hear. "Fritz was very patient. And he was so confident that we could do it that he wanted to announce on April 27, 2010, even before the deal was signed."

"Fritz was very definitive in what he wanted—incredibly so," Tony recalls. There was no horse-trading. Tony remembers him saying, "The price is the price, and I care about my employees, and I care about the beer, and I care about San Francisco—so you will not move." Keith and Tony agreed to keep all the employees for a minimum of two years, with no reduction in salary or benefits. And everyone involved was ecstatic that Anchor would remain in San Francisco.

The sale was final on August 4, 2010. Keith and Tony each owned 25%; London's Berry Bros. & Rudd, a fine wine and spirits merchant since 1698, 40%; and a group of investors called the Griffin Group, 10%. But the day-to-day decision making and direction at Anchor Brewers & Distillers would be up to Keith and Tony. The winery still belonged to Fritz, but much to everyone's surprise, Fritz decided not to reestablish it elsewhere. He was serious about retirement. Rather than haggle over long lists of other assets, Tony suggested to Fritz, "Just take what you want when you want it." And that's how Tony and Keith ended up with a car they didn't know they owned. After the sale, I casually asked my new boss, marketing director Lynn Lackey, "Who's going to drive the Suburban?"

"What Suburban?" she replied.

"You know, under the brewhouse, behind the kegs. The 1950 Chevy Suburban with the Anchor logos on it."

"We bought a Suburban?"

It didn't take long for Keith and Tony to see what the brewery was all about. "It's real," said Tony. "I can touch it. I can feel it. When you go around here, that's craft. The employees here are engaged. It's got authenticity, it's got a heritage, and it's got a story that you can tell there's no gaps, no holes in it. And it's all about quality." Their goals were to be accepted as the new owners of Anchor; to increase efficiency, productivity, and capacity; and to grow the business without compromising quality.

On November 18, 2010 at the Palace Hotel, the San Francisco Museum and Historical Society presented the William C. Ralston Award to Anchor Brewing Company, "a business which has made significant contributions to the collection, preservation and interpretation of San Francisco history." The guests included Jane Cunningham, the great-great granddaughter of Gottlieb Brekle, as well as Mark Carpenter, Linda Rowe, and Mike Lee, plus Tony Foglio and Keith Greggor. I introduced Fritz Maytag, who would accept the award on Anchor's behalf, as "someone who is always interesting—a Renaissance man, a visionary, a pioneer, and a sort of historical alchemist, who rescued an all-but-forgotten little piece of San Francisco history and transformed it into a San Francisco icon." Fritz, who had reached what he calls "the age that is humorously known as my anecdotage," paused a moment and then improvised an absorbing five-minute talk on alchemy, from his first microscope to his last day at Anchor.

The next morning, I brought the framed award to the brewery. "Where shall we hang it, Keith?" "In the most prominent place," he replied, as he walked the few steps from Fritz's old office to the door through which every visitor since 1979 had seen the brewhouse for the first time. "Right here." It's been there ever since.

NEW DIRECTION

There were fifty full-timers and ten part-timers at the brewery when Fritz left. To do what Keith and Tony hoped to do would require not only more than a hundred additional people, but new equipment. The game changer was the new Krones filler in 2011, which made it possible to speed up the bottling line from 270 bottles per minute to nearly 450. Now, Anchor could bottle 7,000 cases in the same shift it had taken to bottle 4,000. And the new filler reduced the "airs" in the bottle, improving the beer's shelf-life. There would be a new malt mill in 2012 and new cellar tanks in 2013. Anchor's legacy brews would continue to be open-fermented and dry-hopped with hop bags, as always, but in 2014 Anchor added vertical closed fermentors called *unitanks* for some of its new beers. By hooking up

Anchor's new custom-made external hopping device (EHD) to a unitank, they could dry-hop an IPA, for example, in two days instead of two weeks. Also in 2014, Anchor added its very first canning line, which would be instrumental in getting Anchor beers out to a new audience.

Though most of these changes were unseen—if not unheard—they represented a huge investment in Anchor's future. Soon the brewery's capacity grew well beyond what Fritz ever dreamed could be achieved in one building. And there was a new website and social media presence, a new online reservation system for tours, and a new retail store. Underlying all the changes was the conviction to make the brewery even more of a destination, an expansion of Fritz's philosophy that this Palace of Steam Beer—along with a pint or two—beautifully expressed what Anchor was all about.

With Fritz's departure, John Dannerbeck was promoted to president/CEO and Mark Carpenter to brewmaster. Mark's first of many new beers with Keith and Tony was Brekle's Brown. The year 2011 was Mark's 40th anniversary at Anchor, bottled beer's 40th anniversary at Anchor, Anchor Brewing's 115th anniversary, and Golden City's 140th anniversary. So there was a lot to celebrate, which Mark did

with a brew that looked both to where Anchor had been and where it was going. He used the recipe for the 1986 Christmas Ale—a delectable all-malt brown ale—as his inspiration, but with a twist: a relatively unknown floral-citrusy hop called Citra. I was now heading up the Design Committee, so for the label I asked Jim Stitt to draw the word *Brekle's* in the same cursive style the brewery used for the word *Anchor* in 1909. Brewed on December 15, 2010, Brekle's Brown was released during 2011's SF Beer Week and poured at the GABF that fall in honor of brewmasters Gottlieb, Fritz, and Mark.

In addition to continuing Anchor's legacy beers, Keith and Tony wanted to focus on a variety of innovative brews to help Anchor better connect with a younger audience. So over the next four years, Mark and his team created over two dozen new beers. There were contemporary takes on classic brews, from dry-hopped Brotherhood Steam to double-hopped Double Liberty IPA. There were new barrel ales. There was a new IPA every year. There were new seasonals, like Anchor Saison, Summer Wheat, BigLeaf Maple Autumn

Red, and Winter Wheat. There was Flying Cloud San Francisco Stout and California Uncommon Kölsch. Mark also spearheaded a no-holds-barred, eight-beer, four-year series, which I named Zymaster (from the Greek word *zymē* [a leaven] + master). Down the road, for the first time at Anchor, there would be fruit beers, including Meyer Lemon Lager and Mango Wheat Ale.

Everything was about *new*. Of course, Keith and Tony secretly hoped, like any self-respecting Californian, that Anchor would strike gold. And it didn't take long. In Fritzian fashion, the strike was a great beer that told a true but obscure story. It was California's first genuine lager, Boca Beer, reborn in 2012 as Zymaster Series #1–California Lager, and born again in 2013 as Anchor California Lager.

Mark's idea for Anchor California Lager arose from his many years of telling people the story Anchor Steam. Just as Fritz had created Old Potrero 18th-Century-Style Rye to help tell the story of Old Potrero 19th-Century Rye, wouldn't it

be great, he thought, if there was an Anchor California Lager to help tell the story of Anchor Steam Beer? Mark shared his idea with me, and I couldn't wait to delve into the history of Boca Brewing, Boca Beer, and the original recipe for California's first genuine lager.

It didn't take Anchor's staff long to drink the first keg of Zymaster #1–California Lager. By the time somebody hooked up the second, everyone was excitedly discussing the possibility of turning this unique brew into a year-round product. Like Boca Beer, Anchor California Lager (4.9% ABV) is an all-pale-malt brew, made with the finest California 2-row barley. And it is a single-hop beer, using only fresh, whole-cone Cluster hops, descended from an old line originally grown in California. Cluster, America's premier nineteenth-century hop, has a long history as a dual-purpose hop for both bittering and aroma, creating a flavor profile like no other. Brewed with San Francisco tap water—fresh from Yosemite—and fermented with Anchor's own special strain of lager yeast, Anchor California Lager is kräusened in the traditional manner and lagered in Anchor's cellars. The result is a uniquely sessionable lager that is somewhat maltier, hoppier, and stronger than modern American lagers, a delightful tribute to the rich heritage and traditions of California brewing.

The inspiration for Anchor California Lager's original 2013 label was the original Boca Lager Beer label, as it appears on an extremely rare 1880s trade card in the Anchor Brewing Collection. I showed it to Jim, asking him to reimagine this label as a horizontal oval. But in California, of course, it's all about the bear. The California grizzly on Boca's EXPORT label appears to be heading east (well, at least to the right), probably because Boca exported its products by rail to the eastern states. Anchor's California grizzly is from a woodcut by Durbin Van Vleck, first published in 1856 in *Hutching's California Magazine*. Van Vleck modeled

it after an original illustration by Charles Christian Nahl, who drew the bear from life in Grizzly Adams's San Francisco menagerie. Nahl's bear would later serve as inspiration for the bear on the California state flag. Although that bear is heading west, Anchor's bear—like Van Vleck's and Boca's bears—is heading east.

Following California Lager's release, Anchor initiated a partnership with the California State Parks Foundation, whereby the brewery donates a portion of the proceeds from the sale of this beer to the Foundation, holds volunteer park cleanup/conservation days for Anchor employees with Foundation staff, and provides free beer for park fundraisers and membership drives. In 2014, Anchor inaugurated its new canning line with Anchor California Lager, perfect for a day at the beach or a hike in the woods.

Anchor Distilling continued to grow, taking full advantage of a cocktail renaissance fueled by groundbreaking products like Old Potrero and Junípero Gin. Soon there were new products in the Anchor portfolio that held special appeal for mixologists, including Hophead Hop Vodka; Old Tom Gin, a historical product sweetened with stevia; and Christmas Spirit, a distilled Christmas Ale. With all the variety on the beer side, Anchor's bottle and can variety-packs took off.

In 2015, to celebrate the golden anniversary of Fritz's purchase of the brewery, I asked Jim to give a little refresh to Anchor Steam's packaging, which

gave both the beer and the brewery a boost. In August, city hall took notice of "the 50th anniversary of Fritz Maytag's investment and the beginning of an American craft beer tradition" with a proclamation from Mayor Lee: "Our City takes pride in being home to tens of thousands of businesses that make up our diverse business community and the backbone of San Francisco's economy, and the many years of dedication and partnership of Anchor Brewing Company represent San Francisco values at their best."

GRAND SLAM

Brews and baseball go together hand and glove. And Steam Beer and baseball go back long before the San Francisco Giants, to the days of the Pacific Coast League's San Francisco Seals. One of their stars was sandlot phenom Oscar Vitt, who would go on to play with Ty Cobb's Detroit Tigers. The Seals signed Vitt by giving him the bonus he asked for: "one glass of steam beer." In 2009, Anchor had celebrated the hundredth anniversary of the Seals' first San Francisco championship with reproductions from its collection of original Seals baseball cards. In 2010, the Giants made the playoffs, on their way to their first World Series victory since moving to San Francisco in 1958. At game time, Anchor employees grabbed their radios and headed to the roof, where the scoreboard was visible and the crowd audible. Although Anchor Steam was still on draught and in plastic bottles at the ballpark, the brewery had no formal relationship with the team. So, being very careful not to use any Giants or MLB trademarks, Anchor cheered on the Giants with a series of full-page playoff and World Series ads in the *Chronicle*. Some featured Seals players. Some featured the view from Anchor's rooftop.

After the Series, the Giants called to thank Anchor for its support, which led to a winning "Brews & Baseball" partnership—from Scottsdale

Toasting the Giants, L to R: Rich Carvalho, Mark Carpenter, Keith Greggor, Belle Rosin, Tom Holmes, Ollie Lagomarsino, Eric Svendberg

to San Francisco—including the opening of Anchor Plaza at AT&T Park in 2011 and Anchor's "Catch a Brew!" campaign. Apparently, it was good luck for the Giants, Anchor, and the City. In 2014, in addition to Giants 12-packs of Steam, there would be Giants World Series magnums with which to celebrate their *third* championship in SF.

Working with the Giants on two collaboration brews was a treat for everyone at Anchor. After a successful tryout on draft in September 2015, Orange Splash Lager was the Anchor/Giants lead-off hitter in the 2016 season. This brew's scouting and development, like Meyer Lemon Lager, had been managed by Scott Ungermann. Born in 1967, a year and a half after Fritz bought the brewery, Scott, a UC Davis grad, was brewmaster at ABI Fairfield prior to joining the Anchor team in 2012 as production director. He was promoted to brewmaster upon Mark's retirement in early 2016.

Mark Carpenter played a key role at Anchor for more than forty-four years, almost breaking Fritz's record. Linda Rowe had retired in 2015, after her own amazing forty-plus-year Anchor career. Mike Lee was the sole remaining 8th Street

alumnus at Anchor when he left in 2016, after thirty-nine years of faithful service. Their contributions to Anchor, their co-workers, and craft beer are immeasurable. Ask them what their three "shipwrecked on a desert island" beers would be, and they'll all give you the same answer: Steam, Steam, and Steam.

Batting second in the Anchor/Giants lineup was Los Gigantes Mexican-Style Lager, which debuted in the 2017 season. Anchor brewer Ramon Tamayo created the recipe for Los Gigantes, a smooth, easygoing lager crafted to be all about baseball and San Francisco—with their equally strong connection to the Latino community.

Anchor's partnership with the Giants also resulted in the 2015 Opening Day for the Anchor Beer Garden at the Yard. Directly across McCovey Cove from the ballpark, this pop-up was a great place for fans to enjoy Anchor's hall-of-fame and rookie brews. The Yard welcomed beer drinkers into the Anchor world, reawakening San Francisco's longtime connection to its hometown beer in a new and different way. And at the end of each day, all Anchor had to do was look at the receipts to learn which of its beers were a hit and which a swing and a miss.

Building on the success Anchor was having with the Giants, Anchor initiated a partnership with the Golden State Warriors in the 2013–14

Malisha Robinson and Mike Thompson canning Los Gigantes

Anchor beer would be, appropriately enough, Anchor California Lager, "the golden lager for the Golden State."

SEA CHANGE

From brewhouse to bottle shop, Anchor's indefatigable production team sustained the brewery's unprecedented growth to an all-time high of 159,162 barrels in 2014. Anchor was riding another craft beer wave, and it was a record-breaking one. In 1896, there had been 136 breweries in California, 30 of them in San Francisco—including Anchor. Now, California had more than 518 *craft* breweries, and as many in San Francisco as in 1896. It was a far cry from 1978, when Anchor was the only brewery in the City. San Francisco had come full circle.

And San Francisco was a microcosm. In 2010, craft beer in the US was growing at a healthy annual rate of 11.8%. In 2014, the wave crested at 17.8%, after which it tumbled down to 2.66% in 2018. But even as craft beer sales fell, the total number of breweries in the US continued to rise. In 2015, it reached 4,847—716 more than the previous high *in 1873*. By 2018, that number would climb to 7,686, of which 841 were California craft breweries.

It was a sea change. Goliaths like ABI were playing in craft beer's sandbox, either by acquisition or imitation. And the craft beer market itself

season. The Warriors, whose final season in Philadelphia is best remembered for Wilt Chamberlain's 100-point game, moved west at the start of the 1962–63 season. They became the Golden State Warriors in 1971—the same year, coincidentally, that Anchor began bottling Steam Beer. For the Warriors partnership, the featured

was maturing, even as hundreds of very small, very local breweries were still opening all over the country—95% of them making fewer than ten thousand barrels a year. And with thousands of breweries came tens of thousands of beers. That created a challenge for flagship beers like Anchor Steam. And how could Anchor's classic brews— Steam, Porter, Liberty, Foghorn, Christmas, and now California Lager—thrive in this increasingly complex and challenging environment? And how, alongside them, could Anchor's new innovation brews take off and avoid one-and-done fates in a fickle world where drinkers, retailers, and wholesalers buy a pint, a case, or a pallet and, rather than reorder, ask, "What's new?" And with Anchor's own plethora of new beers, how could they reassure customers that the company hadn't lost its way, its identity? The answer would be the creation of a new environment altogether, in which Anchor's history of creativity and its future of creativity could flourish as one.

Anchor had the power all along. In 1871, Brekle's Golden City Brewery was a tiny local brewery, neighborhood beer bar, and gathering place. In 1965, Kuh's Old Spaghetti Factory was a great good place, a place that a twenty-something like Fritz Maytag could call his local. And in 2015, the Anchor Beer Garden at the Yard had tapped into San Francisco's palpable hometown spirit of camaraderie and community. Anchor's great idea that proved to be a good idea would be Anchor Public Taps. On Potrero Hill, right across the street from Anchor Brewing Company, it would be the neighborhood's pilot brewery and beer bar, the cornerstone of Anchor's rise.

In the summer of 2017, with a green light from Keith, the northwest corner of 495 De Haro Street—where Fritz's York Creek winery once stood—underwent another transformation, making way for Anchor Public Taps. It would be an expensive job, especially because the San Francisco fire marshal, even without knowing Anchor's fiery history, said the entire building would have to be sprinklered. On August 2, while construction at Public Taps was still underway, Keith let everyone at Anchor in on some important news, inviting them to gather in the taproom the next morning to discuss it with some people from the Sapporo Group. The news would become official August 4 and the paperwork finalized September 1, 2017. Sapporo had bought Anchor.

TRANSITION

Keith and the Anchor Brewers & Distillers board had witnessed the maturing of the craft beer business during their tenure, with thousands of new breweries as well as major non-craft players joining the fray. In 2016, the impact of these changing times had led to a search for the right new owner for Anchor's future. In 2017, after the closure of San Francisco's Speakeasy Brewery and Heineken's buyout of Lagunitas, they made their decision.

The sale included the brewery property, buildings, equipment, brands, and most important of all, its legacy. Anchor Distilling was not part of the sale, but rather retained by Keith and Tony's investment group. The distillery itself would remain at Mariposa Street through 2020, but as a completely separate entity renamed Hotaling & Co., where Bruce, Kendra, and the distilling team would continue making great craft spirits.

The criteria for the sale were essentially the same as Fritz's had been seven years before: Keep Anchor in San Francisco, respect and preserve its rich legacy and tradition, invest in its future— locally, domestically, and internationally—and take care of its employees. My fellow employees and I did not need much reassurance. At the end of the day, Anchor and Sapporo were both brewers, with rich histories and a sunny forecast.

GOLDEN FUTURE
(2017–)

Integrity is doing the right thing when you don't have to—when no one else is looking or will ever know—when there will be no congratulations or recognition for having done so.

—Charles W. Marshall, *Shattering the Glass Slipper* (2002)

Sapporo and Anchor have a lot in common, including Fritz Maytag, who enjoyed a Sapporo or two in Hokkaido in '59. Anchor has Fritz's beer label collection, which includes what Sapporo's historian describes as "a very, very precious one and valuable for our history." It's a Sapporo Lager Beer label from between 1908 and 1936, featuring the traditional symbol of Sapporo Beer, the North Star.

Sapporo's humble beginnings are a lot like Anchor's. In 1873, an enthusiastic young man from Japan, Seibe Nakagawa, began brewing in Fürstenwalde, Germany at the Berlin Beer Brewing Company. After two years of training, he returned home in 1875. Hisanari Murahashi, in charge of developing Japan's beer business during the Meiji Reconstruction, hired Nakagawa to open a lager

incorporated as the Sapporo Brewing Company, Ltd. The latter occasion marked a departure by which the brewery became a modern plant, ice machine and malting and bottling apparatus being imported from Germany. At first, on account of the limited demand, the output was only about 2,500 barrels annually; but with the increased demand came a corresponding expansion of the brewery's facilities, until now it is run to its full yearly capacity of 25,000 barrels. . . . The kinds of liquors now brewed are lager and kuro, or black beer—the former being light colored like Pilsener and the latter resembling the Kulmbacher beer of Germany.

SAPPORO TODAY

Sapporo began exporting beer from Japan to the United States in 1964, and Sapporo USA was established in 1985. Sapporo Premium, the brewery's flagship, has been the #1 Asian brand beer in America for over thirty years. In Canada, Sapporo Group has four breweries, including Canada's third largest beer company, Sleeman Breweries, as well as Unibroue, Okanagan, and Wild Rose. With the addition of Anchor in 2017, there have been many opportunities for these breweries to work together. In 2016, emblematic of its long-range vision, the Sapporo Group had launched its "SPEED 150" initiative to build the company toward its golden future in 2026, its sesquicentennial year.

GETTING ACQUAINTED

After the sale, I had a chance to get to know my Sapporo colleagues better. All of us love baseball and the Giants, but I was surprised that everyone at Sapporo rooted for the Los Angeles Angels. I was reminded that its rising star, Shohei "Shotime" Ohtani, who would be the American League's

beer brewery in Tokyo. Knowing from his German training that making genuine lager beer required plenty of ice, Nakagawa convinced Murahashi to build the brewery in the northern city of Sapporo, on the island of Hokkaido. Nakagawa oversaw the construction of the brewery, beginning June 27, 1876. The Kaitakushi Beer Brewery, Japan's first, opened on September 23, 1876, marking the start of Sapporo Beer.

Anchor also has Fritz's library, which includes a 1903 first edition of *One Hundred Years of Brewing*. Surprisingly, this old book about American brewing devotes its final pages to the global future of the beer industry. It includes this history of Sapporo:

The Sapporo Brewery, at the place of the same name, was founded in 1876 by the Colonial Government of Hokkaido, with a view to encourage the industry and to furnish a market for the barley which was being successfully grown in the vicinity. In 1886 the plant passed to private proprietors, in the persons of Messrs. Okura & Company, and two years later the business was

Rookie of the Year in 2018, had gotten his start in 2013 with Hokkaido's Nippon-Ham Fighters baseball club. Sapporo's goal for Anchor, I was told, was like the Giants' goal: to win the home game. To do so would require continuous improvement, *kaizen* (改善), whose kanji characters signify good change, change for the better. Though I wasn't familiar with the word, I was very familiar with the concept—how quality never slips when you're always trying to make it better—which Fritz had instilled in Anchor long before it moved to Mariposa Street. From another Giants/Angels fan, I learned another word: *kaitaku* (開拓), as in Kaitakushi Brewery and Hokkaido Kaitaku no Mura (the Historical Village of Hokkaido). It means "pioneering spirit," which has been fundamental to the ethos of both Anchor and Sapporo since the 1870s.

Pilot brewers Dan Volek and Ramon Tamayo

ANCHOR PUBLIC TAPS

In that spirit, Anchor Public Taps had its grand opening on Saturday, October 21, 2017. There were over a thousand visitors that day, curious to see what it was all about. Anchor's new seven-barrel pilot brewery wasn't quite ready for prime time yet, so two of Anchor's fellow San Francisco breweries offered to help. Anchor collaborated with Thirsty Bear to create Barbary Coast Rye, a hoppy, red rye beer with cassia. And two brews flowed from a collaboration with Local Brewing: Anchored at Local, which was dry-hopped with old-school, whole-cone Nelson Sauvin and new-school Mosaic pellets and Mosaic Cryo Lupulin Powder; and Locally Anchored, a hazy IPA brewed with Denali hops and dry-hopped with Hallertau Blanc, Galaxy, and Mosaic lupulin powder.

Brewmaster Scott Ungermann, whose Fog Breaker IPA would be the first brew to get scaled up from the pilot brewhouse at Public Taps to the main brewhouse at Mariposa, believed that Anchor Public Taps represents "a really important moment in our history, as far as our ability to connect locally with people in San Francisco and to develop new beers. Anchor Public Taps is going to help us get better at making new beers and enable us to see every day what connects with our customers." This new concept meant that Anchor now had its own designated mad scientist/alchemist (aka pilot brewer) right across the street from the brewery, who was fearless and unconstrained by convention

Sensory session. L to R: João Alameida, Otis Morgan, Tom Riley, Scott Ungermann, Jen Jordan, Kevin West, and Dane Volek

THE ANCHOR BREWING STORY

or economics. It's a place where beer is made for its own sake and failure is just part of the process.

In November 2017, Anchor's first pilot brewer, Dane Volek, got to make the first brew at Public Taps. Dane had gotten his start at Anchor in the racking room in 2008 before moving to the bottle shop and then fermentation. He became a shift brewer in 2012, just in time to be on the very first brew of California Lager. His brewhouse mentor was Tom Riley, who had been a brewer since 1991. Following a trial brew on November 11, the first official Brew Day at Anchor Public Taps was November 21, 2017. The beer was named Admiral Nelson—but not for historical reasons. This single malt and single hop (SMaSH) IPA featured local-farm-to-local-malthouse malt from *Admiral* Maltings, the Bay Area's first malthouse since Prohibition, which had opened in the summer of 2017. The hops were *Nelson* Sauvin, which had been pioneered by Anchor in Humming Ale.

Spring 2018 welcomed the debut of Anchor Steam Beer in cans, which brought a sleek, contemporary feel to the classic Steam look. That same year, Anchor was the recipient of the Art Deco Society of California's award for the preservation of its building, as well as the San Francisco History Association's award for the preservation of its history. And Mayor London Breed nominated Anchor to San Francisco's Legacy Business Registry, noting how the brewery "has contributed to the history and identity of the city and fostered civic engagement and pride."

AT THE SMITHSONIAN

In 2017, Anchor, Fritz, and I had donated his De Clerck books, an original, signed 1968 press sheet of Anchor Steam labels, and his white Anchor coveralls to the National Museum of American History in Washington, DC. But there was something missing: Fritz's microscope. I screwed up my courage and asked him if, after nearly sixty-five years, he'd be willing to part with it. I was not surprised that he said yes.

For many years, Fritz and I had gotten tag-team haircuts every five weeks at Flo Cimino's old-school barber shop on Potrero Hill. Then we'd walk down the street to the Thinker's Café for our "haircut lunch." After one such meal, Fritz said he had something for me. He got in his Tesla and

In the foreground of the *Brewing a Revolution* exhibit is a museum label with a picture of Fritz. Its title says it all: "The Alchemist."

swung it around next to my car. Then he got out, opened the back door, and slowly pulled out an ancient-looking wooden box with a big metal handle. As he handed it to me, Fritz cautioned me about how heavy it was, and that the handle might not be the best way to carry his microscope. I carefully cradled it in my arms. Fritz turned away quickly and said, "Thanks, Dave. I'll see you soon."

When the time came to make the donation on Fritz's behalf, determined not to be the guy that lost or damaged Fritz's most prized possession, I packed the microscope in bubble wrap, placed it gently in a carry-on bag, and flew to DC. The next morning, after bringing it down to breakfast with me at my hotel, I delivered it to Theresa McCulla at the Museum, where it will forever be enshrined.

In November 2018, Fritz and I, along with our wives Beverly and Deb, were in Washington, DC, for the fifth annual Smithsonian Food History Weekend at the National Museum of American History. There, Fritz participated in a panel discussion with Ken Grossman, Charlie Papazian, and Michael Lewis, moderated by the curator of the Museum's American Brewing History Initiative, Theresa McCulla. But the highlight of the trip was seeing Fritz's microscope and other Anchor memorabilia on display, just a few yards from Julia Child's kitchen.

UNION-MADE IN SAN FRANCISCO

In late 2019, I asked Jon Ezell, who worked in the bottle shop just like I had twenty-eight years before, about the "Union-Made in San Francisco" catchphrase that would soon grace Anchor's packaging.

I've never met Fritz Maytag, but have been regaled with stories around the bar, more times than I can count. I have also spent time in his former office, browsing and reading through the library of brewing books he left behind. I imagine him a passionate brewer who cared about the welfare of his employees as much as the company he dedicated his career to. His efforts allowed the company and its employees to thrive and be a proud example of what a brewery and a workplace could be. It is no surprise that such a vibrant craft beer industry grew out from such an unassuming seed on Potrero Hill. On March 13, 2019, over two-thirds of the Anchor workforce voted to preserve and protect what we think is the best job in SF—making Steam Beer! In doing so we aligned ourselves with another historic San Francisco organization, the International Longshore and Warehouse Union (ILWU).

The new collective bargaining agreement between the ILWU and Anchor Brewing took effect January 1, 2020. It had been nearly 128 years since the incorporation of Anchor's union predecessor, Co-operative Brewing Company. Now, the pioneer of the craft beer movement had become the pioneer of the craft beer *union* movement. Today, Jon is still working at Anchor, a proud brewer of Anchor Steam Beer.

PANDEMIC

More than a century ago, Anchor survived the influenza outbreak. And Anchor, resilient as ever, has survived COVID-19. Out of an abundance of caution, its historic brewery was closed to the public in 2020. Draught beer had been well over half its business, but when bars and restaurants shut down, Anchor stopped shipping kegs altogether. Many employees worked from home, while a stalwart few kept doing what Anchor does best—working together to brew and bottle beer. That way, at least Anchor's core line of beers could make it to market. Once Public Taps was permitted to sell beer to go, Dane came up with the idea of pilot brewing a hard seltzer, something completely unexpected from Anchor but welcomed by its loyal San Francisco followers. Kristyn Carter, a graduate of the Culinary Institute of America who had left her job at the

Fairmont Hotel in 2019 to become general manager of Public Taps, had one of those great ideas that's also a good idea: "How 'bout if we call it Seltzer in Place?" In April 2020, Dane created the first of three Seltzers-in-Place: Piña Colada, followed by Lemon Raspberry and Pomegranate Habanero.

In September 2020, Anchor collaborated with local artist Jeremy Fish to reimagine San Francisco's original city flag for the pandemic, with its motto—*Oro en Paz, Fierro en Guerra* ("Gold in Peace, Iron in War")—and rising phoenix. These symbols were as apropos in 2020 as they had been after the 1906 earthquake and fire. Jeremy's masked phoenix is an especially relevant symbol of the abiding strength, resilience, and optimism San Francisco shares with its oldest brewery. The beer, developed at Public Taps, was Stay Strong San Francisco Pilsner. Anchor donated 35% of the proceeds from its sale, plus 100% of the proceeds from T-shirt sales, to the United States Bartenders'

Guild, whose members were especially hard hit by the pandemic.

In 2021, Anchor Public Taps expanded its outdoor seating and reopened, much to the delight of its thirsty neighborhood.

A NEW BREWMASTER

Tom Riley became Anchor's new brewmaster in August 2020, the seventh since Prohibition. Tom is a third-generation San Franciscan who grew up right on Potrero Hill. His mother, Bette, had gotten a job in the bottle shop in 1980. Tom started in 1984, followed by his twin brother Dan in 1985. Tom worked in the racking room and bottle shop before becoming warehouse manager/forklift driver. In 1991, he started training with Richard to be a brewer. In those days, there was Fritz, brewmaster; Mark, assistant brewmaster; Tim Herring, head brewer; and the four shift brewers—Richard Gossett, Bruce Joseph, Bob Anders, and Tom—who worked ten-hour shifts, four days a week, rotating every five weeks. When it came to teachers, Tom says, "Richard was the best." Totally unflappable, even during earthquakes, Richard always had a coffee cup full of wheat beer in his hand and a good story for you, told in his inimitable KSAN-radio DJ voice.

You don't train at Anchor from a manual. You train, Tom remembers, by shadowing a brewer "on the first half of the brew and then you start working alone and then you do a five-week stretch of that, and then you learn the cooling shift." The training is hands-on, and the coolest cucumbers make the best students. Tom says the hardest thing about brewing is

the multitasking. You've got three, four, five balls up in the air—or plates spinning. And they're all important. And what sometimes ends up happening to a novice is that one thing goes wrong and takes your attention, and then, because we're such a hands-on brewhouse, your timing on all the other things starts to go, all of that multitasking and keeping track in your head of what's going on, what valves are open, what valves are closed, what valves are supposed to be open and vice versa. You know, you leave one valve open, you could dump the whole brew down the drain.

A good multitasker makes for a good manager, so when Anchor's fermentation manager retired in 2015, Tom got the job. "We were wanting to make more IPAs, so we were getting unitanks and EHDs and needed to figure out how to really put this equipment into service." After three years he was promoted to assistant brewmaster and then to brewmaster. I asked him, "Did he have his dream job now?" He replied,

It's just always been a dream job working here. It's a San Francisco–born thing; I'm a San Francisco–born thing. But it's really humbling, knowing the people I follow. I have the utmost respect for Scott and all the brewers before him. I worked for Mark for *years*, and he *hired* me. And working for Fritz, well, I always knew that was special. Being here and really being immersed in and seeing the vision of the company back in those days, and now being tasked with carrying on that tradition, I feel a lot of responsibility on my shoulders. The quality of the beer is the most important thing to me. And Sapporo just wants us to make our beer the best it can be. They're fantastic people. They don't want to change us. But they are here to support us and make us better.

Soon it was time for Anchor's forty-sixth Christmas Ale. Although I had stepped back from the Design Committee to work on this book, I got to choose the Christmas Ale tree again. And it had to be just right. For years, Anchor has talked about how "trees symbolize the winter solstice when the earth, with its seasons, appears born anew." In this spirit of hope, renewal, and community, I chose not one but three giant sequoias—what John Muir called "columns of sunshine"—in California's Mariposa Grove. Together, they are the Three Graces, representing radiance, joy, and flowering. At ninety-two, Jim Stitt had taken "early retirement" after forty-seven years of designing Anchor labels. No one could ever replace him, but illustrator Nathan Yoder did a beautiful job of continuing

Anchor's enduring Christmas tradition, inspired in 2020 by Civil War–era lithographs of the Mariposa Grove. In the spirit of giving, Anchor's 2020 Christmas Ale helped support Meals on Wheels America.

SESQUICENTENNIAL

The year 2021 marked the sesquicentennial of Gottlieb Brekle's Golden City Brewery, the 125th anniversary of Anchor Brewing Company and Anchor Steam Beer, and the 50th anniversary of the first bottling of Anchor Steam Beer in modern times—all in San Francisco. To celebrate, Anchor would introduce three brand-new beers as well as brand-new packaging for its pioneering Steam, Porter, Liberty, California Lager, 2021 Christmas Ale, and (in 2022) Old Foghorn.

For half a century, Anchor's labels and logos served the brewery with beauty and distinction. In 1971, when the brewery bottled Anchor Steam Beer for the first time since the 1930s, its award-winning label was easy to spot on the shelf—it sat next to Budweiser, Miller, Coors, Lucky Lager, and maybe Heineken. There were just 133 breweries in all of America. Fast forward to 2021 when—thanks in many ways to Anchor—there are some 9,000 breweries in the US, each with up to a dozen beers or more. The beer aisle has become the noisiest aisle in the supermarket, with hundreds of beer labels screaming for attention and very little clarity about who makes what—if they make it at all. To be heard through the cacophony, Anchor opted not to change the beer or start shouting, but rather to appeal more directly and succinctly to its current and potential fans with a new, more unified look that was both rooted in Anchor's unique history and looking ahead to its golden future.

Together, Tom, Dane, and the Anchor team developed three brand-new beers for 2021: Little Weekend Light Golden Ale is a low-cal, low-carb, low ABV, reduced-gluten ale with natural mango. Tropical Hazy IPA, inspired by Dane's trip to the hop harvest in Yakima, is all about the Strata hops, but for their fruitiness rather than bitterness. And Crisp Pilsner—bright, clean, and refreshing—features Czech Saaz hops, which Anchor has been using since the 1980s. I asked Dane what he would want people to say after a glass of any of these brews. "More please," he replied.

Once perfected on the Public Taps pilot brewery in 2020, these new beers needed to be scaled up from a modern, stainless steel, two-vessel brewhouse to a more antiquated, all-copper, three-vessel system that's manually operated. Tom and Dane (who would be promoted to assistant brewmaster in October 2021) worked side-by-side to help make that happen. "Obviously," Dane told me, "Tom's been around a long time. He knows things in and out around here. He's a pleasant guy to work with and we share laughs all the time, but I would just say it's been a learning process from him from day

one. He's always impressed me with his ability to just jump in, you know, feet first, and get his hands dirty and know right away that this is the way."

Hearing Dane extol Tom's "just jump in" attitude reminded me immediately of Fritz's story about how Lucky Lager's Otto Wiesneth "climbed up and jumped into the mash/lauter tun, right there in front of my eyes. Now I'd been in that damn thing I don't know how many times. But when he jumped into the lauter tun, I thought *Now there's a man who loves brewing*. He did it with *enthusiasm!* I just loved it. Yeah, a lot of engineers, you know, they keep their hands clean, but he just jumped in. I couldn't believe it. I loved him."

These two vivid examples of enthusiasm, fifty-four years apart, reveal a meaningful through line of the Anchor story. Enthusiasm is the fountainhead from which flows the optimism, determination, teamwork, and can-do/jump-in attitude that still speaks for itself at Anchor every day. "It was a joy," Fritz reflects. "People ask me whether I miss the brewery and I say no, but I do miss one thing: sitting down with the people I had trained and worked

with—who had taught me, and we'd learned together, and that I trusted totally—and dealing with a crisis. I would sit there, and I would know: *We are the Anchor Brewing Company. We can do anything.*"

There are two additional words that help convey what Anchor is all about: *pioneer* and *quality*. A hundred and fifty years ago, Gottlieb Brekle, "the old pioneer brewer" (he was fifty-two) invited all of San Francisco to visit his "new and magnificent" Golden City Brewery and spend time in the public taproom that was so integral to it. He "always has the best" beer, and it is of "excellent quality." Fast-forward to Anchor Brewing and Fritz Maytag. What appealed to his abiding curiosity in 1965? A "medieval" San Francisco brewery that hadn't lost enthusiasm but—in its struggle to survive—had lost its pioneering spirit and sacrificed the quality of its legendary beer. In the process of recharting Anchor's course from one of surviving to one of thriving, Fritz discovered his own enthusiasm for and joy in "making wonderful beers and pioneering a world brewing renaissance."

Like a Sherpa at base camp, Fritz guided his brewery and its beer to the mountaintop and, with a winding queue of climbers behind him, to even higher peaks beyond. The "wholistic" philosophy he pioneered at his 8th Street brewery has become Anchor's enduring company philosophy: You must have a deep reservoir of quality—both inside and outside the bottle. "Ninety-five percent of what you've done will literally never be seen or appreciated by anyone other than maybe your employees or your wife." And to do that requires integrity, what Charles W. Marshall calls "doing the right thing when you don't have to—when no one else is looking." Integrity has always been in Fritz's DNA. Thanks to him, it will forever be in Anchor's DNA.

Anchor's unique story is why its beers taste good "here," as Fritz likes to say, pointing to his mouth, and "here," pointing to his forehead. Take a tour of Anchor Brewing Company, and you will learn about its pioneering spirit and be guided, from start to finish, through its hands-on process of making unique beers of excellent quality—*with enthusiasm!* Sample the classic brews that fomented the craft beer revolution: Anchor Steam, Anchor Porter, Liberty Ale, Old Foghorn, and Our Special Ale. Then cross the street to Anchor Public Taps to see the evolution of the revolution.

Anchor Public Taps is a great good place to sample all of Anchor's beers. Try time traveling from Anchor Steam to California Lager to Crisp Pilsner. Or sample West Coast IPA or Easy Weekend Lo-Cal Hazy IPA or the latest innovation—all in a relaxed, family-friendly, dog-friendly atmosphere. And take a good, hard look at the pilot brewery from which, in its first three years, over 120 distinct, experimental beers emerged. A few pilot beers will be chosen for brewing across Mariposa Street, where they can join ranks with Anchor's legendary brews. And at Public Taps, you are not just an observer of that selection process; you are a participant.

Now squint your eyes a bit and take another look at the tiny brewhouse in this vibrant San Francisco building. Perhaps you see it in a new way. Perhaps it is 8th Street reborn.

APPENDIX
ANCHOR HOMEBREW RECIPES

As a homebrewer you give yourself and the people who you know a choice: not only to brew the kind of beer that you like, but also the opportunity to feel and understand what beer is all about.

—**Charlie Papazian,** *The Complete Joy of Home Brewing* (1984)

Homebrewer turned Anchor brewer Bruce Joseph believes that "homebrewers recognize in Fritz and Anchor a commitment to the product that comes from having integrity. They have great respect for that and for Fritz's role in the evolution of beer." In 1984, a member of the San Andreas Malts, Allan Paul (who would open San Francisco's first brewpub in 1985), approached Fritz about sponsoring a California Homebrew Club of the Year Award. In 1984, the Gold Country Brewers became the first of a long line of clubs to have their names inscribed on the handmade trophy, which is on display at Anchor.

The development of these homebrew recipes began years ago with Mark Carpenter (since 1971) and continued with an ad hoc Anchor homebrew team comprised of Bruce Joseph (since 1980), Andrea DeVries (since 1994), Dane Volek (since 2008), Jen Jordan (since 2014), and me (since 1991), ably assisted by Emma Christensen, author of *True Brews* and *Brew Better*, and a team of recipe testers. There are both partial mash/extract and all-grain recipes for each beer. Feel free—one of the great joys of homebrewing!—to tweak them to match your sensory perception of these classic brews. To paraphrase Charlie Papazian: Relax. Don't worry. Have a homebrew—or have an Anchor and repurpose the empties!

ALL-GRAIN BREWING: GENERAL DIRECTIONS

(See specific recipes for temperature, volume, and time details)

Remove the yeast from refrigeration and allow it to come to room temperature as you make the wort. If necessary, activate according to package instructions.

MASHING

Mixing dry, milled grains with warm water creates an oatmeal-like mixture called the mash. Mashing breaks down proteins to amino acids, which creates yeast food, while leaving some protein to help create a great head on your beer. Mashing also breaks down starch to simple sugars, which the yeast converts to alcohol and CO_2.

What to do: Mix the milled grains evenly with the warm mash water and gypsum in your mash/lauter tun. Stir to break up dough balls. Apply heat if needed (or stir to cool) until target mash temperature is reached for the specific recipe you are brewing. Cover the mash and hold temp. for 60 minutes. During the mash rest, in a separate pot, warm up the sparge water that you will use to rinse the grain bed.

LAUTERING

Lautering allows the sweet, hot, syrupy liquid called wort (we don't call it beer until later, when we *pitch* [add] the yeast) to drain from the mashed grains.

What to do: When the mash rest is complete, drain off a few quarts of wort and very gently pour this back over the top of the mash, being careful not to disturb the grain bed. Repeat several times until the wort being drained looks less cloudy. The mash should also start to look more compact and form a grain bed 1 or 2 in. below the surface of the wort. Slowly drain the wort into the boil kettle.

SPARGING

Sparging involves gently pouring warm water over the grains—think Mr. Coffee.

What to do: When the surface of the remaining wort falls to within an inch above the grain bed, begin pouring the warmed sparge water over the top of the grains to rinse. Go slowly and steadily, disturbing the grains as little as possible and maintaining 1 to 3 in. of liquid above the grain bed. Continue adding sparge water until you have collected 6 US gal. (22.7 L) of wort. If you run out of warmed sparge water, just add additional water directly to the wort to top it off.

BOILING

Boiling sterilizes the wort, precipitates proteins and tannins, and produces color, flavor, and aroma. Adding hops to the boil provides bitterness to balance the sweetness of the wort, and mid to late additions of hops provide aroma.

What to do: Bring the wort to a rolling boil. Boil vigorously for 60 minutes, adding hops as listed in the ingredients for your recipe.

COOLING AND FERMENTATION

Cooling is essential because yeast will not survive in hot wort. During fermentation, the yeast converts simple sugars to alcohol and CO_2 and reproduces.

What to do: Use a wort chiller or an ice bath to cool the wort as quickly as possible to slightly below fermentation temperature. Transfer the wort to a sanitized fermentation container, add the yeast, and churn the wort vigorously with a sanitized whisk to aerate. Attach the lid and insert a sanitized airlock.

Follow the fermentation time and temperatures for each specific recipe.

PACKAGING AND STORAGE

After primary fermentation, the finished beer should be packaged in bottles and naturally carbonated before serving. *Priming* (adding a small amount of dissolved sugar to the beer just before bottling) helps the yeast create CO_2 in the sealed bottles, carbonating the beer.

What to do: Be sure your bottles are clean and sanitized. To prepare your priming sugar, first bring 2 cups of water to a boil. Turn off the heat. Stir to dissolve 4 oz. (113 g) anhydrous (powdered) dextrose into the hot water. Cover and cool the solution to room temperature. Gently pour the cooled priming solution into the finished beer and let it settle for 15 minutes. Fill bottles with primed beer and *crown* (cap) them with sanitized *crowns* (bottle caps). Store the crowned bottles out of the light at approximately 70°F (21°C) for 2 weeks to naturally carbonate the beer. Check carbonation level before cold storage. For *racking* (kegging), skip the priming and shoot for 2.5 volumes of CO_2. You may want to use an online keg carbonation (PSI) calculator to help you determine the proper setting for your regulator at a given temperature. Be sure you are adequately trained in the use of tapping equipment before you begin. Safety first.

PARTIAL-MASH BREWING WITH EXTRACT: GENERAL DIRECTIONS

(See specific recipes for temperature, volume, and time details)

Remove the yeast from refrigeration and allow it to come to room temperature as you make the wort. If necessary, activate the yeast according to package instructions.

Note: If you are brewing Liberty Ale or Anchor California Lager with extract only (no grain at all), please follow the extract-only directions within those specific recipes.

What to do: Place the milled grains in a muslin bag and add to heated steep water. Meanwhile, fill a second pot with 1 US gal. (3.8 L) of water for

rinsing and heat until steaming (approx. 160°F (71°C) for 20 minutes). Once steeped, transfer the grain bag to the pot of rinse water. Gently dunk and swish the bag a few times to rinse. Do not squeeze. Compost the spent grains.

Transfer the steeping water and the rinse water to the boil kettle. Add additional water to reach a volume of 5.6 US gal. (21.2 L). Bring to a boil, then turn off the heat and add the liquid malt extract. Stir until the extract is completely dissolved.

If necessary, top up with extra water to obtain 6 US gal. (22.7 L) of wort, and bring to a rolling boil. Add the hops following the schedule on the ingredients list for the specific brew. Total boil time: 60 minutes.

For wort cooling, fermentation, storage, and packaging, follow the All-Grain Brewing General Directions.

ANCHOR STEAM BEER®

We've been making Anchor Steam Beer, our flagship brew, since 1896. It is the archetypal California common beer. The way we make it has evolved over time, and for many decades Anchor alone has used the quaint nickname "steam" for its beer. Today, steam is a trademark of Anchor Brewing. This recipe enables the homebrewer to create a delicious version of Anchor Steam, without coolships, open fermentation, or kräusening.

TASTING NOTES

Appearance

Deep amber color; creamy, light-tan head. Lingering laciness.

Aroma

Rich, caramel maltiness followed by fresh, herbal spiciness. Subtle fruity and floral esters (see page 15).

Taste

Caramel, malt, and biscuit, balanced by herbal-hop spice.

Mouthfeel

Smooth and velvety, with lively bubbles.

Finish

Lingering caramel sweetness, balanced by mellow bitterness and thirst-quenching dryness. Süffigkeit!

5 US gal. (19 L)

OG = 1.050

Pre-boil Gravity = 1.041

FG = 1.013

IBU = 35

SRM = 9

ABV = 4.9%

INGREDIENTS FOR ALL-GRAIN RECIPE

8 lbs. 8 oz. (3.9 kg) 2-row pale malt, milled

1 lb. 5 oz. (0.6 kg) caramel 40L malt, milled

0.25 oz. (7 g) gypsum (optional if using soft [very-low-mineral] water)

4 US gal. (15.1 L) mash water at 158°F (70°C)

3.33 US gal. (12.6 L) sparge water at 168°F (76°C)

0.75 oz. (21 g) US Northern Brewer pellet hops at 9.6% alpha acids for bittering, added at the beginning of the 60-minute boil

0.25 oz. (7 g) US Northern Brewer pellet hops at 9.6% alpha acids for flavor/aroma, added with 20 min. left to boil

0.5 oz. (14 g) US Northern Brewer pellet hops at 9.6% alpha acids for aroma, added at the end of the boil

White Labs WLP810 (San Francisco Lager) or Wyeast 2112 (California Lager) or Imperial L05 (Cablecar Lager) yeast

Infusion mash temp. target = 149°F (65°C)

Yeast pitch temp. = 59°F (15°C)

Ferment at 61°F (16°C) for 10 days (or until final gravity is reached)

Ferment at 66°F (19°C) for 3 days (diacetyl rest)

Lager at 40°F (4.4°C) for 14 days

4 oz. (113 g) anhydrous (powdered) dextrose for bottling (see General Directions)

INGREDIENTS FOR PARTIAL-MASH/ EXTRACT RECIPE

1 lb. 5 oz. (0.6 kg) caramel 40L malt, milled

6 lbs. (2.7 kg) golden light liquid malt extract OR 5 lbs. (2.3 kg) light dried malt extract

3 US gal. steep water (11.4 L) at 149°F (65°C) plus 1 US gal. (3.8 L) warm rinse water

0.25 oz. (7 g) gypsum (optional if using soft [very-low-mineral] water)

Hops, yeast, and fermentation schedule: same as All-Grain Recipe

ANCHOR CALIFORNIA LAGER®

We first brewed Anchor California Lager in 2011 and released it in 2012, inaugurating our Zymaster Series. It is our re-creation of California's first genuine lager, which was first released by Boca Brewing Company in 1876, just in time for America's centennial celebration. Anchor California Lager makes for a delightful counterpoint to Anchor Steam. This recipe enables the homebrewer to create a delicious version of this brew, without icehouses, open fermentation, or kräusening.

TASTING NOTES

Appearance
Vibrant golden color; tight, white head with tiny bubbles that last in the glass.

Aroma
Fresh lager-yeast, followed by light citrus, herbal, and floral hoppiness.

Taste
Crisp, clean, and refreshing. Biscuity malt, perfectly balanced with Cluster-hop earthiness and bitterness.

Mouthfeel
Smooth, with an effervescing, subtle bite.

Finish
Slightly dry, back-end bitterness, balanced by a hint of sweetness. Clean. Thirst quenching.

5 US gal. (19 L)

OG = 1.047

Pre-boil Gravity = 1.039

FG = 1.011

IBU = 32

SRM = 6

ABV = 4.9%

INGREDIENTS FOR ALL-GRAIN RECIPE

9 lbs. (4.1 kg) 2-row pale malt, milled

0.25 oz. (7 g) gypsum (optional if using soft [very-low-mineral] water)

3.75 US gal. (14.2 L) mash water at 157°F (69°C)

3.45 US gal. (13 L) sparge water at 168°F (76°C)

0.65 oz. (18 g) Cluster pellet hops at 7.5% alpha acids for bittering, added at the beginning of the 60-minute boil

0.35 oz. (10 g) Cluster pellet hops at 7.5% alpha acids for flavor/aroma, added at the end of the boil

White Labs WLP830 (German Lager) Wyeast 2206 (Bavarian Lager) or Fermentis SafLager™ S-23 or Imperial L05 (Cablecar Lager) yeast

Infusion mash temp. target = 149°F (65°C)

Yeast pitch temp. = 48°F (9°C)

Ferment at 50°F (10°C) for 14 days (or until final gravity is reached)

Ferment at 66°F (19°C) for 3 days (diacetyl rest)

Slowly lower the temperature to 34°F (1°C) and lager for at least 14 days before packaging

4 oz. (113 g) anhydrous (powdered) dextrose for bottling (see General Directions)

INGREDIENTS FOR EXTRACT RECIPE

6 lbs. 8 oz. (2.9 kg) golden light liquid malt extract OR 5.75 lbs. (2.6 kg) light dried malt extract

0.21 oz. (6 g) gypsum (optional if using soft [very-low-mineral] water)

Bring 5.5 US gal. (21 L) of water and gypsum (if using) to a boil. Turn off the heat and add the malt extract. Stir until the extract is completely dissolved. If necessary, top up with extra water to obtain 6 US gal. (22.7 L) of wort. Boil for 60 minutes.

Hops, yeast, and fermentation schedule: same as All-Grain Recipe

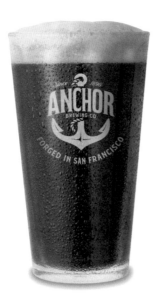

ANCHOR PORTER

There were no extant English porters when we brewed our first modern Anchor Porter in 1972. We originally made this all-malt porter with lager yeast and kräusened it with Anchor Steam. Since the early 1990s, we have been making Anchor Porter with our own strain of ale yeast, though it is still kräusened with Steam. This recipe enables the homebrewer to create a delicious version of Anchor Porter, without open fermentation or kräusening.

TASTING NOTES

Appearance
Intimidatingly deep, dark brown, almost opaque, with mahogany accents, topped with a thick, tan head. Lingering laciness.

Aroma
Roasty, toasty, caramel, toffee, burnt sugar, with a hint of earthy, grassy hops.

Taste
Slight sweetness, plus astringency and subtle, back-end bitterness.

Mouthfeel
Surprisingly smooth, silky, and full, without being heavy or chewy.

Finish
Very subtle smokiness, slight bitterness and astringency, with a hint of lingering sweetness.

5 US gal. (19 L)

OG = 1.065

Pre-boil Gravity = 1.054

FG = 1.019

IBU = 35

SRM = 38

ABV = 5.6%

INGREDIENTS FOR ALL-GRAIN RECIPE

10 lbs. (4.5 kg) 2-row pale malt, milled

1 lb. 6 oz. (0.62 kg) caramel 40L malt, milled

8.5 oz. (0.24 kg) black malt, milled

8.5 oz. (0.24 kg) chocolate malt, milled

0.28 oz. (8 g) gypsum (optional if using soft [very-low-mineral] water)

5.6 US gal. (21.2 L) mash water at 162°F (72°C)

2.5 US gal. (9.5 L) sparge water at 168°F (76°C)

0.9 oz. (26 g) US Northern Brewer pellet hops at 9.6% alpha acids for bittering, added at the beginning of the 60-minute boil

0.35 oz. (10 g) US Northern Brewer pellet hops at 9.6% alpha acids for flavor/aroma, added after 30 minutes of boiling

White Labs WLP051 (California Ale V) or Wyeast 1272 (American Ale II) or Omega OYL-004 (West Coast Ale I) or Imperial A07 (Flagship Ale) yeast

Infusion mash temp. target = 152°F (67°C)

Yeast pitch temp. = 65°F (18°C)

Ferment at 67°F (19°C) for 7 days

Ferment at 72°F (22°C) for 3 days or until final gravity is reached

Slowly lower temp. to 40°F (4°C) and store for 7 days before packaging

4 oz. (113 g) anhydrous (powdered) dextrose for bottling (see General Directions)

INGREDIENTS FOR PARTIAL-MASH/EXTRACT RECIPE

1 lb. 6 oz. (0.62 kg) caramel 40L malt, milled

8.5 oz. (0.24 kg) black malt, milled

8.5 oz. (0.24 kg) chocolate malt, milled

0.21 oz. (6 g) gypsum (optional if using soft [very low mineral] water)

7 lbs. 4 oz. (3.3 kg) golden liquid malt extract OR 6 lbs. (2.7 kg) light dried malt extract

1.5 US gal. (5.7 L) of 149°F (65°C) steep water, plus 1 US gal. (3.8 L) warm rinse water

Hops, yeast, and fermentation schedule: same as All-Grain Recipe

LIBERTY ALE®

We first brewed Liberty Ale on April 18, 1975, in celebration of the two-hundredth anniversary of Paul Revere's historic ride. This iconic brew introduced America and the world to the distinctiveness of an all-malt, single-malt, single-hop pale ale. Dry-hopped in our cellars, it is the forerunner of and model for today's American IPAs. This recipe enables the homebrewer to create a delicious version of Liberty Ale, without open fermentation or bunging.

TASTING NOTES

Appearance
Rich golden color; cream-colored head, with fine carbonation and good retention.

Aroma
Crisp, fresh, citrusy, piney, evergreen. Fresh Cascade hops and subtle ale-yeast aromas.

Taste
Classic hop-forward, medium bitterness, with a touch of malty sweetness and toasted bread.

Mouthfeel

Effervescent carbonation, with light-medium body.

Finish

Bitterness that doesn't bite or linger; crisp, clean, dry, and refreshing.

5 US gal. (19 L)

OG = 1.060

Pre-boil Gravity = 1.049

FG = 1.015

IBU = 50

SRM = 7

ABV = 5.9%

INGREDIENTS FOR ALL-GRAIN RECIPE

11 lbs. 8 oz. (5.2 kg) 2-row pale malt, milled

0.28 oz. (8 g) gypsum (optional if using soft [very-low-mineral] water)

4.7 US gal. (17.8 L) mash water at 158°F (70°C)

2.8 US gal. (10.6 L) sparge water at 168°F (76°C)

1.25 oz. (35 g) Cascade pellet hops at 8.2% alpha acids for bittering, added at the beginning of the 60-minute boil

0.75 oz. (21 g) Cascade pellet hops at 8.2% alpha acids for flavor/aroma, added 30 minutes into the boil

0.5 oz. (14 g) Cascade pellet hops at 8.2% alpha acids for aroma, added at the end of the boil

2 oz. (57 g) Cascade pellet hops at 8.2% alpha acids for dry-hopping, added to fermentor after 6 days of fermentation

White Labs WLP051 (California Ale V) or Wyeast 1272 (American Ale II) or Omega OYL-004 (West Coast Ale I) or Imperial A07 (Flagship Ale) yeast

Infusion mash temp. target = 149°F (65°C)

Yeast pitch temp. = 65°F (18°C)

Ferment at 67°F (19°C) for 6 days, then add the 2 oz. (57 g) Cascade pellet hops to fermentor

Ferment at 72°F (22°C) for 3 more days

Slowly lower temp. to 40°F (4°C) and store for 7 days before packaging

4 oz. (113 g) anhydrous (powdered) dextrose for bottling (see General Directions)

INGREDIENTS FOR EXTRACT RECIPE

8 lbs. 3 oz. (3.7 kg) golden light liquid malt extract OR 7 lbs. (3.2 kg) light dried malt extract

0.21 oz. (6 g) gypsum (optional if using soft [very-low-mineral] water)

Bring 5.4 US gal. (20.4 L) of water and gypsum (if using) to a boil. Turn off the heat and add the malt extract. Stir until the extract is completely dissolved. If necessary, top up with extra water to obtain 6 US gal. (22.7 L) of wort.

Hops, yeast, and fermentation schedule: same as All-Grain Recipe

ACKNOWLEDGMENTS

The Anchor Brewing Story could never have been written without my wife, Deb Shidler, whose love, support, and "You're doin' it!" faith in me was unwavering right up until her untimely passing in 2021. Our shared passion for history, genealogy, and research led to many discoveries for this book, including Gottlieb Brekle's birthplace, birth date, and incredible journey from Ossweil to Valdivia to San Francisco, as well as Gottlieb and Marie's secret adoption of his nephew, future brewer Frederick, as their son.

To the entire 8th Street gang, including Fritz Maytag, Gordon MacDermott, Mark Carpenter, Linda Rowe, Chris Solomon, Mike Lee, Phil Canevari, and Dennis Kellett, who were especially helpful.

To the entire Mariposa Street gang, including Bruce Joseph, Tom Riley, Darek Ochtera, Bob Brewer, Kevin West, Andrea DeVries, John Dannerbeck, Keith Greggor, Tony Foglio, Lynn Lackey, Teagan Thompson, Matt Davenport, Scott Ungermann, Dane Volek, Ramon Tamayo, Jen Jordan, Jon Ezell, Wolfgang Salger, Rhys Carvolth, Michelle Muhme, Gideon Bush, Jiro Ohkawa, and Scott Pederson, for all their help and support. To honorary Anchorite Peter Kollnberger, who knows everything about brewing and so graciously helped me decipher old German text. And to my Anchor partners in rock 'n' roll crime, the Hysters, featuring the Old Fog Horns.

To Elizabeth Brekle, Jane Cunningham, and Jacque Turner, my earliest direct connections to the Brekle family. And to Fred and Sue Brekle and all future generations.

To all the amazing artists, illustrators, and graphic designers with whom I've collaborated, including Jim Stitt, Jack Martin, Richard Elmore, Elaine Kwong, Grace Woo, Susan DeSmet, Eric Sabee, Brian Bisio, David Williams, and Jim Phillips. And to still-local artist Dennis Ziemienski, whose mid-1970s illustration of a bottle and glass of Anchor Steam inspired this book's cover art.

To the incredible photographers with whom I've worked: Andree Abecassis, Kirk Amyx, Erin Conger, Allen D. Johnson, and Terry McCarthy. And to Bill Brach and Norman Seeff—what a treat to see your photos and hear your stories about Janis and Steve.

To Ken Hepler, Charles Ruble, Frits Kouwenhoven, and all the wonderful printers who taught me so much about their craft.

I owe a huge debt of gratitude to the fine staffs of these institutions, which both preserve history and bring it to life: the American Philosophical Society; the Art Deco Society of California; The Bancroft Library and Doe Library, UC Berkeley; the Brewers Association; the California Historical Society; the California State Archives; California State Library and Sutro Library; the Chicago History Museum; the Family History Library (Salt Lake City & San Bruno, CA); Landesarchiv Baden-Württemberg, Stuttgart; the Library of Congress; the Mechanics' Institute Library; the National Archives (Washington, DC & San Bruno, CA); the National Museum of American History, Smithsonian Institution; the San Francisco History Association; the San Francisco History Center, San Francisco Public Library; the San Francisco Historical Society; the Shields Library, UC Davis; The Society of California Pioneers; the Truckee-Donner Historical Society; and the Verdi History Center.

A special shoutout to Axel Borg, Susan Goldstein, John Hogan, Patricia Keats, and Susan Snyder, as well as my fellow company historians: Lynn Downey, Historian Emeritus, Levi Strauss & Co.; and Bob Chandler, Historian Emeritus, Wells Fargo.

To Paula Johnson and Theresa McCulla at the National Museum of American History, Smithsonian Institution, Washington, DC, for their unstinting support of craft brewing in America.

To Miguel Civil and Sol Katz (the Ninkasi Project), Marcia Jervis (Anchor Distributing), Myrna Ver Ploeg (Maytag Dairy Farms), Paul Draper (Ridge Vineyards), Peter Albin (Big Brother and the Holding Company), Chet Helms, Tom ("The Iceman") Macaulay, Balloonist Deke Sonnichsen, Tom Dalldorf, Lew Bryson, Jay Brooks, Kari Schutty, Sara Ferguson, and the Blowup Lab—what an eclectic joy to work with all of you!

To the Tougas family, for their generous donation of the Oasis's vintage Anchor sign (see page 87), as well as an Oasis table and benches. To Greg Goss, who rescued August Maritzen's original 1906 Anchor blueprints (see *The Anchor Brewing Story*'s endpapers) from a dumpster and graciously gave them to me for the Anchor archive. And to Bob Welch, a true gentleman, for the gift of his vivid memories of the Crystal Palace Market and Anchor Brewing in the 1950s.

To Tom Acitelli, Charlie Bamforth, Bo Burlingham, Natalie and Vinnie Cilurzo, Ken Grossman, and Charlie Papazian for their encouraging words.

Thanks to Emily Timberlake for asking me to write this book. And special thanks to Julie Bennett and her super team at Ten Speed Press—especially Annie Marino, Betsy Stromberg, and Kimmy Tejasindhu—as well as homebrewer/author Emma Christensen and freelance editor Chris Hall—for their invaluable contributions to *The Anchor Brewing Story*.

CREDITS

(*Right, Left, Top, Bottom = R, L, T, B*)

Andree Abecassis, photographer: 176–177, 217R.

Kirk Amyx, photographer: 10, 16T, 17 (Steam Beer/Anchor sign), 30B, 39, 43R, 49, 50T, 53, 54, 55L, 58R, 59 (sign and bottle), 68, 78, 86, 87, 95, 113, 114T, 116, 124, 125, 129, 130, 136, 140, 142, 143, 151, 156T, 161, 180, 191L, 193, 196, 204L, 205, 206B, 207, 209 (bottle), 211, 212B, 218, 222, 224, 230R, 231R, 232, 233, 234, 236, 237T, 239T, 241, 246, 249, 251, 252B, 253R, 254R, 259L, 268 (trophy), 270, 271, 273, 274.

The Bancroft Library, © The Regents of the University of California: 21 (Wimmer Nugget, BANC PIC 19xx.031:066—OBJ); 36: Executive Committee United Brewery Workmen's Union of the Pacific Coast logo, *Statement of the United Brewery Workmen's Union of the Pacific Coast* (1891); 38 (detail), x F862.6.U6; 37: International Union of the United Brewery Workmen of America logo, *Konstitution und Nebengesetze der Brauer und Mälzer Union No. 7 des Internationalen Verbandes der Vereinigten Brauerei-Arbeiter von Amerika*, Revidiert und angenommen den 18 April 1907, x F851.L18, no.17; 38B: Co-operative Brewery advertisement, *The Coast Seaman's Journal*, F850.C7, v. 5, no. 24, p. 12, March 23, 1892; 63T (L to R): (1) Joe Allen, 68 years, brewmaster, truck driver, and chief cook and bottle washer of Anchor Brewing Corp. at work, (2) Brewmaster Joe Allen smelling hops, (3) Brewmaster Joe Allen brewing, *San Francisco News-Call Bulletin* photograph archive (BANC PIC 1959.010—NEG part 3, BOX 90 [07-30-56.06])

Brian Bisio: 253R.

David Björkman, photographer, © Brewers Association (Used with permission): 204R.

Justin Blair: 11.

Bill Brach, photographer, © Bill Brach: 98–99.

Peter Breining, photographer: 63B (platform), 67B: Peter Breining/*San Francisco Chronicle*/Polaris.

David Burkhart: 8, 15, 18, 22, 23, 25, 27–30, 39, 43R, 47L, 48B, 49–51, 52B, 53–55, 58–59 (labels and bottles), 65B, 68, 74T, 76, 78, 80, 113, 116, 129, 130, 136, 137B, 140, 142, 155, 161, 191L, 193L, 196, 200T, 206T, 207, 209 (bottle), 211, 219T, 231R, 232, 233, 237 (decanter and stereoview), 239T, 246, 249, 251, 252B, 253R, 254, 258L, 259, 260, 262R.

California State Archives, Trademark Registrations and Specimens, Old Series, 1861–1900, Office of the Secretary of State, Sacramento, California: 35 (#TM_1840_united_brewery_workmen_001), 38T (#TM_2190_coop_brewing_002), 44R (#1457B_cal_soda_works_trademark).

James Chen, photographer: 173.

Chicago History Museum: 47R, *The Western Brewer and Journal of the Barley, Malt and Hop Trades* (June 1906).

Erin Conger, photographer: 11, 244, 256, 258R, 266, 267.

Keith Dennison, photographer: 71, 75.

Richard Elmore: 150, 197, 200R (labels), 204L.

Howard Erker, photographer: 16, 62T, 70, 72T.

Kaffe Fassett: 79, Kaffe Fassett, textile artist (born 1937).

Jeremy Fish: 261.

John Gorman, photographer: 97.

Gene X Hwang, Orange Photography: 247.

Bill Hyde: 110, 113.

Marcia Jervis: 124.

Library of Congress, National Photo Company Collection: 83, Maytag Co. display (ca. 1926), glass negative.

Nicholas R. Lobuglio Jr: 157.

David Lyon: 205.

Jack Martin: 232, 233, 239T, 249, 251, 252B.

Mauritshuis, The Hague: 9.

Fritz Maytag: 67T, 82, 84, 86, 88, 188, 229, 230L.

Terrence McCarthy, photographer: 4, 104, 170, 175L, 195, 219T, 226–227, 242–243, 253L, 262L, 265.

Tom Meyer: 220R.

Alan Paterson, photographer: 172, 175R.

Jim Phillips: 220L.

Rayment & Collins (photography and retouching): 262R, 263, 264.

Redtail Media: 20.

David Rumsey Map Collection, Stanford Libraries: 46, Sanborn-Perris Map Company, Limited, fire insurance map (1905).

Eric Sabee: 15 (cutaway view).

San Francisco History Center, San Francisco Public Library: 48T (AAC-3939), 60 (AAC-6439), 62R (AAC-6436).

Kari Schutty: 44L, Norddeutscher Verein Silver Anniversary program book, 1899).

Norman Seeff, photographer, © Norman Seeff: 186.

Lars Speyer, photographer: 94, 107, 109, 115, 122, 127, 148B, 152, 153, 178.

James Stitt: 128, 130, 134T, 136, 140, 142, 161, 166, 189T, 191, 196, 200L (label), 207, 211, 212B, 217R, 218L, 219B, 222, 224, 230R, 231L, 234, 236, 237T, 239B, 249, 251, 252.

Truckee-Donner Historical Society, TDHS Collection: 32, 34.

Jacque Turner: 26.

Verdi History Center, Verdi History Preservation Society, Inc: 33.

Bob Welch, photographer: 57, 64, 65T, 66.

Rollo Simpson Wheeler: 228.

Dennis Ziemienski: 13 (black and white illustration), 112.

INDEX

Award-winning author and historian **David Burkhart** is an honors graduate of Yale. In 1991, he joined the small staff of Anchor Brewing Co., where he worked side-by-side with owner and brewmaster Fritz Maytag. In his thirty-plus years at Anchor, Burkhart has done nearly every job at the brewery, adding Anchor brewery historian to his many titles in 2010. His books on the 1906 San Francisco Earthquake and mixologist William T. "Cocktail" Boothby have won numerous awards, including the Benjamin Franklin, Independent Publisher, National Indie Excellence, and USA Best Books Awards in History. Burkhart is also a professional trumpeter; a founding member of the Grammy-nominated Bay Brass; a performer with San Francisco's Symphony, Opera, and Ballet; and a professor at the San Francisco Conservatory of Music.

Fritz Maytag grew up in Newton, Iowa. He graduated from Deerfield Academy in 1955 and Stanford in 1959, where he subsequently studied Japanese. The owner of York Creek Vineyards and chairman emeritus of Maytag Dairy Farms, Anchor Brewing Co., and Anchor Distilling Co., Fritz is the recipient of the James Beard Foundation's Outstanding Wine and Spirits Professional and Lifetime Achievement Awards.

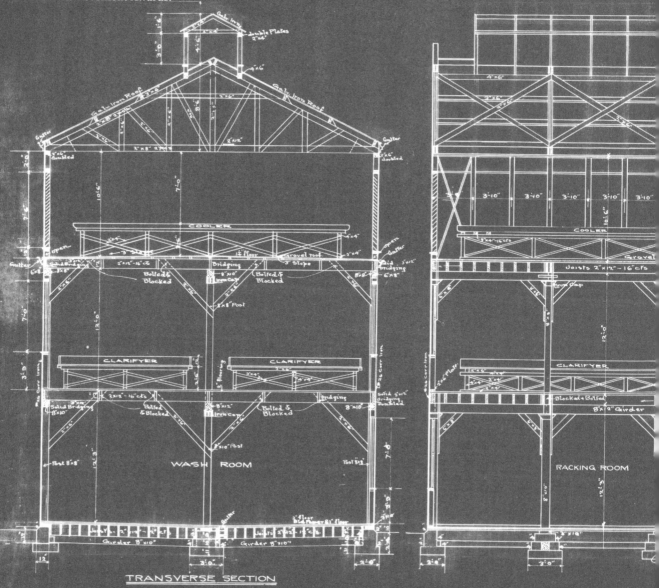